CIVIL-MILITARY RELATIONS ON THE FRONTIER AND BEYOND, 1865–1917

CIVIL-MILITARY RELATIONS ON THE FRONTIER AND BEYOND, 1865–1917

CHARLES A. BYLER

In War and in Peace: U.S. Civil-Military Relations
David S. Heidler and Jeanne T. Heidler, General Editors

Praeger Security International
Westport, Connecticut · London

Library of Congress Cataloging-in-Publication Data

Byler, Charles A.
   Civil-military relations on the frontier and beyond, 1865–1917 / Charles A. Byler.
      p. cm. — (U.S. civil-military relations, ISSN 1556–8504)
      Includes bibliographical references and index.
      ISBN 0–275–98537–7 (alk. paper)
   1. Civil-military relations—United States—History.   I. Title.   II. Series.
   JK330.B95   2006
      322'.5097309034—dc22   2006008231

British Library Cataloguing in Publication Data is available.

Library of Congress Catalog Card Number: 2006008231
ISBN: 0–275–98537–7
ISSN: 1556–8504

First published in 2006

Praeger Security International, 88 Post Road West, Westport, CT 06881
An imprint of Greenwood Publishing Group, Inc.
www.praeger.com

Printed in the United States of America

The paper used in this book complies with the
Permanent Paper Standard issued by the National
Information Standards Organization (Z39.48–1984).

10 9 8 7 6 5 4 3 2 1

65187277

To my mother and father

Contents

Illustrations

Series Foreword

No other aspect of a nation's political health is as important as the relationship between its government and military. At the most basic level, the necessity of protecting the country from external and internal threats must be balanced by the obligation to preserve fundamental civil liberties. The United States is unique among nations, for it has successfully maintained civilian control of its military establishment, doing so from a fundamental principle institutionalized in its Constitution and embraced by its citizens. The United States has thus avoided the military coup that elsewhere has always meant the end of representative government and the extinguishing of individual freedom. The American military is the servant of citizens, not their master.

This series presents the work of eminent scholars to explain as well as assess civil-military relations in U.S. history. The American tradition of a military controlled by civilians is venerable—George Washington established it when he accepted his commission from the Continental Congress in 1775— but we will see how military leaders have not always been sanguine about abdicating important decisions to those they regard as inexperienced amateurs. And while disagreements between the government and the military become more likely during wars, there is more to this subject than the institutional arrangements of subordination and obedience that mark the relationship of government authorities and the uniformed services. The public's evolving perception of the military is also a central part of this story. In these volumes we will see explored the fine line between dissent and loyalty in war and peace and how the government and the armed forces have balanced civil liberties against national security. From the years of the American Revolution to the present, the resort to military justice has always been an option for safeguarding domestic welfare, but it has always been legally controversial and generally unpopular.

The United States relies on civilians to serve as most of its warriors during major conflicts, and civilian appreciation of things military understandably changes during such episodes. Opinions about the armed services transform accordingly, usually from casual indifference to acute concern. And through it all, military and civilian efforts to sustain popular support for the armed forces and mobilize enthusiasm for its operations have been imperative, especially when the military has been placed in the vague role of peacekeeper, far from home for extended periods. The changing threats that America has confronted throughout its history have tested its revered traditions of civil-military relations, yet Americans have met even the most calamitous challenges without damaging those traditions. The most successful representative democracy in the world has defended itself without losing its way. We are hopeful that the volumes in this series will not only explain why but will also help to ensure that those vital traditions Americans rightly celebrate will endure.

David S. Heidler and Jeanne T. Heidler,
General Editors

Preface

The period between the end of the Civil War in 1865 and the American entry into World War I in 1917 was a time of dramatic change for the United States. The nation experienced unprecedented economic growth. It endured the social upheaval that accompanied rapid industrialization and urbanization. It acquired an overseas empire and exerted its influence more forcefully in Asia and Latin America. These developments had a profound effect on the nation's military, which served the government as an instrument of expansion and as a means of keeping order on the frontier, in the strife-torn industrial cities, and in the growing American empire. The military underwent a remarkable transformation during this period. The army grew from a constabulary of around 25,000 soldiers scattered across the country in small frontier outposts and crumbling coastal fortifications to a force of over 100,000, capable of operating in such distant places as China and the Philippines. The navy's growth was even more impressive. What in the 1870s had been an embarrassing collection of obsolete vessels—most still made of wood and powered by wind—developed into a navy that ranked among the world's largest and most technologically advanced.

Americans looked upon the striking transformation of their military with a mixture of pride and uneasiness. While many celebrated the development of the armed services as evidence of the nation's rising power and hailed each new battleship as a symbol of American wealth and ingenuity, others worried that the creation of a large military in a time of peace represented a troubling departure from the American practice of shunning a standing military and relying instead on citizen soldiers who took up arms only in time of war. For Americans brought up to regard the standing army as a tool of monarchs and a threat to liberty, the rise of a larger, more professional military with responsibilities around the globe raised some disquieting questions. Would the expanded military remain subordinate to the authority of civilian leaders? Would it exercise undue influence in the making of government policies? Would it be used to advance the interests of a particular party or a particular political leader? Would military attitudes regarding obedience to authority and the privileges of rank seep out into the larger society and undermine the cherished American values of individualism and egalitarianism?

Members of the military, in turn, had concerns of their own. Even as the armed services began to grow, officers expressed their frustration with a political system that had, in their view, shamefully neglected the military for decades. Officers complained that the old American prejudice against a professional military caused the country's political leaders to refrain from taking the steps necessary to prepare the United States for modern warfare. Some officers wondered why they—with their years of training and experience—so often had to submit to the decisions of civilians who had little understanding of military matters.

Despite the military's frequent complaints about the neglect it suffered at the hands of civilian leaders, it actually fared reasonably well once the nation had moved beyond the contentious period of Reconstruction. The government did not move as quickly as many in the military desired, but the fact remained that civilian leaders sanctioned the creation of the largest peacetime military that Americans had yet seen, and over time they approved many of the measures that military reformers had advocated to make the administration of the services more efficient and to improve the living conditions and the training of officers and enlisted men. Although the military continued to draw criticism from a considerable number of politicians, journalists, and intellectuals, by the early twentieth century the public image of the armed services had improved significantly. More Americans, it seemed, looked upon the larger peacetime military as a source of national pride rather than a cause for anxiety.

Likewise, many of the warnings issued by critics of the military during the late nineteenth and early twentieth centuries seem overblown in retrospect. Contrary to the predictions of some critics, civilian control of the military survived both Reconstruction and the establishment of an American empire overseas. Although officers often grumbled about government policies, they accepted civilian control as an essential element of the American political system and, with very few exceptions, did as civilian leaders told them to do. The military as a whole never sought to serve the interests of a particular political party or leader, and most officers followed the advice of General William Tecumseh Sherman to stay out of politics. Outside of purely military affairs, the military's influence on the making of policy remained limited and haphazard—a number of individual officers gained the attention of civilian policymakers, but civilian leaders seemed content to keep the military in its longstanding role as an instrument rather than an architect of the nation's foreign policy.

This study aims to provide a broad overview of major developments in civil-military relations during the period between the Civil War and World War I. It is organized thematically rather than chronologically. Chapter 1 discusses how the American public viewed the military during the period. It explains how dissatisfaction with the role of the army in Reconstruction and the traditional American suspicion of standing armies, among other factors, caused many Americans to have an unfavorable opinion of the military in the late nineteenth century, and how successes in war and empire-building improved the public image of the armed services by the early twentieth century. Chapter 2 analyzes the complex relationship between the military and Congress. It discusses the reasons behind the efforts of members of Congress to restrict the size and limit the responsibilities of the army in the 1870s and the increased willingness of Congress in later decades to approve larger military appropriations. Chapter 3 looks at the experiences of officers and enlisted men during the period, with a particular focus on three key issues of the time—the desertion problem, the role of African Americans in the military, and the intense dissatisfaction of officers with the slow rate of promotion. Chapter 4 considers the military's subordination to civil authority and reasons for the military's acceptance of the principle of civilian supremacy. It explains how, over time, presidents succeeded in exercising greater control over military operations both inside and outside the United States. Chapter 5 discusses the partially successful efforts of military reformers to persuade civilian leaders to approve legislation creating a general staff for the army and navy, and relates those efforts to the rise of professionalism in the officer corps. Chapter 6 assesses the reasons for the often strong discontent within the military regarding the political system and aspects of civil society. It also discusses the relatively rare instances when military officers openly defied civilian leaders.

Many people deserve recognition for helping to make this work possible. The series editors, David and Jeanne Heidler, provided much-appreciated encouragement and advice. My editor at Praeger Publishers, Heather R. Staines, was unfailingly patient and helpful. To my undergraduate advisor and mentor—G. Thomas Edwards—I owe a continuing debt of gratitude for inspiring me to pursue a career in history and for providing a model of how a historian can be both an active scholar and a dedicated teacher. My family, I hope, understands how much I appreciated their patience while I was writing this book. I am especially grateful to my wife, Kim Wilson, for her perceptive editorial advice and constant support.

Chronology of Important Events

1865

April   The Civil War ends. The U.S. army occupies the defeated South.
         President Abraham Lincoln is assassinated. Vice President
         Andrew Johnson becomes president.

1866

         Congress establishes the size of the regular army at about
         54,000 officers and enlisted men.

January General Ulysses S. Grant issues General Order No. 3, which di-
         rects commanders in South to protect U.S. soldiers, Freedman's
         Bureau agents, and loyalists from prosecution by civil authori-
         ties for acts committed under military authority and to protect
         blacks from prosecution for offenses that would not apply to
         whites.

July   General Grant issues General Order No. 44, which permits sol-
         diers to arrest persons charged with crimes against citizens
         when civil authorities either cannot or will not do so.

1867

March   Congress overrides President Johnson's veto to approve the Re-
         construction Act. The act makes the civilian governments in
         southern states provisional, reinstates martial law, and divides
         the South into five military districts.

Congress passes the Command of the Army Act; a measure designed to protect General Grant. The act prohibits the president from removing or reassigning the commanding general without congressional approval. It also requires that all orders from the president and the secretary of war go through the office of the commanding general.

July   Congress passes the Third Reconstruction Act, which authorizes commanders of the military districts to remove uncooperative state officials from office and gives the commanders greater authority to determine voter eligibility.

President Andrew Johnson replaces General Philip Sheridan as the commander of the Fifth Military District (Louisiana and Texas) following Sheridan's decision to remove Governor James Throckmorton of Texas from office.

1868

November   The army's attack on a Cheyenne village along the Washita River in the Oklahoma Indian Territory brings condemnations from eastern humanitarians.

General Ulysses S. Grant, the Republican candidate for president, wins the election.

1869

William T. Sherman replaces Grant as commanding General of the Army. Congress votes to reduce the size of the regular army to a maximum of 37,313.

The Grant administration initiates the "Peace Policy" in Indian affairs. In an effort to improve conditions on the Indian reservations, the administration consults with church leaders in determining the appointments of Indian agents. The army may not enter Indian reservations without the permission of officials of the Indian Bureau.

1870

January   Humanitarians denounce the army's attack on a village of peaceful Piegan Indians along the Marias River in Montana. News of the attack eliminates the possibility that Congress might approve a bill transferring the Indian Bureau from the Interior Department to the War Department.

July   Georgia is the last of the former Confederate states to be readmitted to the Union, thereby ending military government in the South.

Congress passes legislation forbidding army officers on active duty from holding civilian appointments in the government.

1871

April   The Ku Klux Klan Act becomes law. It permits the army to assist federal officials in arresting individuals for conspiring to deprive citizens of their constitutional rights.

July   Congress reduces the base pay in the regular army to $13 per month. Partly as a consequence, the army loses nearly one third of its enlisted men to desertion in 1871.

1874

Congress establishes the size of the regular army at 27,000 officers and men.

1875

January   General Philip Sheridan directs federal soldiers to intervene in a dispute over election results for seats in Louisiana's legislature. The troops enter the legislative chamber and help the Republicans establish themselves as the majority.

1876

June   Sioux and Cheyenne warriors destroy much of the U.S. Seventh Cavalry under George A. Custer at the Battle of the Little Bighorn. The defeat leads Congress to authorize the enlistment of 2,500 additional cavalry troops.

1877

Henry O. Flipper becomes the first African American to graduate from the U.S. Military Academy at West Point.

July   President Rutherford B. Hayes orders the army to intervene in the nationwide railroad strike.

The failure of Congress to pass an army appropriation bill leaves the service without pay until November, when Congress approves an appropriation during a special session.

1878

June   Congress passes Posse Comitatus Act, which places limits on the use of federal troops in domestic law enforcement. The act makes it unlawful to use the army "for the purpose of executing the laws, except in such cases and under such circumstances as such employment of said force may be expressly authorized by the Constitution or by Act of Congress."

1880

January   The House Naval Affairs Committee issues a report criticizing the decrepit state of the navy and calling for it to be rebuilt.

April   Controversy over treatment of African Americans at the Military Academy erupts after Johnson C. Whittaker, a black cadet, is found bleeding and tied to his bed in his room at West Point. Army officials accuse Whittaker of staging the incident, but the charges against him are eventually dismissed.

1882

August   Congress passes an act that temporarily limits the number of commissions awarded each year to graduates of the Naval Academy and that establishes limits to the number of officers at each rank, thereby reducing promotion opportunities for junior officers.

1883

March   Congress approves funding for the construction of three steel cruisers, the first American warships to be made of domestically produced steel.

November   General Philip Sheridan replaces William Sherman as Commanding General of the Army.

1885

March   Congress establishes the Endicott Board to examine the nation's coastal defenses. The board eventually recommends that the nation spend $126 million to improve coastal fortifications.

1888

August   Commanding General Philip Sheridan dies. General John Schofield replaces him.

1890

October   Congress attempts to open more opportunities for advancement
             in the army by enacting legislation that permits the promotion
             of officers by seniority within their branch (i.e., infantry, ar-
             tillery, and cavalry) rather than only within their regiment. The
             law also requires examinations to ensure that all lieutenants
             and captains seeking promotion meet basic physical and profes-
             sional standards.

December   Attempts by army troops to disarm a band of Sioux near
             Wounded Knee, South Dakota, result in violence, and the sol-
             diers kill over 100 Sioux men, women, and children. Humani-
             tarians condemn the army's actions.

1894

July   President Grover Cleveland orders federal troops to intervene in
             the Pullman strike.

August   Congress votes to require the army to enlist only American cit-
             izens or immigrants committed to going through the naturaliza-
             tion process.

1895

October   Commanding General Schofield retires. President Cleveland ap-
             points General Nelson Miles as his replacement.

1897

             The navy opens recruiting stations in inland cities and begins to
             recruit "landsmen," men without maritime experience who re-
             quire training before being assigned to ships.

1898

March   Congress appropriates $50 million to spend on the military and
             authorizes the president to expand the regular army to 104,000
             men in time of war.

April   The Spanish-American War begins.

September   President William McKinley establishes the Dodge Commission
             to investigate the War Department's handling of the army's mo-
             bilization during the Spanish-American War.

December   The Paris Peace Agreement ends the war with Spain and gives
            the United States possession of Puerto Rico, Guam, and the
            Philippines.

1899

February   Fighting begins between U.S. troops and Filipino nationalists
            led by Emilio Aguinaldo.

April   President William McKinley orders regular troops to intervene
            in the labor dispute between miners and mine owners in the
            Coeur d'Alene region of northern Idaho. The use of the soldiers
            to arrest union members causes outrage in the labor movement.

1900

March   Secretary of the Navy John D. Long creates the General Board
            of the Navy, a group of senior officers who would advise the
            secretary and plan for war in peacetime.

June   U.S. forces join with those of Great Britain, Japan, Russia, and
            other powers to intervene in the Boxer Rebellion in China.

1901

March   U.S. troops capture nationalist leader Emilio Aguinaldo in the
            Philippines.

1902

January   A U.S. Senate committee begins investigation of allegations of
            atrocities committed by American soldiers in the Philippines.

May   U.S. military government in Cuba comes to an end with the es-
            tablishment of an independent Cuban government.

July   President Theodore Roosevelt declares the end of the Philippine
            War.

December   A group of retired officers joins with interested businessmen to
            form the Navy League, an organization devoted, in the words
            of one officer, to the "important missionary work of spreading
            the naval propaganda among the people at large."

1903

February   The Army General Staff Act becomes law. The act gives the
            army a general staff, headed by a chief of staff, and eliminates
            the position of commanding general.

August   Commanding General Nelson Miles retires. President Theodore
          Roosevelt appoints General Samuel B. M. Young as the first
          chief of staff.

1906

August   Citizens of Brownsville, Texas, blame black soldiers of the
          Twenty-fifth Infantry Regiment stationed at Fort Brown for a
          shooting incident that left a town resident dead. When members
          of the unit refuse to name any of their fellow soldiers as perpe-
          trators of the crime, President Theodore Roosevelt orders the
          discharge of all of the 167 enlisted men present at Fort Brown
          on the night of the shootings.

1907

December The sixteen battleships of the "Great White Fleet" depart
          Hampton Roads, Virginia, to begin their fourteen-month cir-
          cumnavigation of the globe.

1912

          Secretary of War Henry Stimson forces the resignation of Adju-
          tant General Fred Ainsworth. The resignation represents a vic-
          tory for Stimson and General Leonard Wood, the army's chief
          of staff, in their struggle to increase the authority of the chief of
          staff over the bureaus of the War Department.

1914

April   President Woodrow Wilson backs the demand of Admiral
          Henry T. Mayo that Mexican officials offer a salute to the
          American flag as an apology for the brief detention of some
          American sailors in Tampico. When Mexico refuses, Wilson or-
          ders U.S. forces to occupy the port city of Vera Cruz.

August   World War I begins in Europe.

December President Woodrow Wilson announces to Congress his determi-
          nation to stay out of the European war and his belief that the
          United States should continue to rely on citizen soldiers rather
          than a large standing army.

1915

March   Congress approves legislation establishing the position of chief
            of naval operations. The CNO is to advise the secretary of the
            navy and supervise "the operations of the fleet."

July   President Woodrow Wilson drops his opposition to the pre-
            paredness campaign and asks the War Department and the
            Navy Department to devise plans for the buildup of the armed
            forces.

1916

            Secretary of the Navy Josephus Daniels amends the U.S. Navy
            Regulations so that no commander can issue an ultimatum to
            foreign officials "without first communicating with the Navy
            Department, except in extreme cases where such action is nec-
            essary to save life."

March   A raid by Pancho Villa's band on Columbus, New Mexico,
            prompts President Woodrow Wilson to order army troops un-
            der the command of General John Pershing to enter Mexico
            with orders to destroy, capture, or disperse the raiders.

May   Congress approves the National Defense Act, a measure that
            expands the size of the regular army and clarifies the role of the
            National Guard as a reserve force.

June   A violent clash between U.S. soldiers and troops of the Mexican
            government at Carrizal, Mexico, increases tensions between the
            United States and Mexico. The Wilson administration rejects
            General Pershing's call for retaliation and begins a gradual
            withdrawal of American forces from Mexico.

1917

April   The United States enters World War I.

1

Americans Look at Their Military, 1865–1917

In the fall of 1873, Major General John Pope, commander of the army's Department of the Missouri, spoke to a group of Civil War veterans gathered for a meeting of the Society of the Army of the Tennessee. Along with the expected reminiscences about the war, Pope included in his remarks words of concern about what he saw as the potential for a significant rift between the military and the rest of American society. The well being of both the army and the people, he said, demanded that there be "a common sympathy and a common interest between them." The Civil War had given the regular army and American civilians a shared purpose, but now, Pope warned, relations between the two groups threatened to return to the state of "unhappy and well-nigh fatal divorce" that had existed before the war. Pope blamed the problem on the army's geographical isolation in frontier posts and its stubborn adherence to tradition. If this physical and psychological separation from the rest of society continued, soldiers would no longer be citizens in the "highest and truest sense" and the army would "properly and naturally become an object of suspicion and dislike."[1]

General Pope's concerns about an estrangement between civilians and the military in the years following the Civil War were far from unusual. Civilians and military officers alike noted that the American public seemed to hold the armed services in low regard. As William Tecumseh Sherman, the army's commanding general, wrote to a friend in 1873, "it is now the fashion to abuse the Army and Navy." A decade later the editor of the *Army and Navy Journal* complained that a "democratic atmosphere is not congenial to the profession of arms, and the spirit of the age is unfriendly."[2]

The military's unpopularity had many sources, including the long-held American suspicion of professional armies and the army's involvement in

such controversial tasks as enforcing Reconstruction measures in the southern states. By the 1890s, however, the standing of the military began to improve. The swift victory over Spain in 1898 and the military's increasingly
important role as an instrument of American foreign policy helped it gain a
more positive reputation. Still, a substantial segment of the American public
continued to look upon the military with indifference or even hostility. The
determined opposition to a large and professional military that was so widespread after the Civil War was still very much in evidence on the eve of
America's entry into World War I.

THE IDEAL OF THE CITIZEN SOLDIER

An important article of faith in American political ideology was that standing armies—that is, permanent armies composed of professional soldiers—
posed a threat to individual liberties and representative government.
Americans favored the militia over regular troops and the volunteer "citizen
soldier" over the professional. That preference had deep roots in American
history. The colonists had relied primarily on militia forces for their defense.
Influenced by the ideology of Britain's Radical Whigs, patriots had made the
presence of British army regulars in the colonies one of the principal grievances against the Crown during the revolution. Distrust of the professional
military became a central political principle for many Americans, especially
those who, like Thomas Jefferson and his followers, opposed the creation of a
strong central government. In political rhetoric and schoolbook versions of
history, the standing army, usually represented by the despised Redcoats, almost always appeared as an instrument of tyranny. The idea that a large standing army endangered liberties "has been repeated diligently on the stump and
in the press since 1775," noted an army officer in 1906, "[I]t has grown into
the crevices in our foundation and cannot be eradicated."[3]

Many Americans also looked on the regular military with disfavor
because its practices seemed so much at odds with mainstream American
values. The military's rigid hierarchy violated egalitarian ideals, and its centralized structure contradicted the traditional American emphasis on local
control. Most Americans cherished individualism and were skeptical of authority; the military, in contrast, emphasized the unquestioning submission
to superiors. The military "converts citizens into machines," wrote one critic
in 1893, "unintelligently obeying the master mechanic who pulls the wires
and moves the pieces." Carl Schurz, a former U.S. senator and a leading
critic of imperialism, argued in 1899 that an army's obligation to follow the
commands of "a superior will" without question made it in "nature and
spirit an essentially monarchical institution."[4]

As an alternative to the regulars stood the citizen soldier, who either
served in the state-run militia or volunteered for national service in time of
war. These volunteers had a powerful hold on the American imagination.

The nation's independence had been won, many Americans believed, because of the willingness of the minutemen and other militia members to leave behind their plows and shop counters to fight the British regulars. The Civil War, during which hundreds of thousands of Americans had served as state volunteers, created even greater confidence in the efficacy of the citizen soldier. In this somewhat romanticized view of the past, not only did such soldiers win wars, but they also did so without sacrificing the qualities—such as independence and initiative—that made them good Americans. As part-time or temporary soldiers, they avoided the mentality of obedience and dependence that some believed characterized the regular.[5]

During the late nineteenth century, a large number of books, articles, and political speeches extolled the citizen soldier and, either explicitly or implicitly, condemned the regulars. Senator John Logan of Illinois, himself a prominent volunteer general during the Civil War and one of the leading critics of the regular army, sought to distinguish between the motives of the volunteer and the regular. The volunteer, he asserted, fought for "a principle, for right, for justice," in contrast to the man who was a soldier "by mere occupation or by force." Members of the state militia, or National Guard as it came to be known by the 1880s, also received favorable comparisons to the regulars. The regular army was "separated in interest and aspirations from the great body of the people," one congressman declared in 1887, whereas the guardsman "stays at home and does a citizen's work while he keeps alive his sympathies with his fellow citizen." The more fervent advocates of the citizen-soldier ideal went further in their rhetoric, calling the regulars "hirelings" and comparing them to mercenaries.[6]

WASTE, INDOLENCE, AND ARROGANCE

Another problem with the military, as many Americans saw it, was its cost. Although officers of the army and navy complained that Congress was far too stingy in its military appropriations in the years following the Civil War, many political and business leaders resented spending by the government for a purpose that seemed so unproductive, particularly at a time when the United States was not threatened by external enemies. A current of thought popular in business and intellectual circles in the late nineteenth century held that industrialization and increased international trade made war illogical, obsolete, and, not incidentally, bad for business. Many agreed with the Social Darwinist philosopher Herbert Spencer that Western society was evolving beyond the primitive competition of warfare to the higher realm of economic competition. If war had become increasingly unlikely in the new industrial economy, then spending good money on weapons and soldiers in peacetime struck many Americans as especially wasteful. Yale professor and Social Darwinist William Graham Sumner put it succinctly: "Industrialism builds up; militancy wastes."[7]

Defenders of the military carried an additional burden as they tried to fend off attacks on the military's excessive cost and undemocratic nature: the decidedly negative public image of the men in the enlisted ranks of the regular army and the navy. Many Americans saw the enlisted men as social misfits lacking the initiative to take advantage of the opportunities presented by the expanding economy. A New York newspaper captured that point of view in 1877 when it characterized the army as a collection of "bummers, loafers, and foreign paupers." Even the *Army and Navy Journal*, a steadfast supporter of the military, advocated efforts to "elevate the character of the service" so that "the Army shall cease to be looked upon as merely a refuge for the disappointed and the unworthy."[8]

Soldiers and sailors were associated in the public imagination with numerous vices—drinking, gambling, profanity, and prostitution above all. One former soldier who had served in the army in the 1880s suggested that the image was justified. He stated that soldiers were "the most debased in manner of living" of all the men he had known. The fact that some judges allowed convicts to choose between enlistment and jail added to the military's poor reputation. The lyrics of "The Regular Army O!" a popular ballad of the 1870s, referred to the practice: "We had our choice of going to the army or to jail, / Or up the Hudson River with a cop to take a sail." Critics of the military may have exaggerated its status as a refuge for shirkers, criminals, and the dissolute, but enough ne'er-do-wells of various types joined the service to make descriptions of its moral deficiencies seem credible.[9]

Both the army and the navy relied heavily on the urban poor and immigrants to fill the enlisted ranks, a practice that, given the ethnic and class prejudices of the era, contributed to the low standing of the military. In the 1880s as many as half of the navy's enlisted men were foreign-born; in the army, the foreign-born made up from a third to a half of the enlisted soldiers in the three decades following the Civil War. Humorist Mark Twain wrote of the recruits in 1901, "[N]o American-born person can pronounce their names without damage to his jaw nor spell them without a foreign education."[10]

Officers of the army and navy generally had a better image than the enlisted men, but many Americans still looked upon them with disfavor. In the era of rising fortunes and no-holds-barred competition, the career of an officer—characterized as it was by low pay, promotion through seniority, and, in the absence of war, few opportunities to make a mark—struck some as a path fit only for the untalented and unambitious. The view of officers as social drones, enjoying a leisurely existence without important responsibilities, was widespread. Captain Charles King, returning to his home state of Wisconsin to heal from wounds inflicted by Indians, was asked by a businessman: "Well, old fellow, how do you manage to kill time out in the army—nothing but play poker and drink whiskey?"[11]

To some critics, the status and privileges of the officer class seemed to contradict the American values of equality and fairness. Detractors could

1. "The Regular Army O!" A disreputable-looking set of enlisted men on the cover of sheet music for the popular song of the 1870s, "The Regular Army O!" USZ62-68232, Library of Congress.

point to the officers' demands of absolute obedience from subordinates and the inclusion of officers among the social elite in many localities as characteristics of a group that was more aristocratic than democratic. Senator Logan warned that the "feeling of caste-distinction" among the graduates of the Military Academy at West Point posed a potential threat to the American system of government. An army colonel writing in 1906 dismissed the notion that officers formed a special caste, but he observed that Americans looked at military leaders with suspicion in part because they detested "any appearance of assumed or real superior class, of aristocratic clanism or distinction. The public press have pounded the service from time immemorial with the unjust charge of privileged class, putting on airs, assuming superiority over their fellow citizens."[12]

The resentment that many Americans had toward officers became apparent in the public reaction to the case of an army private who disobeyed an order to help with a domestic chore at an officer's home. The army's decision in 1889 to discharge Private Dell P. Wild for refusing that order received national attention. Wild became something of a celebrity, perhaps because the words he was said to have uttered in disobeying the order—"I did not enlist to do any such work. I enlisted as a soldier and not as a servant"—struck a responsive chord. An advertisement for a public appearance by Wild praising his defiance of the "popinjays" and the "military snobocracy" suggested how some Americans perceived officers.[13]

Americans were willing to elect soldiers to office, but they seemed to prefer those who had served as volunteers to the professionals. Most of the presidents of the period had been soldiers—Ulysses Grant, Rutherford Hayes, James Garfield, Benjamin Harrison, and William McKinley had fought in the Civil War, and Theodore Roosevelt gained renown with the Rough Riders in Cuba—but only Grant had been a professional. Even in Grant's case supporters emphasized his civilian experiences; his campaign touted his status as a war hero and also his roots as a tanner from Ohio. Only one other regular officer, General Winfield Scott Hancock, captured the presidential nomination of a major political party during the period between the Civil War and World War I. When Hancock ran as a Democrat in 1880, Republicans and their supporters hastened to distinguish him from Grant. "Hancock is not a soldier in the sense that Grant was a soldier," stated the *New York Tribune*. "He represents the regular army and West Point alone. Grant was of the people, for he entered the army at the beginning of the war from civil life." Hancock lost the election to a volunteer general, James Garfield.[14]

DISAGREEABLE TASKS

The army's direct involvement in two of the most contentious issues of the late nineteenth century—Reconstruction and federal Indian policy—added to the military's poor image. In both cases, the army received criticism not only for its role in the matter but also for its conduct in carrying out federal policies.

Reconstruction brought the wrath of many Americans upon the regular army because Congress made it the main instrument for implementing the federal government's controversial policies in the defeated South following the Civil War—no other agency of the government had the size and strength to take on that role. In the immediate aftermath of the war, the army was present in the southern states as an occupying force, and even after President Andrew Johnson permitted the reestablishment of state governments, federal soldiers remained to preserve order. Army officers also provided the leadership and much of the personnel for the Freedman's Bureau, an agency created by Congress to aid the emancipated slaves. Relations between the soldiers and the white population of the South were generally tense. The whites, already inclined to detest the army as the agent of the Confederacy's defeat, resented the continuing presence of the soldiers, many of whom were black. The occasional mistreatment of civilians by the troops, as when some soldiers burned down a Texas town in 1866, added to the tension.[15]

The antagonism of southern whites toward the U.S. military grew even greater when Congress increased the army's authority over the South. In 1867 the Republican Congress, having refused to recognize the state governments that President Johnson had sanctioned, divided the southern states into five military districts, each commanded by an army general. The Reconstruction Act made the existing state governments provisional and subject to the district commander, whose responsibilities included the registration and protection of eligible voters—in particular the newly enfranchised blacks—and the supervision of elections for delegates to state constitutional conventions. Congress gave the commanders the power to remove uncooperative state officials from office and to use military courts for law enforcement when, in the commander's judgment, the civil courts failed to act or to treat all citizens equally. The responsibilities of the district commander would end in a given state once Congress had voted to admit its representatives.[16]

The district commanders used their authority with varying degrees of enthusiasm. Some clearly sympathized with the southern whites and did little to help the blacks. Nevertheless, many of those whites, angry over policies that brought the former slaves into the political process while excluding many former Confederate leaders, complained of military repression. They objected when military commanders removed from office recalcitrant elected officials—including the governors of Louisiana, Texas, and Georgia. When the commanders stationed their soldiers close to polling places on election day in order to protect black voters from violence, many whites protested that the military was trying to overawe Democratic voters. The heavy-handed actions of some officers stirred even more ill feeling against the army. For instance, commanders closed down a number of newspapers that had been critical of the army, and one general ordered the suspension of an Alabama bishop who had encouraged clergy to omit prayers for "all in civil authority" from Sunday services. The suspension drew protests from both southerners and northerners, and the general eventually revoked it.[17]

Opponents of Congressional Reconstruction made the role of federal troops in the southern states a central part of their rhetorical attack on Republican policies and played upon traditional American worries about the threat to liberty and democracy posed by a standing army. President Johnson warned that the policies of congressional Republicans had brought the South under the "absolute despotism" of military rule. Of the Reconstruction Act of 1867, he made the hyperbolic declaration, "No master ever had a control so absolute over the slaves as this bill gives to the military officers over both white and colored persons." Frank Blair, the Democratic candidate for vice president in 1868 and a volunteer general for the Union during the war, claimed that the Republican policies would lead to a military dictatorship. Democratic newspapers in both the South and the North regularly attacked Congressional Reconstruction for placing civilian authorities under "bayonet rule."[18]

Although such language was politically motivated, it raised questions about the role of the military that made many Americans uneasy. That uneasiness grew more acute after 1870, when all of the southern states had been readmitted to the Union and the military districts had ceased to function, yet federal troops remained in the South. The troops were there to preserve law and order, said the Radical Republicans, and to protect the civil rights of African Americans; Democrats insisted that the soldiers were present to ensure that southern Republicans stayed in power. Opponents of Reconstruction pointed to the Ku Klux Klan Act of 1871, which authorized federal officials to employ the army to aid in arresting individuals who used violence to deprive citizens of their rights, as additional evidence of the Radicals' penchant for bayonet rule. The dire warnings of the critics aside, the South was in no danger of falling under military tyranny. The army had only about 8,000 soldiers stationed in the region, and the Grant administration, sensing the increasing weariness of northerners regarding Reconstruction, had little appetite for the aggressive use of troops. Outside of South Carolina, where federal soldiers played an important role in breaking up the Ku Klux Klan, the army acted only sporadically against the white conservatives who were using terror to drive blacks and white Unionists out of politics.[19]

The growing distaste for military measures became apparent in the public response to General Philip Sheridan's deployment of federal troops to resolve a political quarrel in Louisiana in 1875. Disputed results in the state's fraud- and violence-filled legislative elections of 1874 left it unclear which party would control the legislature when it met to organize in January 1875. When Democratic legislators used appointed sergeants-at-arms to claim the speaker's chair and declare their candidates the winners of the disputed seats, the Republican governor requested assistance from General Sheridan, who had recently been placed in command of the Department of the Gulf by President Grant. Sheridan authorized a detachment of soldiers to enter the statehouse and remove the legislators not approved by Louisiana's Returning Board, thereby restoring the legislature to the Republicans. This action, coupled with Sheridan's statement that the members of the state's White League were "banditti" who should be tried by military commissions, provoked outcries not only in Louisiana but throughout the nation as well. Newspapers denounced Sheridan in their editorials, state legislatures passed resolutions condemning the action, and the governors of Ohio, Georgia, and Wisconsin issued statements of censure. Even many Republicans were troubled by the image of armed soldiers marching into a legislative chamber in support of one faction in a political dispute. President Grant offered only a halfhearted defense of Sheridan, and the administration, which had already become hesitant to approve military intervention in the South, became even more reluctant to use troops.[20]

FRANK LESLIE'S ILLUSTRATED NEWSPAPER

No. 1,008—Vol. XXXIX.]   NEW YORK, JANUARY 23, 1875.   [Price 10 Cents.

WE ARE IN THE MIDST OF A REVOLUTION TENDING FAST TO THE CONCENTRATION OF ALL POWER IN THE HANDS OF ONE MAN.

2. "Grant's Last Outrage in Louisiana." A political cartoon on the cover of the January 23, 1875 issue of *Frank Leslie's Illustrated Newspaper* depicts Uncle Sam protesting as President Ulysses S. Grant, dressed in his old military uniform, directs a group of armed soldiers who are escorting legislators out of a government building. The cartoon, which appeared a few weeks after federal troops had entered the Louisiana state house to help the Republicans establish control of the legislature, evokes the concerns about military despotism and "bayonet rule" that the Democrats often raised in response to the government's use of the military in Reconstruction. LC-USZ62-127921, Library of Congress.

Reconstruction service damaged the army's reputation considerably. It entangled soldiers in a contentious political struggle, with the result that their actions inevitably seemed partisan in nature. When the army acted vigorously to protect the rights of southern blacks, conservatives asserted that it had become a tool of the Republicans for preserving their party's control of the southern states. When it acted cautiously, on the other hand, Radical Republicans accused officers of complicity with the southern Democrats.[21]

The army also drew condemnations from many Americans for its efforts to carry out the nation's Indian policy. Frontier whites blasted the army for failing to conduct a ruthless war against the western tribes, while humanitarians criticized it for being too aggressive. General Sherman reflected the military's frustration with its position when he wrote that there existed "two classes of people, one demanding the utter extinction of the Indians, and the other full of love for their conversion to civilization and Christianity. Unfortunately the army stands between and gets the cuff from both sides."[22]

Those who believed the army was not doing enough pointed to the continuation of Indian attacks on whites in the West despite years of campaigning by federal troops. They criticized the failure of the army to keep open the Bozeman Trail against the Sioux in the late 1860s, the seemingly inept attempts to defeat a small group of Modoc Indians besieged in northern California's lava beds in the early 1870s, and the tardy pursuit in 1877 of the Nez Perce led by Chief Joseph. The inability of the army to stop raids by Apache bands until the capture of Geronimo in 1886 also injured its prestige among frontier whites.[23]

For other Americans, though, the problem with the army was its rough, and sometimes brutal, treatment of the Indians. A small but influential group of humanitarians in the East kept up a steady verbal attack on the army for its conduct of the Indian wars. Army officers, they asserted, deliberately goaded the tribes into conflict, and the soldiers stationed near reservations corrupted tribal members. The humanitarians were especially critical of what they regarded as the army's readiness to kill Indian noncombatants as well as warriors. The killing of women and children by soldiers in attacks on the Cheyenne along the Washita River in 1868, on the Piegans near the Marias River in 1870, and on the Sioux at Wounded Knee in 1890 brought an outpouring of denunciations of the army. Commanders such as Sherman and Sheridan defended the soldiers and contended that such deaths were an unavoidable result of Indian warfare, but some critics charged the army with carrying out a conscious campaign of extermination.[24]

By the late 1880s, with Reconstruction over and the Indian wars largely at an end, the army's reputation began to rise. Relieved of two controversial duties, the army no longer attracted the criticisms of civilians upset with what it had done or failed to do in the South or on the frontier. A revival of interest in the Civil War—indicated by an increase in published writings on the subject as well as in membership in the main organization of Union veterans, the Grand Army of the Republic—suggested a growing acceptance of things military. So did the popularity of Charles King's novels about army life in the West. A former army captain, King countered the common view of indolent officers and debauched enlisted men with depictions of frontier soldiers as active, resourceful, and morally upright. By the 1890s a critic of the military expressed alarm at the resurgence of public interest in the armed services. "Like other agues that shake the body politic," he wrote, "militarism is intermittent. After our civil war a chill set in. Men had had enough soldiering for one generation. Now again a rising temperature bespeaks a strong accession of military fever."[25]

The regular army's success in restoring order in several major conflicts between management and labor helped explain its improved standing with many civilians. In 1877 President Rutherford B. Hayes, responding to calls for assistance from state governors, ordered federal troops to intervene in the massive railroad workers' strike that tied up rail traffic and sparked violence through much of the nation. In 1894 President Grover Cleveland used the army to break up a strike by employees of the Pullman Palace Car Company and the boycott of Pullman cars by the American Railway Union, and the government dispatched federal soldiers to the Coeur d'Alene area of northern Idaho periodically during the 1890s to keep order during a struggle between mine owners and unionized miners. In each of these episodes the army won praise for carrying out its duties with efficiency and restraint. To those Americans made anxious by the rioting that accompanied the labor unrest, the army became a comforting presence.[26]

Many observers compared the regulars' conduct in the strikes favorably with that of the state National Guard troops. In 1877 many members of the National Guard had sympathized with the strikers and refused to move against them—a number of Guard units in Maryland, Pennsylvania, Iowa, Indiana, Missouri, and West Virginia simply fell apart in the face of the upheaval. A similar collapse of portions of the Guard occurred in California during the 1894 strike. Other National Guard units were too quick to respond with force and opened fire on strikers and rioters. In 1877 the efforts of Guard units and the police to quell riots in Chicago, Pittsburgh, and other cities left dozens of civilians dead and wounded. In contrast, the regulars were not responsible for a single death. In 1894 the army used more force— regular troops shot at protesting crowds in California, Indiana, and Illinois and killed five men as a result—but still was less likely than the police or the Guard to open fire.[27]

Not all Americans were pleased with the army's performance. Labor unions and their supporters pointed out that the interventions favored management over the striking workers. The railroad and mining companies, they complained, used the soldiers as tools to protect their interests. The critics denounced the close cooperation between army officers and company managers—in some cases the managers directed the disposition of troops—and noted that regulars were used to guard the private property of the railroad and mining companies. In the 1894 railroad strike, the army escorted trains carrying replacement workers. Moreover, by arresting or driving away the strikers, the soldiers helped ensure that the strikes would fail. "The capitalist and the scab are on top," commented labor leader Eugene Debs in 1892, "and the armies of the Union, with shotted guns, stand guard to see that they remain on top."[28]

At first the union movement directed little of its anger against the soldiers themselves but kept the focus of its criticism on the company owners and political leaders who, in labor's view, misused the army. By the 1890s, however, the federal government's more aggressive use of the regulars to stop the railroad workers' and miners' strikes caused many in the labor movement to take a more disapproving view of the army. Warnings of the dangers of standing armies and "military despotism" began to appear in the labor press. Some labor organizations and journals also began to disparage the regulars in language that Americans had long used to express their distrust of the professional military. They described soldiers as "hirelings" and "lackeys" who lived lives of dissipation at the public's expense. Governor John Peter Altgeld of Illinois, a strong supporter of organized labor, followed the well-established rhetorical tradition of comparing the virtuous volunteer soldier with the heartless professional. "The volunteer carries a conscience as well as a gun," Altgeld said, making the volunteer less than perfectly dependable when called upon to do "dastardly work." For such tasks, said the governor, the government relied on the regulars. Officers, many of whom had worked closely with company managers during the strikes, came in for particular abuse. One labor journal described the "strutting gilt lace, sword jingle and circus trapping that makes every West Point cadet and small officer swell up in pompous arrogance, as if he were a little tin god looking down in sneering contempt on the whole work-a-day world below!"[29]

Most middle-class Americans, however, appreciated the army's role in halting the disorder that accompanied the strikes. With few exceptions, the popular press applauded the army's conduct in responding to the unrest. "One thousand [regulars] are worth all the militiamen . . . brought into service," the *New York Times* declared in 1877. "Mobs appreciate the difference so clearly," said a Boston newspaper in 1894, "that as a rule regulars are able to effect without firing a shot what militia could not accomplish without severe fighting." Some in the press saw in the strikes a reason for the country to maintain a large peacetime army; rather than endangering liberties, they argued, such a force would protect lives and property from rampaging rioters.[30]

EXPANSION, WAR, AND SCANDAL

The navy largely avoided the level of criticism that the army experienced. Certainly the small and dilapidated navy of the two decades following the Civil War enjoyed little respect, but the nature of the navy's mission left it out of the sight and therefore out of the thoughts of most Americans. While the army grappled with the politically charged problems of Reconstruction and the conflict between whites and Indians, the navy quietly went about its business of showing the flag in foreign ports and occasionally protecting American citizens and property overseas. In addition, there existed no tradition of fearing the peacetime navy as a threat to liberties and democracy in the way that some Americans feared standing armies. As a naval officer observed in 1881, "an increase of the navy is not considered by either political party as dangerous to the institutions of the country." One congressman in 1886 even promoted a strong navy as means of safeguarding the country from the dangers posed by a standing army. A navy capable of protecting the nation's shores, he suggested, made a large army unnecessary.[31]

By the 1880s the navy's relatively positive image brought benefits in the form of increased congressional appropriations. Supporters of the navy pointed to the abysmal condition of the fleet—it consisted mostly of outmoded Civil War–era craft and ranked below the navies of such nations as Egypt and Brazil—and argued that national pride as well as the national interest demanded a larger and more modern force. The increased appropriations gave the navy new steam-powered steel ships. These new ships, in turn, brought more favorable attention to the navy. In 1889 Secretary of the Navy Benjamin Franklin Tracy, recognizing the public interest in the modern vessels, ordered the navy's first steel cruisers—the *Atlanta*, *Boston*, and *Chicago*—to make well-publicized visits to American ports as the "Squadron of Evolution."[32]

As the squadron's tour suggested, the navy and its civilian advocates were making deliberate efforts to popularize the service. A growing number of articles on the navy, many of them written by naval officers, appeared in the nation's popular magazines. Widely read books by Theodore Roosevelt and Captain Alfred Thayer Mahan emphasized the vital role of navies throughout history in winning wars and developing national power. Navy supporters took advantage of the public's interest in new technologies to promote the building of faster, stronger, and more technologically advanced cruisers and battleships. The best example of the navy's increasing skill at public relations was its exhibit at the Columbian Exposition in Chicago in 1893. At an earlier opportunity for public recognition, the Centennial Exhibition in 1876, the navy had provided only some uniforms, weapons, and small-scale models of historic ships for display. For the 1893 Exposition, however, the navy constructed an impressive full-scale model of a battleship. The 348-foot-long *Illinois*, resting on stilts in Lake Michigan, drew large crowds of exposition-goers, who watched in fascination as the crew of real sailors fired the ship's guns and conducted drills.[33]

The navy's popularity increased dramatically when the United States went to war with Spain in 1898. Credit for the quick American victory in the conflict went largely to the navy, which won decisive victories over its Spanish counterpart at Manila Bay in the Philippines and Santiago in Cuba. The navy's feats of skill and daring delighted the public, especially the arduous voyage of the battleship *Oregon* from its West Coast port around Cape Horn to join the main fleet in the Caribbean, and Commodore George Dewey's attack on the Spanish fleet at Manila. Dewey became the war's leading hero. His image seemed ubiquitous, appearing even in advertisements, and tens of thousands of citizens gathered in New York City to greet him upon his return to the United States in 1899.[34]

The army contributed to the victory too but gained far less positive publicity than the navy. The army's capture of San Juan Hill outside of Santiago and its successful campaigns to take Manila and Puerto Rico from the Spanish were overshadowed by the failures of its supply system early in the war and its inability to deal effectively with outbreaks of disease among soldiers serving in Cuba and in camps within the United States.[35]

Early in the war, the army's supply problems captured the attention of the press and the public. The War Department's supply bureaus were ill prepared for the sudden mobilization of the army, which swelled in size from 28,747 officers and enlisted men before the war to nearly 300,000 by its end. To be fair, the bureaus had received little guidance from the McKinley administration about what the army's role in the war would be, and the congressional appropriation for the wartime buildup came only a month before the start of the hostilities. Those factors, coupled with the inefficiencies of the bureaus, meant that the army faced embarrassing shortages of important materials in the first months of the war. At the camp near Tampa, Florida, that served as the assembly point for the invasion force headed for Cuba, a mere two rail lines brought in train cars carrying a hodgepodge of supplies, and many cars arrived without a bill of lading to indicate what they contained. The inadequate system for unloading cargo at Tampa created congestion that had cars full of freight languishing on sidings as far north as Columbia, South Carolina. At other camps, volunteers went without uniforms, tents, and weapons for weeks or months. With many of the soldiers writing to family members or their hometown newspapers to complain about the shortages, the failings of the supply system became widely known.[36]

A more deadly problem was the army's failure to cope with the spread of disease among the troops. Poor sanitation in many of the camps in the United States caused typhoid and dysentery to spread at alarming rates. The army's Medical Department proved unequal to the challenge, and the press provided shocked Americans with accounts of the miserable conditions in camp hospitals. Malaria afflicted the soldiers in Cuba in the weeks following the American victory at Santiago, something most Americans back home first learned about when the press obtained and published a bluntly worded letter written by a group of officers to their commander demanding that their troops be returned to the United States before disease wiped them out. The War Department scrambled to withdraw the soldiers and transport them to a hastily established camp on Long Island. There the ailing soldiers stumbled off the "fever ships," as the press called the vessels that carried them from Cuba, only to find a camp lacking adequate provisions and medical facilities. Disease killed most of the American servicemen who died in the war—only 379 of the 5,462 military deaths in the conflict resulted from combat. Some of the deaths from disease may have been unavoidable, especially considering the state of medical knowledge at the time, but in the eyes of many Americans the army's incompetence and indifference had added to the high death toll.[37]

President McKinley, seeking to quiet the public's anger over the mismanagement of the army, appointed a special commission to investigate the matter. The commission, headed by Grenville Dodge, a prominent businessman, and composed of both army officers and civilians, conducted its inquiry in late 1898. The Dodge Commission's work helped to dampen the controversy to a degree; it concluded that the problems resulted not from corruption and malfeasance but from outdated procedures and poor organization within the War Department. The army could take some solace in the fact that much of the blame fell on the civilian head of the War Department, Secretary of War Russell Alger, but many uniformed officers serving in the department's staff bureaus received criticism as well.[38]

The aspect of the commission's work that attracted the most attention, however, was its investigation of the sensational charges made by Major General Nelson Miles, commanding general of the army, about the beef supplied to troops during the war. General Miles—Civil War hero, famed Indian fighter, and a critic of the administration's handling of the war—asserted that the army's Commissary Department had procured canned and refrigerated beef that was at best unpalatable and at worst hazardous to the health of those who ate it. The refrigerated meat, he said, had been treated with chemicals, or "embalmed," as he put it, to help preserve it from spoiling. The head of the Commissary Department, Brigadier General Charles P. Eagan, denied the charges and used abrasive language to denounce Miles in a public hearing. Miles's accusation, Eagan declared, was a lie, and "I wish to force the lie back into his throat, covered with the contents of a camp latrine." The Dodge Commission determined that the canned beef was edible, though perhaps not tasty, and that the refrigerated meat had received no chemical treatment. Even so, the "embalmed beef" scandal, with its spectacle of squabbling and name calling among high-ranking officers, cast the army in a poor light.[39]

NEW ROLES, OLD CONCERNS

With its victory over Spain, the United States joined the ranks of the world's imperial powers. For the first time in its history the United States held overseas colonies, and the initial responsibility for governing these possessions fell to the army and the navy. The task of administering the former Spanish island of Guam went to the navy, while the army took charge in Cuba, Puerto Rico, and the Philippines. In the case of the latter three places, military rule did not last long—the army handed over authority to American civilians in Puerto Rico and the Philippines in 1900 and 1901 respectively and to a Cuban government in 1902. During that brief period, however, officers earned high marks in much of the American press for their work as colonial administrators. Americans read in their newspapers and magazines about the army's efforts to build schools and roads, improve sanitation in towns and villages, provide inoculations against disease, and establish the structures of representative government. Such projects helped improve the military's public image.[40]

The aftermath of the Spanish-American War also found the army, navy, and marines playing a new role as agents of a more assertive American foreign policy. The expansion of American economic interests abroad, as well as the rise of potential adversaries such as Germany and Japan, caused American leaders to look to the military not only to protect American citizens and property overseas—something it had always been asked to do—but also to safeguard strategic points such as the Panama Canal and the Philippines. The leaders also called upon the military to intervene in Caribbean and Central American countries experiencing political upheaval with the goal of establishing stability and discouraging other powers from getting involved. Between 1900 and 1917, the government gave the army and navy such responsibilities in Panama, Cuba, Haiti, the Dominican Republic, Nicaragua, and Mexico. The interventions were controversial within the United States, and many Americans deplored the use of the military for such ends. To those who viewed the interventions as necessary and desirable, however, the idea of U.S. soldiers, sailors, and marines taking charge and restoring order in foreign lands had considerable appeal. During China's Boxer Rebellion of 1900, for instance, army and marine units received much favorable publicity for their efforts as part of an international force that marched from the coast to Peking in order to rescue the foreign citizens trapped there by the anti-Western Boxers.[41]

The army's campaign against Filipino nationalists who resisted American control of the archipelago also drew favorable attention, but it attracted criticism as well, in part because not all Americans believed that the United States should retain the Philippines as a colony, and in part because of the harsh methods some in the army used to defeat the nationalists. The insurgency, which began in 1899 and lasted for three years, sought to force the withdrawal of the Americans and establish the Philippines as an independent nation. Determined to hold on to the colony, Presidents William McKinley and Theodore Roosevelt sent over 125,000 U.S. soldiers to the islands during the three-year period. Despite periodic setbacks, the army conducted a successful fight against the insurgents. After destroying the army of nationalist leader Emilio Aguinaldo in 1899, the Americans spent the next two years battling Filipino guerilla forces in the countryside. The daring mission that resulted in the capture of Aguinaldo in 1901 made its leader, Brigadier General Frederick Funston, a national hero.[42]

Other stories that came out of the Philippines, however, were less pleasing to Americans. Accounts of U.S. troops destroying foodstuffs, burning down villages, and killing Filipino noncombatants provoked a controversy similar to that surrounding the army's practices in the earlier Indian wars. Journalists also reported that some U.S. soldiers were torturing suspected insurgents. Much of the press coverage focused on the soldiers' use of the "water cure," a procedure that involved forcing dirty water down the throat of a prisoner until he agreed to tell interrogators what they wanted to know. Critics of American policy in the Philippines argued that the army's methods shamed the country and showed how a war of conquest brutalized those involved. The army and its defenders countered that the anti-imperialists had exaggerated the accounts of cruelty to undercut public support for the war, and that the atrocities committed by Filipino guerillas were far worse than anything the Americans had done.[43]

Commanding General Nelson Miles, never one to shy away from controversy, gave the atrocity allegations greater credibility when he asserted after a tour of the Philippines that some troops had committed acts "which are not in accordance with the rules of civilized warfare and are detrimental to the honor and discipline of the army."[44] In 1902 a Senate committee examined the accusations. Republicans supportive of the Roosevelt administration's Philippines policy controlled the inquiry, and the result was mostly favorable to the army. Not so favorable were the highly publicized court-martial trials of Major Littleton Waller of the marines and General Jacob Smith of the army, both accused of giving orders that led to the torture and killing of prisoners and civilians during the campaign to pacify the island of Samar. A military court acquitted Waller, but General Smith, alleged to have commanded subordinates to kill all males on Samar over the age of ten and to turn the island's interior into a "howling wilderness," was convicted. Although with the end of the insurgency the atrocity allegations gradually faded from the headlines, stories of soldiers administering the water cure and laying waste to Filipino villages were powerful and colored the way Americans viewed the army. Like the accounts of "fever ships" and "embalmed beef" in the war against Spain, such scandals kept the army's reputation from rising as far as success in defeating its enemies might otherwise have carried it.[45]

Although the army and navy had new responsibilities and greater resources following the Spanish-American War, they found that many of the concerns civilians had about the military remained the same. Some Americans continued to warn of the dangers presented by standing armies and professional soldiers, and many continued to hold a low opinion of the men who served in the army and navy. Anti-imperialists took the lead in expressing uneasiness about the military. One of the dangers of owning an overseas empire, they argued, would be the increase in the size and influence of the nation's armed forces that the empire would necessitate. They made fears of militarism—the predominance of military values and military interests in society—a central part of their case against holding colonies. The anti-imperialist leader Carl Schurz warned that the large military necessary to hold colonies and compete with the other powers would harm the nation's economy and undermine democracy. Nothing was more likely to weaken a nation's adherence to constitutional government, he said, than "warlike excitements, which at the same time give to the armed forces an importance and a prestige which they otherwise would not possess." Democratic candidate William Jennings Bryan sounded a similar theme in his campaign for the presidency in 1900: "The army is the personification of force, and militarism will inevitably change the ideals of the people, and turn the thoughts of our young men from the arts of peace to the science of war. The government which relies for its defense upon its citizens is more likely to be just than one which has at call a large body of professional soldiers."[46]

Defenders of the military, more vocal than they had been in the 1870s and 1880s, dismissed such characterizations. "There is no more danger that military training and the military spirit in our country will develop militarism," wrote an army major, "than that any boy who learns how to box is going to become a professional prize-fighter, ready to hit anything in sight." Theodore Roosevelt, the Republican candidate for vice president in 1900, criticized those who saw the army as a threat to democracy. During the election campaign he asked audiences to stamp their feet if they disapproved of what he characterized as Democratic insults against the nation's military heroes; in one speech he called for veterans and "boys in blue" in the audience to join him on the stage, and then, pointing to the men, exclaimed, "Behold your tyrants!" William Jennings Bryan's decisive loss in the 1900 presidential election suggests that most Americans did not share the Democratic candidate's concerns about the army. Nevertheless, the persistent warnings about militarism by Bryan and others helped keep the Jeffersonian distrust of the military alive and fairly healthy.[47]

The old notion of soldiers and sailors as reprobates in uniform also proved durable. A booklet published by the army in 1904 noted the prevalence of "the idea that to be a soldier of our Regular Army is to be in a position which is below that of the ordinary citizen, and which entails duties and labors degrading to an American." Opponents of militarism, eager to paint the army and navy in unflattering hues, wrote of the "pollutions of camp life" and the "vile festival" of sexual practices that allegedly occurred aboard naval ships. Officers complained frequently about such stereotypes and other evidence of civilian prejudice against members of the military, such as the failure of most states to pass laws allowing soldiers and sailors to establish residency for purposes of voting or the exclusion of enlisted men from some places of business. In 1906 a sailor's lawsuit against a Rhode Island amusement company that had sold him a ticket to a dance while he was dressed in civilian clothes but denied him admission when he returned later in uniform gained nationwide attention, especially after the sailor received $100 to help with legal fees from a sympathetic Theodore Roosevelt. The harassment of enlisted men by the local police also irritated members of the military. In 1907 the *Army and Navy Journal* accused the police in San Antonio, Texas, and other cities with military posts nearby of arresting soldiers on "the slightest provocation" and keeping them in jail under false charges.[48]

As these examples suggested, Americans of the early twentieth century remained ambivalent about the military. Certainly it had risen significantly in public regard since the 1870s, but traditional suspicion of the regular military persisted, and many Americans still preferred to rely on the volunteer rather than the professional for their defense. The nation's political leaders either shared those attitudes or at least had to pay them some deference, with results that strongly affected the size, structure, and purpose of the American armed forces.

2

Congress, Popular Opinion, and the Making of Military Policy

The typical member of Congress in the late nineteenth century had little reason to spend much time thinking about the nation's military policy. With the natural defensive barrier provided by the Atlantic and Pacific oceans and with friendly neighbors on its borders, the United States faced no danger of invasion by a hostile power. All that the country seemed to need was a navy of sufficient size to provide assistance to the occasional American missionary or merchant in trouble in foreign lands, and an army large enough to deal with the diminishing number of Indians still resisting the expansion of whites into the West. The military need not cost much, most members of Congress agreed, and it required little in the way of new technology or new forms of organization. The military matters most likely to hold the attention of senators and congressmen concerned the opportunities for patronage and other benefits to constituents that the army and navy could provide. But while most members of Congress welcomed the presence of a navy shipyard or army post in their home state or district, they shared with most Americans a degree of suspicion of the military and looked to keep spending on the armed services to a minimum.

By the turn of the century, however, attitudes in Congress began to change. Hostility to the military decreased, and appropriations for the services rose significantly. A number of developments explain the shift in attitude, chief among them, the expansion of the American economy, the perceived importance of international trade, the realization that improvements in naval technology made the United States more vulnerable to attacks from abroad, and, after the Spanish-American War of 1898, the existence of an overseas American empire. Equally important was the fact that officers had become more adept at finding ways to build support for the armed services among the public and within Congress. While members of Congress continued to view the military as an important source of patronage, they also became more inclined to see the army and navy as essential to the nation's security and as vital instruments of foreign policy. The military still had many critics in Congress, and the legislators certainly did not grant the services everything they wanted, but by the early twentieth century the relationship between Congress and the military had improved considerably.

CONGRESS AND THE MILITARY: PATRONAGE, POSTS, AND SHIPYARDS

Under the Constitution, the president, Congress, and the states shared responsibility for the nation's military. The Constitution gave both the executive and legislative branches authority over the military on the national level; at the state level both the president and the state governments could exercise control over the militia. The division of authority had its advantages—for one, it kept any one part of the civilian government from gaining complete control over the military. The authority of Congress to pass laws, approve appointments, and determine appropriations, for instance, counterbalanced the president's substantial authority as commander in chief. The main disadvantage of the system of divided authority was that it made the creation of a coherent and consistent military policy difficult to achieve. Presidents and Congress were frequently at odds over such matters as the size of the military budget or promotion policies. Many in the military found it frustrating to have to answer to Congress as well as the president, and they grew impatient with the system's inefficiency.[1]

Although Congress played a limited role in the day-to-day management of the armed services, its influence pervaded almost every aspect of the military's existence. Congress established the size of the military through the appropriation process. It passed laws that determined the organization of the services, promotion policies, pay rates for military personnel, and the regulations that governed conduct within the military. The Senate had the authority to approve or turn down officers nominated for promotion by the president. In addition, Congress largely controlled access to the service academies. Each year, young men nominated for admission by members of Congress filled most of the available openings in the entering classes at the Naval Academy in Annapolis and the Military Academy at West Point. Members of Congress also intervened in the affairs of the War or Navy Department in the interest of friends or constituents serving in the military. The member might pester the departments or even the White House to transfer a favored officer to a more desirable ship or post or to a coveted staff position in Washington. Secretary of the Navy Richard W. Thompson complained in the 1870s that he had been "annoyed almost to death" by the congressional demands on behalf of particular officers. Loath to disappoint influential members of Congress, the departments often agreed to the requests.[2]

Within Congress, members tended to look to a handful of senators and representatives for guidance on military issues. Both the House and the Senate had a committee on military affairs and a committee on naval affairs, and members of those bodies exercised tremendous influence on matters regarding the army and navy. The chairmen of the committees were especially important. They possessed a combination of authority and expertise that made them a crucial part of the policymaking process. Most of them had spent years as junior members of the committee before rising to the chair, and they often held the chairman's position for long periods as well. Pennsylvania Republican James D. Cameron, for example, chaired the Senate Committee on Naval Affairs for all but two of the years between 1881 and 1897. Cameron's successor, Maine Republican Eugene Hale, ran the committee for the next twelve years. Joseph Hawley of Connecticut presided over the Senate Committee on Military Affairs for sixteen years, while Congressman John A. T. Hull of Iowa spent an equal number of years as chairman of the House Committee on Military Affairs. Legislation concerning the military—including spending bills and measures to authorize promotions—could rarely make headway in Congress without first gaining the approval of such powerful chairmen.[3]

A significant portion of the senators and congressmen of the late nineteenth and early twentieth centuries had served in the military during the Civil War. Chairmen Hawley and Hull had both fought for the Union, as had such prominent members as James Garfield of Ohio and John Logan of Illinois. Service in the war did not necessarily mean that such men became advocates of the regular army, however. Most of the veterans had been volunteers, and as such they often had great confidence in the fighting ability of the citizen soldier and little regard for the regulars. Many noted that professional soldiers had not always performed well in the war—here they pointed to lackluster performances by West Point graduates such as George McClellan and Ambrose Burnside. Some of the former volunteers expressed the belief that elitist West Pointers had favored their own during the war and failed to recognize deserving volunteers. Senator John Logan's resentment over General William T. Sherman's decision in 1864 to pass him over for command of the Army of the Tennessee in favor of a graduate of the Military Academy undoubtedly contributed to the fervor with which the senator sought to reduce military expenditures in the 1870s.[4]

For most members of Congress, regardless of party, the military represented a welcome source of patronage and pork-barrel spending. Members understood that an Army Corps of Engineers project to improve a harbor or waterway in their state or district boosted the local economy by providing an infusion of dollars and making it easier to transport goods. An army post in the area offered not only security but created business for local concerns

3. USS *Baltimore* in dry-dock at Mare Island Navy Yard, 1890s. Members of Congress valued navy shipyards and army posts for the economic activity they generated and the opportunities for patronage they provided. Members worked hard to bring shipyards and posts to their home states or districts and, once they were established, to keep them open. The Mare Island Navy Yard, located in San Francisco Bay, was the navy's main facility on the West Coast. #NH 71055, Naval Historical Center.

ranging from livestock breeders to saloon owners. An active navy shipyard—requiring an abundance of labor and construction material—could be especially important to the economy of a port city. Some members of Congress used the posts or shipyards in their districts to reward political supporters. A congressman might see to it that a local businessman received the contract to supply food to an army post or lumber to a shipyard. A number of shipyards were notorious for providing hundreds of jobs to local men during election years. Military facilities located in the states and districts of powerful members of Congress often thrived. Senator Henry Cabot Lodge of Massachusetts made sure that the Boston Naval Yard remained one of the nation's busiest, and Francis E. Warren of Wyoming, chairman of the Senate Military Affairs Committee, pushed the army to make Fort D. A. Russell, located near Cheyenne, a major post.[5]

The political value of posts and shipyards meant that members of Congress worked hard to protect them. Periodic efforts by the War and Navy

Departments to economize by closing facilities they deemed unnecessary often faced strong opposition from the members of Congress representing the affected states and districts. The army wanted to close many of its small frontier posts as the Indian wars came to an end, and as the expansion of railroads made it easier to move troops from place to place. The effort met with political resistance, but by the 1890s the War Department had succeeded in shutting down a good number of the more isolated and insignificant posts. In 1895 troops were stationed at only 77 posts, far below the 197 that had existed in 1870. The posts that remained, however, were often politically well defended. In 1911 the plans of General Leonard Wood, the army's chief of staff, and Secretary of War Henry L. Stimson to make further reductions in the number of posts stirred the wrath of congressional Republicans and Democrats alike. Stimson's announcement that eighteen "obsolete" posts could be abandoned immediately without harming army operations led alarmed members to attach a rider placing a moratorium on closings to the army appropriation bill.[6]

THE CAMPAIGN AGAINST THE ARMY

In 1874 the political cartoonist Thomas Nast published a series of cartoons in the magazine *Harper's Weekly* on the subject of military appropriations. One of the cartoons depicted two skeletons standing at attention before the Capitol Dome, one representing the navy and the other the army, with the caption "What Congress proposes to reduce our Army and Navy to." Another cartoon showed a skeleton in a soldier's uniform guarding the gate of a frontier fort while a group of Indians in war regalia approached. Nast's main point came through clearly—congressional parsimony in spending on the army and navy threatened to starve the military to the point that it would become useless. Nast and other friends of the military were concerned because during the late 1860s and 1870s, Congress seemed determined to make significant cuts in the size of the armed services. Led by congressional Democrats irate over the army's involvement in Reconstruction, the drive to trim military appropriations and limit the role of the army in domestic affairs reached the peak of its strength in the 1870s. Representative James Garfield noted in 1878 that there existed in Congress a rising "spirit of unfriendliness, if not positive hostility, toward the Army." The omnipresent threat of reductions and restrictions left the army, in the words of General Philip Sheridan, "in a condition of constant panic all the time."[7]

The shrinking of the army following the Civil War, while certainly expected, was nevertheless dramatic. With the demobilization of volunteer regiments, the army dropped in size from over a million men in May 1865 to fewer than 200,000 by the end of the year. As the demobilization continued in 1866, Congress decided to establish the army's postwar strength at just over 54,000 officers and enlisted men. The army had reason to be pleased with that decision—it authorized a force considerably larger than the 18,000 soldiers serving in army before the war. The willingness of Congress to approve a larger army arose from the desire of the Republican majority to ensure that there would be enough troops available to carry out occupation duties in the defeated South and to protect white settlements and railroad construction crews from the increasingly restive tribes of the Great Plains. Not all Republicans were content with the army's new size, however. In 1867 John Logan of Illinois and Benjamin Butler of Massachusetts, both newly elected Republican congressmen who had served as volunteer generals in the war, sponsored legislation to cut the number of officers in the army substantially. Congressman James Garfield led the successful resistance to this measure. The hatred of congressmen like Logan for the regular army, Garfield noted, "amounts almost to insanity."[8]

Garfield and other friends of the army could not contain the budget-cutting impulse for long. In 1869 Congress voted to reduce the army to a maximum of 37,313. Five years later, Congress had set the size of the army at 27,000 officers and enlisted men, and the number would remain below 30,000 for the next quarter century. The measures to reduce the size of the army had the enthusiastic support of most Democrats, who accused it of propping up Republican governments in the southern states. "During the last ten years not one half of our Army has been employed for legitimate purposes," said an Ohio Democrat. "Its use has consisted mainly of running elections and keeping the dominant party in power." Republicans became more accepting of the cuts as the demands of Reconstruction duty began to diminish. By the end of 1870, all of the southern states had been readmitted to the Union and only about 8,000 troops remained in the South, with the number dwindling even more in subsequent years. A segment of the Republican congressional contingent supported the reduction of the military for economic reasons. Excessive government spending, they believed, would drive prices upward. As the economizers saw it, Congress had to exercise fiscal discipline in order to prevent such inflation, and the military seemed like a reasonable place to limit expenditures. The reductions also had the backing of those members of both parties who distrusted the "elitist" officer corps and believed the volunteer militia provided adequate protection for the nation.[9]

In the 1874 congressional elections, the Democrats, having returned to power in most of the southern states, gained a majority of the seats in the House. Although the Senate remained in Republican hands, the Democrats now had the means to advance legislation that would further reduce the army's strength and authority. General Philip Sheridan's decision in January 1875 to send armed troops into Louisiana's legislative chambers, an action that allowed the Republicans to maintain control of the state legislature, enraged Democrats and made them more determined to strike a blow at the army. Led by the new chairman of the House Committee on Military

Affairs, Henry B. Banning of Ohio, the Democratic House passed measures to reduce the army's size yet again and to decrease officers' pay. The Republican Senate blocked the legislation. In 1876, the shocking news of the victory of the Sioux and Northern Cheyenne over George A. Custer and his Seventh Cavalry at the Battle of the Little Bighorn derailed the effort to cut army appropriations for a time. Distressed by the disaster, Congress even approved a temporary increase in the number of cavalry troops.[10]

The army enjoyed only a brief respite. When Congress reconvened following the election of 1876, Democrats were again ready to take aim at the army. Many of them were irritated that the Grant administration had, at the request of Republican governors, stationed federal troops near polling places in Louisiana and South Carolina during the election. The governors argued that the soldiers were needed to protect black voters from acts of violence by whites, but the Democrats contended that the troops were meant to intimidate opponents of Republican rule. The House approved legislation to reduce the army to 17,000 soldiers—smaller than it had been in 1860—and to prohibit the use of federal troops to guard polling places. When the Republican Senate declined to accept those measures as provisions of the army appropriation bill, an impasse resulted. Unable to resolve their differences, the House and Senate made no appropriation at all for the army in the second session of the Forty-fourth Congress. The troops went without pay from July to November 1877, when Congress, in a special session, approved an army appropriation bill.[11]

Voting on bills related to the army did not fall entirely along party lines. Some Democrats from western states, aware that their constituents wanted an army strong enough to protect them against Indians, voted in favor of larger appropriations. Army leaders especially appreciated the support they received from the Democratic members of the Texas congressional delegation. As representatives of a former Confederate state, the Texans shared with other southern Democrats resentment of Reconstruction, yet they valued the army's efforts to halt attacks by Indians on white settlements in their state. Texans applauded General E.O.C. Ord, commander of the Department of Texas, for his willingness to send troops across the border into Mexico in pursuit of Indian raiders, initially even without clear authorization from his superiors. Sherman gave the Texas delegation credit for preventing Congress from approving the bills to reduce the army despite the strong support for the measures among other congressional Democrats.[12]

The haggling over the army continued in 1878. The House voted to reduce the army to 20,000 men, but the Senate refused to concur, and the size of the army remained unchanged. The Senate did go along with the House, however, in passing the Posse Comitatus Act, a measure that emerged in reaction to the army's role during Reconstruction and the nationwide railroad strike of 1877. The act forbade federal marshals and other civilian officials from using troops as a posse to assist in making arrests—a common practice during Reconstruction and the strike—unless such action had been "expressly authorized by the Constitution or by act of Congress."[13]

By 1879, with Reconstruction abandoned and few soldiers stationed in the South, the campaign against the army had lost some of its steam. That year the Senate finally agreed to the House measure banning the use of federal troops to protect polling places, but supporters of the legislation failed to gather enough votes to override President Rutherford B. Hayes's veto. Army leaders realized, however, that the danger of further restrictions and reductions would exist as long as the public perceived that the regular army had no important function. In the 1880s, with the Indian wars drawing to a close and no powerful enemies threatening the United States from without, officers struggled to find a purpose for the army that would convince Americans of its indispensability.[14]

Some officers seized upon the regular army's role in putting down domestic disorders to argue that the army could serve as a well-disciplined constabulary, with the suppression of such disturbances as its main purpose. Many Americans, however, were dubious about such a role for the army, and the passage of the Posse Comitatus Act in the year following the railroad strike of 1877 indicated that a majority in Congress favored limitations on the army's participation in law enforcement. Even many in the army seemed unenthusiastic about making strike duty a central mission of their service. In addition, the revitalization of the National Guard in many states following its poor performance in the 1877 strike made the army appear less essential as a guardian of domestic order.[15]

The campaign to improve the nation's coastal defenses provided a more promising rationale for building a larger army. Army engineers asserted that the antebellum-era fortifications protecting American port cities were woefully inadequate. The old masonry forts would not withstand shells fired from the rifled guns of modern warships, they said, nor would the smooth-bore guns located in the forts have much effect on the armor plate of those vessels. Presidents Rutherford Hayes and Chester Arthur took up the call to rebuild the fortifications and provide them with rifled guns, and in 1885 Congress directed President Grover Cleveland to establish a board to study the issue. The board, chaired by Secretary of War William C. Endicott and containing both civilian and military members, produced a report warning that the nation's seaports lay dangerously open to attack from hostile warships. The Endicott Board called upon Congress to spend $126 million to build up the defenses at nearly thirty points along the coastline.[16]

At first glance, the potential for congressional support for the project seemed strong. For the members of Congress representing the coastal cities, there was the prospect of pleasing constituents, who would be grateful for the extra protection and for the money coming into their communities as construction projects got under way. The politically influential steel industry, which stood to receive large contracts to produce the steel that would go into the guns and armor plating required by the fortifications, could be counted on to push for the rebuilding project. Some army officers lobbied aggressively in favor of improved defenses. The Coast Defense Convention, attended by nineteen state governors, chose General John Schofield to head a committee charged with forming a permanent organization to campaign for more money for coastal fortifications. General Nelson Miles, commander of the Division of the Pacific, made the case for rebuilding the fortifications to members of Congress from the West Coast states and reported that many had promised to vote for the appropriations measures.[17]

Despite these favorable prospects, Congress was slow to act on the Endicott Board's recommendations. The board's report appeared in 1886, but Congress provided no substantial funding for coastal defense until 1890. By 1895 Congress had appropriated only about $11 million of the $98 million that the board had called for by that date. The coastal defense project suffered from Congress's continued determination to keep spending in check as well as the perception that the Endicott proposals benefited a few coastal cities rather than the nation as a whole. Above all, the coastal defense campaign lacked a credible enemy. A nation with both the means and the motive to launch attacks on American seaports was difficult to identify in the late nineteenth century, and Congress showed little inclination to spend large amounts of money to defend against a threat that remained mostly hypothetical.[18]

CONGRESS, THE ARMY, AND THE INDIAN BUREAU

As the struggle over appropriations showed, the army and its supporters had limited success in persuading Congress to follow the policies they recommended. The lack of political influence was also evident in the army's failed campaign to win congressional approval for the transfer of the Bureau of Indian Affairs from the Interior Department to the War Department. As the agency responsible for managing the reservations, the Indian Bureau shared with the army most of the responsibility for carrying out the government's Indian policies. The bureau had existed within the War Department until 1849, when Congress moved it to Interior. Many army officers believed that the move had been a mistake. As they saw it, the civilian employees of the Indian Bureau often worked at cross-purposes with the army. The division of authority between the bureau and the army—with the bureau responsible for dealing with Indians living on the reservations and the army responsible for those who did not—led to confusion and conflict. Too many of the bureau's agents, officers complained, were political appointees who had little experience with Indians. In addition, corruption plagued the bureau. Some agents colluded with greedy suppliers who accepted payments from the government but then held back food and materials they had agreed to provide the reservation Indians or, in some cases, sent spoiled food and shoddy goods.

HARPER'S WEEKLY.

A JOURNAL OF CIVILIZATION

VOL. XXII.—No. 1147.] NEW YORK, SATURDAY, DECEMBER 21, 1878. [WITH A SUPPLEMENT. PRICE TEN CENTS.

Entered according to Act of Congress, in the Year 1878, by Harper & Brothers, in the Office of the Librarian of Congress, at Washington.

4. "The New Indian War." Secretary of the Interior Carl Schurz and General Philip Sheridan face off over the issue of whether the Indian Bureau—represented by the small chest of drawers—should be transferred from the Interior Department to the War Department in this Thomas Nast cartoon that appeared on the cover of *Harper's Weekly* in December 1878. William Sherman, Commanding General of the Army, appears in the doorway of the War Department. LC-USZ62-55403, Library of Congress.

Whether attributable to the agents' corruption, indifference, or incompetence, the bureau's mismanagement drove some Indians to leave the reservations. When that happened, the army intervened and fighting often resulted.[19]

Transferring the Indian Bureau to the War Department, many officers argued, had a number of advantages. For one, it would centralize the responsibility for supervising the Indians. It would also open the way for the War Department to replace the political appointees serving as agents with army officers. The army believed it would do a much better job in running the reservations. Proponents of the transfer argued that the War Department would appoint officers as agents based on their experience, not their political connections, and that the officers, realizing that their reputations and their potential for promotion depended on their performance, would work diligently to keep peace on the reservations. Indian leaders often preferred to deal with military men, officers said, because they respected them as fellow warriors. The army would also use a firmer hand in managing the reservations. "Force is the only argument the Indian will heed," said one transfer advocate, "and it is therefore necessary to maintain a display of force in order to preserve his submission. The Interior Department has not such force; the War Department has."[20]

Joining the Interior Department in opposing the transfer were the self-proclaimed "Friends of the Indian," humanitarian reformers living in the eastern cities who wanted the government to come to a peaceful settlement with the Indians and then work to assimilate them into white society. Articulate and politically well connected, the reformers exercised an influence on Indian policy that belied their relatively small numbers. As the humanitarians saw it, the army had a history of provoking unnecessary conflict with the Indians. Soldiers were trained to fight, they observed, and putting them in charge of the reservations would surely lead to more bloodshed.[21]

The arguments against the transfer reflected the unfavorable image of the military in the late nineteenth century. If, as many Americans believed, soldiers tended to be belligerent, dissolute, and incapable of functioning in the civilian world, why should the government give them the responsibility of looking after the Indians? How could army officers teach Indians about such things as reading and farming, skills the Indians needed to learn if they were to assimilate into white society, opponents of the transfer asked? One bureau official, taking advantage of the army's reputation for harboring the indolent, suggested that soldiers would be unable to instruct their charges on the virtues of hard work. "The first lesson to be given the Indian is that of self-support by labor with his own hands—the last lesson which a man in uniform teaches." Furthermore, bureau agents and the humanitarians contended, soldiers would exert a poor moral influence over the Indians. Commissioner of Indian Affairs Nathaniel G. Taylor urged Congress to reject the transfer of the bureau in 1868 in order to save Indians from "the lingering syphilitic poisons, so sure to be contracted about military posts."[22]

Congress took up the debate in the late 1860s, when members introduced legislation to move the Indian Bureau to the War Department. With such prominent army leaders as Generals Sherman, Sheridan, and Schofield calling for the transfer, the House voted to approve the legislation in 1867 and 1868. The measures died in the Senate, however, where the humanitarians had more influence. Prospects for the transfer looked bright when Ulysses Grant entered the White House in 1869. Before becoming president, Grant had endorsed the idea that the Indian Bureau belonged in the War Department, and once in office he appointed active-duty officers to serve as agents at many of the reservations. Congress seemed likely to approve legislation to transfer the bureau, but support for such a bill collapsed when news of the army's attack on a peaceful band of Piegan Indians camped along the Marias River in Montana reached Washington in January 1870. The surprise attack, which resulted in the deaths of over fifty women and children, reinforced the image of the army as an organization determined to destroy the Indians and lent support to the humanitarians' argument that it should not be given the responsibility for the reservations. The transfer legislation failed to pass, and Congress approved a rider to the army appropriations bill that forbade officers from holding civil positions, a measure aimed at both limiting the military's role in Reconstruction and in Indian affairs. Not incidentally, the measure also restored the possibility that positions in the Indian Bureau would remain open as patronage jobs for the civilian supporters of members of Congress.[23]

The army continued its campaign for the transfer of the Indian Bureau throughout the 1870s. In 1876 the House Committee on Military Affairs surveyed sixty high-ranking officers on the issue, and all but two expressed the opinion that the bureau belonged in the War Department. Still Congress declined to approve the transfer. Sherman attributed Congress's stance to concerns about patronage. "We could settle [the Indian troubles] in an hour," the irascible general wrote to his brother, "but Congress wants the patronage of the Indian Bureau, and the bureau wants the appropriations without any of the troubles of the Indians themselves." Perhaps more important, though, were the efforts of successive administrations to improve the bureau's reputation by reducing corruption within it. President Grant, as part of his so-called Peace Policy, appointed men nominated by the Quakers and other religious denominations as agents and superintendents. Under President Rutherford B. Hayes, Secretary of the Interior Carl Schurz had some success in removing corrupt bureau officials. By the late 1870s, even some army officers had to admit that the problem of corruption within the bureau had diminished. Opponents of the transfer plan also prevailed because they tied their apprehensions about the army's involvement in Indian affairs to broader concerns about the role of the military. Secretary Schurz, for instance, argued that permitting the army to supervise the reservations would violate the principle of civilian supremacy over the military, and

Commissioner of Indian Affairs Taylor warned that the transfer of his agency to military control would necessitate a large standing army.[24]

CONGRESS AND THE "NEW NAVY"

In the years immediately following the Civil War, Congress's determination to economize affected the navy as well as the army. The number of naval vessels shrank from 671 at the end of the war to a mere 52 by 1870. The navy's ships were not only few in number but obsolete as well—the United States continued to rely heavily on sailing ships at a time that the European powers were moving ahead with steam-powered vessels. Many Americans nevertheless found the fleet entirely adequate for a nation that had no overseas colonies or foreign foes. They agreed with President Grant's secretary of the navy, George M. Robeson, who maintained that a small navy suited the country's needs in the 1870s.[25]

Naval officers, however, were less complacent about the small size and outdated technology of their service. Many were frustrated by the limited opportunities for promotion in a navy with so few ships. Some also found it embarrassing to have to sail into foreign ports on such old-fashioned vessels—Admiral George Dewey remembered the U.S. fleet of that era as "the laughing-stock of the nations." Discontent over the condition of the navy reached its peak in the *Virginius* incident of 1873. When Spanish officials in Cuba arrested and executed crewmen from the *Virginius*, an American civilian ship that had been carrying munitions to Cuban revolutionaries, the Grant administration ordered the navy to gather warships at Key West, Florida, in order to pressure the Spanish into paying an indemnity. The United States and Spain managed to resolve the issue without violence, but American naval officers were appalled at the state of the assembled fleet. Armed primarily with old smoothbore guns and able to crawl along at only four-and-a-half knots an hour, the fleet impressed no one. "It became painfully apparent to us that the vessels before us were in no respect worthy of a great nation like ours," a commodore said of the fleet afterward. "[W]hat could be more lamentable—what more painful to one who loved his country and his profession."[26]

Many of the discontented naval officers embarked on a campaign to persuade political and business leaders as well as the public at large that the United States needed a larger and more modern navy. Officers wrote articles and gave speeches explaining the importance of the navy in protecting the nation's foreign trade and safeguarding its coastal cities. The message found an increasingly receptive audience. As the navies of other nations developed, the United States seemed less immune to a seaborne attack, a perception reinforced when a dispute between the United States and Chile in 1882 spawned rumors that Chilean warships were steaming northward to bombard cities on the Pacific coast. By the 1880s, proponents of naval expansion began to find more allies in Congress. Officers such as the future admiral Stephen B. Luce cultivated social ties with key members—most notably Congressmen W. C. Whitthorne, a Tennessee Democrat, and Charles A. Boutelle, a Maine Republican, both of whom served as chairman of the House Naval Affairs Committee—and influenced their thinking on naval matters. In 1880 Congressman Benjamin Harris of Massachusetts, Whitthorne's successor as chair of the Naval Affairs Committee, presented a report that detailed the condition of the navy's remaining ships. Noting that almost all of the vessels were antiquated and many of them unfit for service, the report concluded that the time had come to rebuild the navy.[27]

In the following year, the navy offered a possible blueprint for the rebuilding project. The Naval Advisory Board, a panel of officers appointed by Secretary of the Navy William E. Hunt and chaired by Admiral John Rodgers, recommended constructing sixty-eight new ships, most of them to be steam powered, steel hulled, and equipped with modern weaponry. The Rodgers Board estimated the cost of the program at around $30 million. In spite of Secretary Hunt's energetic lobbying and President Chester Arthur's declaration that "every consideration of national safety, economy, and honor imperatively demands a thorough rehabilitation of our Navy," the House Naval Affairs Committee rejected the proposal as too extravagant. With no foreign threat looming to prompt it to loosen the purse strings, the House approved instead only fifteen new ships, none of them innovative in design.[28]

More auspicious for the navy was Congress's decision to create a second advisory board. The authorization of the board, which had the task of determining the navy's needs, suggested that Congress accepted the idea that the navy required at least some rebuilding. In 1883 Congress voted to approve what the advisory board had recommended—the construction of three steel cruisers, the first American warships to be made of domestically produced steel. Urged on by an energetic and talented quartet of secretaries of the navy who served between 1882 and 1897—William E. Chandler, William C. Whitney, Benjamin F. Tracy, and Hilary A. Herbert—Congress passed larger appropriations for constructing more and bigger ships.[29]

As the fleet grew, so did the ambitions of many policymakers. In 1886 the House Naval Affairs Committee called upon the United States to construct a navy equal to any in the world. By the late 1880s Congress had agreed to a shift in naval strategy. The long-standing emphasis on using the navy to guard the coasts and to raid the merchant ships of the enemy in wartime gave way to a focus on constructing fleets of powerful warships capable of destroying enemy vessels far from American shores. Congress balked at funding the construction of the twenty steel-plated battleships called for by Secretary Tracy in 1889, but in 1890 it did approve the construction of three such ships. By the time that William McKinley entered the White House in 1897, the U.S. navy—with six battleships, eighteen cruisers, and around seventy smaller ships—ranked sixth in the world as a naval power.[30]

The increased support in Congress for naval expenditures had several sources. For some members, spending on the navy had political advantages. Senators and congressmen representing coastal states and districts understood that naval construction meant lucrative contracts for local shipbuilding companies and jobs for constituents. Increased ship construction also benefited steel manufacturers, a fact not lost on the members of Congress from steel producing states such as Pennsylvania and Ohio. Manufacturers of the steel plates used to armor the warships depended almost entirely on government contracts. According to some opponents of naval expansion, the "armor and shipbuilding trusts" provided the impetus behind the rising expenditures on the navy. But naval expansion also drew the support of members whose states and districts received no direct benefits from expenditures on the navy. Many members saw a stronger navy as essential for protecting the nation's growing foreign trade. The periodic "war scares" of the 1880s and 1890s influenced some senators and congressmen to vote for a larger navy. Conflicts with Germany over claims to Samoa in 1888, with Chile over the killings of two U.S. sailors in Valparaiso in 1891, and with Great Britain over the Venezuela boundary dispute in 1895 stirred fears that the United States might be drawn into a war against a foe with a superior navy.[31]

For some in Congress, voting for naval expansion was a matter of national prestige as well as of security. Battleships became symbols of the nation's growing industrial power and technological prowess, and by the 1890s Congress favored the construction of such large ships over the less imposing but still necessary smaller vessels such as torpedo boats and light cruisers. Another factor that helped the navy in its bid to expand was that naval appropriation bills, unlike those for the army, were seldom objects of partisan struggle in the late nineteenth century. The concerns that prompted many Democrats to attack the army with such vehemence—Reconstruction and the traditional suspicion of a large standing army—did not apply to the navy. As a group, Democrats tended to be less supportive of expansion than the Republicans, but a number of influential Democrats were among the leaders in pushing for a larger navy, including President Cleveland and members of Congress such as Hilary Herbert, who also served as secretary of the navy during Cleveland's second term.[32]

A MILITARY FOR WAR AND FOR EMPIRE

The Spanish-American War of 1898 put the navy to the test, and it performed well. The navy gave the United States victories over Spain in the two most decisive battles of the war—at Manila Bay in the Philippines and at Santiago in Cuba. Public admiration for the navy soared, and with it, the prospects of greater appropriations from Congress. In fact, even before the war began, the navy had received a large increase in funds; in March 1898, as relations between the United States and Spain deteriorated over the issue of Spain's repression of Cuban rebels, Congress had passed an appropriation bill that provided $50 million for the military, with three-fifths of the amount going to the navy.[33]

The acquisition of the former Spanish colonies of Puerto Rico, the Philippines, and Guam in the treaty ending the war gave the navy another argument for continued growth—now the navy had to have strength enough to defend possessions thousands of miles away from home. The navy added Panama to its list of strategic points requiring protection after President Theodore Roosevelt engineered that country's breakaway from Colombia in 1902 and began the construction across the isthmus of an American-owned canal connecting the Atlantic and Pacific Oceans. Not only did the navy have more responsibilities than in the past, the threat to the United States posed by other powers seemed more plausible than it had previously. Conflict between the United States and Germany or Japan became reasonable to imagine. Both powers had built impressive navies, and both appeared to be intent on expanding their influence and territorial holdings.[34]

When Theodore Roosevelt ascended to the presidency following McKinley's assassination in 1901, the navy gained the most forceful advocate it had ever had in the White House. A former assistant secretary of the navy and author of works on naval history, Roosevelt had long championed naval expansion as an effective form of "peace insurance." As president he called for the continued growth of the navy, with an emphasis on keeping up with the innovations in battleship design introduced by the British. Many naval officers supported the president's campaign by using writings and speeches to educate the public and influence members of Congress. To aid in the campaign for expansion, a group of retired officers joined with interested businessmen in 1902 to form the Navy League, an organization devoted, in the words of one officer, to the "important missionary work of spreading the naval propaganda among the people at large."[35]

Congress, controlled by Roosevelt's fellow Republicans, gave him most of what he asked for. Appropriations for the navy increased from $85 million to $140 million during his presidency. In 1903 alone, Congress authorized the construction of five new battleships. It voted to double the number of midshipmen at the Naval Academy and provided enough money to permit the navy to grow from around 26,000 officers and enlisted men in 1901 to over 45,000 in 1909. By the time Roosevelt left office in 1909, the navy had risen from sixth largest in the world to a position rivaling Germany and lagging behind only Great Britain. The nation's rise as a naval power became obvious to Americans and much of the rest of the world in 1907, when Roosevelt sent a fleet of sixteen battleships on a tour around the globe as a demonstration of U.S. strength. The "Great White Fleet" received abundant publicity and enhanced the navy's already positive public image.[36]

But Congress did not give Roosevelt and the navy everything they wanted. A number of influential members, including some Republicans, questioned

5. President Theodore Roosevelt addresses the crew of the USS *Connecticut*, 1909. Roosevelt had less than a month remaining in his presidential term when he spoke to sailors aboard the USS *Connecticut*, flagship of the Great White Fleet, on the occasion of the fleet's return to Hampton Roads, Virginia after its voyage around the world. #NH 1836, Naval Historical Center.

the size and pace of the buildup. Senator Eugene Hale of Maine, chairman of the Senate Naval Affairs Committee, had been a supporter of expansion in the 1890s but came to believe that the navy's demand for larger appropriations was insatiable. He and other critics observed that the United States faced no true threat from another power and that the U.S. buildup helped fuel a naval arms race that rapidly made current ships obsolete. That position had some support in the business community—the National Association of Manufacturers, for example, opposed Roosevelt's naval program.[37]

Members of Congress concerned about overspending—allied with those who objected to the growth of the armed services on principle—imposed some limits on naval expansion. In 1906 the navy's General Board, a group of officers formed in 1900 to advise the secretary of the navy, recommended the construction of three new battleships, but Congress authorized only one. The General Board's proposal that the United States construct four battleships a year from 1907 to 1914—in order to have a two-ocean, forty-eight battleship fleet by 1920—made little impression on Congress; Roosevelt's call for four battleships in 1907, for instance, resulted in an appropriation for two. Roosevelt had expected some recalcitrance from the legislators. "Congress will not stand for the four battleships," he wrote to the U.S. ambassador to France. "To be frank, I did not suppose that they would; but I knew I would not get through two and have those two hurried up unless I made a violent effort for four." Resistance to spending on the navy grew even stronger after the Democrats regained control of Congress following the 1910 election. Despite the warnings of President William Howard Taft's secretary of the navy in 1912 that a failure to provide for the construction of more than two battleships each year would cause the navy to drop from second to fourth in the world rankings, Congress approved only one.[38]

The Spanish-American War and its aftermath compelled Congress to expand the army as well as the navy, but, as was the case with the navy, Congress refused to give the army all that it wanted. In March 1898, as tension between Spain and the United States grew, the War Department drafted legislation that would permit the president, in time of war, to increase the regular army from its peacetime strength of 27,000 men to 104,000. The McKinley administration planned to supplement that force with an additional 50,000 to 60,000 volunteers. The legislation, introduced in Congress by John A. T. Hull, chairman of the House Military Affairs Committee, quickly ran into trouble. Opposition came from a combination of members of Congress who, for various reasons, were suspicious of the regular army— they included advocates of the volunteer tradition, members upset over the army's recent intervention in labor disputes, and southern Democrats still angry over the army's role in Reconstruction. Also opposed to the Hull bill were congressional supporters of the National Guard. A politically influential organization in many states, the Guard argued that the larger regular army authorized by the bill would leave state units without a significant role to play in the coming conflict. When the House voted down the Hull bill, the War Department worked out a compromise with leaders of the National Guard. After being assured that the volunteers called into service by the president would be drawn mostly from existing National Guard units, the Guard and its congressional supporters dropped their opposition to a bill that expanded the regular army to 61,000. Congress approved the measure on April 25, two days after it had authorized military action against Spain.[39]

Although the law specified that the regular army was to return to its prewar size at the conclusion of the conflict, the acquisition of new territories in the treaty ending the war led the McKinley administration to seek legislation that would keep the army near its wartime strength. The United States needed a large army, administration officials said, to provide the troops necessary to control, protect, and govern Cuba, Puerto Rico, and the Philippines. In November 1898 Congressman Hull introduced a bill, drafted with the assistance of the War Department, authorizing a regular army of

100,000 men. The measure attracted strong opposition from Democrats and from anti-imperialists of both parties. Revelations about mismanagement in the War Department during the war also hurt the bill's chances. Hull successfully guided the measure through the House despite the resistance, but in the Senate Democrats threatened a filibuster to keep the legislation from becoming law. Lacking the votes to overcome the opposition, the administration threw its support behind a Democratic plan to establish a regular army of 65,000 men and a force of federal volunteers numbering 35,000. The bill, which Congress approved in March 1899, provided for only a temporary increase of the army; on July 1, 1901, it was to be cut to a size below 30,000. At the beginning of 1901, however, with the army in the midst of its campaign to quash the nationalist rebellion in the Philippines, Congress authorized the regular army to recruit up to 85,000 men.[40]

During the next decade, the debate over the size of the army became somewhat less contentious, in part because the army's actual strength was often below the figure authorized by Congress. The outbreak of war in Europe in 1914, however, brought the issue to the fore again. Advocates of military preparedness argued that the army, which stood at just under 100,000 in 1914, needed an infusion of new men in case the United States became involved in the worldwide conflict. In Congress, a group of Republicans led by Senator Henry Cabot Lodge attacked the Democratic majority and the administration of President Woodrow Wilson for failing to provide for a rapid increase of the military. Wilson dismissed the accusations as politically motivated and asserted that the United States could continue to rely on the traditional mainstay of its defense—the citizen soldier. Wilson maintained that the United States should anchor its defense not on a standing army but on "a citizenry trained and accustomed to arms." To do otherwise, he suggested, would be "a reversal of the whole history and character of our polity."[41]

By 1915, though, Wilson himself had taken up the preparedness cause. The deaths of American civilians in the sinking of the passenger ship *Lusitania* by a German submarine and the continuing clamor for preparedness caused the president to call for a substantial increase in military spending. He also hoped that by promoting what he called "reasonable preparedness," he would deflate the campaign of the more zealous preparedness advocates for a massive military increase. In October 1915 Secretary of War Lindley Garrison sent to Congress legislation to increase the regular army to about 142,000 soldiers and create a national reserve force—which Garrison dubbed the "Continental army"—of 400,000. Army leaders favored the proposal, but pacifists and many progressive reformers immediately denounced it as a measure that would move the United States closer to war. The Garrison plan also met with opposition from the National Guard, which saw the Continental Army as an organization that would replace the Guard as the nation's principal reserve force. Proponents of states' rights objected as well, noting that the Garrison plan diminished the role of the state-run National

Guard in favor of a body of reserves controlled by the federal government. With many Democrats opposed to the plan and its chances in the House looking dim, Wilson shifted his support to a measure sponsored by the chairman of the House Military Affairs Committee, Congressman James Hay. The new bill established a regular army of 175,000 and dispensed with the Continental Army. The measure designated the National Guard as the first line of reserve and provided Guard units with more federal dollars for training and equipment. In exchange for those benefits, the Guard surrendered some of its independence. The act gave the president the authority to approve or reject any officer's commission issued by a governor, and it allowed the federal government to set standards for equipment, drill, and physical requirements. Despite the accusations of antimilitarists that passage of the bill would pull the United States into the war and warnings by staunch preparedness advocates that it left the country vulnerable—former president Theodore Roosevelt called it a piece of "flintlock legislation"—Congress approved the measure in May 1916.[42]

The passage of the National Defense Act indicated how the attitude of Congress toward the military had changed between the end of the Civil War and early twentieth century. Congress had moved far beyond the idea that the peacetime military should be small, scattered, and devoted to the duties of a constabulary. As the role of the United States on the international stage expanded, Congress became receptive to the notion that in times of peace the military should prepare for war, and that maintaining a large army and navy even in peacetime was an essential part of that preparation. That change in view came partly because of new realities—the need to defend colonies, for example, and the rising power of potentially hostile nations—and partly because of the energetic efforts of the increasingly professionalized officer corps to educate political leaders and the public about the importance of rethinking American military policy. As the rejection of the Garrison plan suggested, however, Congress refashioned the military on its own terms. It remained devoted to the ideal of the citizen soldier—expressed through its preservation of an important role for the National Guard in the country's military system—and it declined to enlarge the army and navy as rapidly as the military thought necessary.

3

The Military Experience, 1865–1917

In 1881 a twenty-two-year-old Virginian named William B. Jett walked the streets of Baltimore, Maryland, in search of employment. He had recently lost his job as a salesman and was nearly out of money. Scouring the pages of the *Baltimore Sun* for notices of job opportunities, he spotted an advertisement announcing that the U.S. cavalry was seeking one hundred men for service on the plains. Excited by the prospect of both employment and a chance to see the West, Jett enlisted. He soon regretted the decision. Sent first to Jefferson Barracks in Missouri, he was appalled by the "despicable" food and rough conditions. Then, assigned to the Fourth Cavalry, he found himself at Fort Huachuca, an isolated post in the desert of southern Arizona. There he endured the stultifying routine of drill, sentry duty, and manual labor, punctuated by a stint in a "filthy" guardhouse and a harrowing battle with Apache warriors. While on guard duty, Jett tried not to think about "what a fool I had been to put myself in virtual slavery for five years at thirteen dollars a month." Unlike many of his fellow soldiers, however, Jett did not desert the army. He suffered through his five-year term of enlistment and, when his discharge finally came in 1886, felt "like a man let out of prison."[1]

Not all enlisted men detested the army as much as Jett—some found life in the service congenial and reenlisted repeatedly—but the high rate of desertion indicated that many shared his negative view of the military. Poor pay, harsh discipline, and dismal living conditions made it difficult for the military to attract and keep recruits. Although officers had some grievances in common with enlisted men—especially regarding inadequate pay and the monotony of service in lonely frontier posts or on long sea voyages—many of their concerns were of a different nature. Above all they complained about the limited opportunities for advancement in the small military establishment of the late nineteenth century.

During the period between the Civil War and World War I, the U.S. government instituted a number of new policies designed to improve the conditions experienced by officers and enlisted men. Leading the effort was a relatively small group of military officers and civilian leaders who saw the improvements as necessary to increase morale and reduce the desertion rate in the armed forces. These reformers cared about such matters because they believed that changes in international conditions required the United States to have a military prepared for war. A military ready for war meant the existence of a stable and well-trained enlisted force—not one plagued by morale and desertion problems. The reformers envisioned an enlisted force composed of fit, intelligent, and highly motivated men who would be capable of handling the new machines of modern warfare. A military prepared for war also required a professional officer corps open to new ideas and devoted to the continuing study of military matters; some reformers even hoped for one in which the talented could rise in rank regardless of seniority.

The advocates of change faced some discouraging obstacles—a Congress reluctant to spend more money on the military, an officer corps disinclined to depart from tradition, and a public largely apathetic about military matters. Despite those impediments, by the early twentieth century the reformers had met with some success. Improved conditions in the military contributed to a decline in desertion rates and an increase in reenlistments. Enlisted men received more training, and officers had more opportunities for professional education. Changes in policies regarding the promotion of officers decreased some of the discontent surrounding that issue. Unfortunately for the cause of racial and ethnic harmony in the United States, the military also became less racially and ethnically diverse, a result of policies intended to reduce the number of society's outsiders—immigrants and African Americans—allowed into the armed services.[2]

ENLISTED MEN IN THE POST-CIVIL WAR MILITARY

The enlisted men of the American armed services in the years following the Civil War generally came from the lower rungs of the social ladder. The poor conditions and low prestige of military service dissuaded Americans with resources and connections from entering the enlisted ranks. The navy found most of its recruits in the waterfront areas of the nation's coastal cities. Until the 1890s, when it had completed the shift from wind-powered to steam-powered vessels, the navy preferred to enlist experienced seamen who knew their way around a sailing ship. Those sailors tended to be tough, hard-drinking men who had few skills beyond those they had learned at sea. Some of them had joined the navy to avoid problems with creditors or the law. Rooming houses in many seaports provided a steady source of new recruits; many landlords pushed boarders unable to pay their rents into the service and took a share of the advance wages that the navy offered as an inducement to enlist.[3]

Like their naval counterparts, the army's enlisted men mostly came from urban areas and joined the military out of economic necessity or to escape troubles in their personal lives. Most of the new recruits, an officer observed in 1885, saw enlistment as simply the least objectionable option among the "choice of evils" that confronted them. A good number of the recruits gave false names upon enlisting, an indication that many of them either wanted to conceal something about their pasts from the army or hide their status as soldiers from friends and loved ones. Many of the enlisted men lacked the skills that could help them advance in civilian life—the most common occupational category listed by those entering the service was "laborer."[4]

Both the army and the navy relied heavily on immigrants to fill the enlisted ranks. In the army the foreign born, mostly Irish and German immigrants, represented around half of the enlisted force in the decade after the Civil War and around a third in the 1880s and 1890s. In the navy immigrants made up about half of the enlisted men throughout the late nineteenth century. On some ships the percentage of immigrants was even higher. When the gunboat *Ashuelot* sank off the coast of China in 1883, news accounts reported that all but 19 of the 111 crew members aboard were foreign born. Naval officers, almost all of whom were native born, fretted about the effect such men—"the dregs of all countries," one officer called them—would have on the efficiency and reliability of their service. How could non-English-speaking foreigners understand the orders of their commanders? Some officers, imbued with the anti-immigrant prejudices of the era, questioned whether foreign-born sailors would be loyal to the United States in time of war. "Our ships go to sea manned by heterogeneous crews, representing nearly every country on the face of the Globe," wrote Commander Stephen B. Luce to the secretary of the navy in 1882. Luce characterized many of the foreign-born sailors as men "utterly destitute of any feeling of attachment for, [or] interest in the navy; whose only care is to earn a present subsistence till something better can be found."[5]

Desertion was a major problem for the military. General Nelson Miles in 1889 identified it as the "principal evil besetting the army." The figures were striking. A report published by the War Department in 1891 indicated that over 88,000 soldiers had fled the army since 1867. Each year during that period the army lost, on average, almost 15 percent of its men to desertion. In 1871, following a decision by Congress to cut military pay, nearly one out of three soldiers deserted. In the navy roughly one out of ten enlisted men deserted annually between 1870 and 1890. Officers complained that a visit by a navy ship to an American port city could result in the loss of dozens of the crew, and some believed that only the marine guards stationed on many vessels kept even larger numbers of sailors from escaping.[6]

The men deserted for a variety of reasons. Some found the pay unsatisfactory. From 1871 until the Spanish-American War, the base pay for an army private was only $13 a month. The equivalent rank in the navy—ordinary seaman, second class—received $15 a month as base pay. Increases in rank and experience brought additional pay for both soldiers and sailors, and enlisted men holding skilled positions, such as machinists or hospital stewards, also received more. In times of economic distress, when civilian jobs were scarce and wages falling, the military's pay rate seemed attractive enough, especially given that the government provided enlisted personnel with clothing, food, and shelter. "Our recruiting officers have never had a better choice of material," noted the *Army and Navy Journal* during the economic slump of 1873. In more prosperous times, however, soldiers and sailors realized that they could make more money in one of the many civilian jobs created by the expanding American economy. Merchant ship captains needing experienced mariners lured a good number of sailors away from the navy, and the higher wages offered to workers in the sparsely populated West induced many soldiers to desert the army.[7]

The abysmal conditions found in army posts and on naval vessels also caused many of the desertions. Aboard ship, sailors contended with cramped living quarters, wretched food, and unpalatable water. The ships had poor ventilation, leaving the air below deck stale and foul smelling. In the army the monotonous diet of beef, bacon, bread, beans, sugar, and coffee left soldiers undernourished and disgruntled. In forts on the frontier the enlisted men often lived in crudely built structures that were crowded, unsanitary, and malodorous. In 1872 General George Crook called the quarters provided for the troops under his command in Arizona "unfit for the occupation of animals." Part of the problem was the army's reluctance to spend much on improving small frontier outposts that might soon be abandoned as the Indian wars came to a close. With members of Congress often determined to keep the posts in their states and districts open, however, a number of the "temporary" posts remained in service for years, and many unlucky soldiers had to live in them.[8]

By the 1880s, military and civilian leaders, recognizing that the existing conditions prompted desertions, damaged morale, and undercut efficiency, began to make improvements in the areas that affected the quality of life for enlisted men. The army started to supply its men with better-fitting uniforms in the 1880s, and some units initiated physical training programs. The soldiers' diet improved after Congress authorized the addition of a pound of vegetables to the daily ration and as the army started to provide extra pay for cooks (Congress did not provide for permanent cooks, though, until 1898). The driving force behind many of the reforms was General John Schofield, who served as the army's commanding general between 1888 and 1895. Working closely with President Benjamin Harrison's secretary of war, Redfield Proctor, Schofield pushed through a number of important changes.

Above all, Schofield and Proctor focused on closing many of the small and poorly constructed army posts scattered across the West. By 1891 they had reduced the number of posts by one-fourth. Money that had gone into maintaining the abandoned posts now went toward improving those that stayed open. The closures permitted the army to concentrate its troops at larger facilities—only a handful of the remaining posts had garrisons of fewer than one hundred men. At the larger posts, maintenance chores could be spread out among more soldiers, and as a result the typical soldier had to spend less time at physical labor and could devote more time to target practice, athletics, and other pursuits.[9]

The reforms of the 1880s and 1890s helped bring about a significant decline in the army's desertion rate. Between 1889 and 1892, the years in which Secretary of War Proctor and General Schofield had introduced numerous reforms, the rate dropped by half. During the 1890s about 5 percent of the enlisted force deserted each year, far below the 15 percent of earlier decades. The severe depression of the early 1890s explained some of the army's greater success in keeping enlisted men, but the improvements in living conditions and changes in recruiting policies contributed to the result.[10]

The reformers also endeavored to improve the quality of the army's recruits. In 1889 Proctor and Schofield ordered recruiting officers to try to get truthful accounts about the backgrounds of potential recruits and to turn away those with a disreputable past. Two years later Congress passed legislation requiring that new recruits be able to read, write, and understand English. In 1894, with the nation in economic depression and anti-immigrant sentiment on the rise, Congress required the army to enlist only American citizens or immigrants committed to going through the naturalization process. By the early twentieth century, the foreign born made up only about 12 percent of the enlisted men, down from nearly a third in the 1880s and 1890s.[11]

Like the army, the navy hoped to lower desertion rates and increase the quality of its enlisted personnel. The naval buildup of the late nineteenth and early twentieth centuries meant that the service needed more men to provide crews for newly constructed ships. Between 1897 and 1909 the enlisted force authorized by Congress more than quadrupled, from 10,000 men to 44,500. The navy wanted a good portion of those new men to be able to understand the technology—electric motors and gyrocompasses, for example—found on modern warships. Improving conditions aboard ship, naval leaders hoped, would help attract and retain capable recruits. Sailors began to receive better food, and many of the newer ships had better ventilation systems and more space for the crew than the older vessels. Naval leaders also discouraged officers from employing some of the severe disciplinary measures—such as punishing sailors by placing them in irons while they served time in solitary confinement—that had been common in the navy.[12]

Sailors appreciated many of the changes, but progress within the fleet was uneven and the navy's desertion rate remained high. In the first eight years of the twentieth century the navy lost over 14 percent of its enlisted force annually. The state of the economy continued to have a profound influence on how many enlisted men fled the service in a given year. Low unemployment and rising prices—characteristics of the economy of the early years of the twentieth century—prompted many sailors to leave the service for higher wages. With the army experiencing an increase in its desertion rate as well, Congress responded by authorizing a moderate increase in the pay for enlisted personnel in both services in 1908. The pay raise, combined with improving conditions aboard ship, contributed to a decrease in the navy's desertion rate beginning in 1909. In 1916 less than 4 percent of its enlisted force deserted. The increased rate of reenlistment also pleased naval leaders. Over 70 percent of eligible sailors reenlisted in 1916, a significant increase from ten years before, when only about half did so.[13]

As the navy moved from the age of sail to the age of steam, it no longer looked for experienced tars able to rig a mainsail but for young men who could be trained to operate steam engines and electrical systems. In the 1870s the navy developed an apprentice program designed to provide boys—most of them poor and many of them homeless—with instruction in nautical skills. Naval leaders intended the program to supply it with a steady source of native-born sailors who would join the service upon reaching the appropriate age and make a career of the navy. Relatively few graduates of the program followed that path, however; one officer estimated that only 10 percent of the apprentices went on to serve as sailors.[14]

The navy also attempted to expand its recruiting base from the seaport cities to the country's interior. In that way it could reduce its reliance on the often unruly and morally suspect professional mariners. A broader recruiting base would also increase the likelihood of bringing native-born Americans into the service, something that many officers thought important. "We want boys who have never seen, and do not know, any other flag than the American, who have good American backgrounds," one officer remarked in 1889. "We want the brawn of Montana, the fire of the South, and the daring of the Pacific slope." The effort to recruit in inland areas began in earnest in 1897, when the Navy Department sent recruiting officers to Chicago and other cities on the Great Lakes. Following the Spanish-American War, with the fleet continuing to grow and experienced seamen in short supply, the navy made greater efforts to recruit "landsmen," men without maritime experience who required training before being assigned to ships. By the 1910s the new recruiting efforts had produced a notable change in the composition of the navy's enlisted force. No longer did the cities of the eastern seaboard provide a majority of the new recruits—now most came from inland recruiting stations. The sailors of the new navy were much more likely to be native-born Americans than their nineteenth-century predecessors. In the 1870s

6. Crewmembers of the USS *Boston*, 1888. In the late nineteenth century, roughly half of the navy's enlisted men were born outside the United States. Some officers expressed concern about the loyalty of the foreign-born sailors. "We want boys who have never seen, and do not know, any other flag than the American," one officer remarked in 1889. #NH 56548, Naval Historical Center.

about half of the enlisted force had been born in the United States—by 1910 the figure had increased to almost 90 percent. Naval crews with a high percentage of immigrants—"mongrel crews," Secretary of the Navy Benjamin F. Tracy had called them in 1889—had become a thing of the past.[15]

RACE RELATIONS AND THE MILITARY

African Americans had reason to look upon the military with ambivalence. On one hand, it presented opportunities that civil society did not. Both the army and the navy accepted black recruits (the marines, though, excluded them) and offered them the possibility of a career as a soldier or sailor. For many blacks, barred from numerous occupations due to racial prejudice, such a career provided a steady paycheck and a degree of respectability. On the other hand, the racism that pervaded American society in the late ninetee7nth and early twentieth centuries existed in the military as well, and blacks in the service faced blatant discrimination and frequent indignities.

In the navy the status of blacks declined significantly as time passed. In the decades immediately following the Civil War, the position of blacks in the navy, while far from equal to that of whites, held some promise. The navy had no restrictions on the recruitment of blacks; they represented 10 percent of the navy's enlisted manpower in 1870 and 14 percent in 1880. Blacks were less likely than whites to be promoted and usually held the less desirable jobs aboard ship, but they worked alongside whites and shared living quarters with them. By the turn of the century, however, blacks made up a smaller percentage of the navy's manpower—in 1910 only 3 percent of the enlisted force was African American—and faced greater restrictions on their roles and their social interactions within the service. Racial segregation, which by the 1890s had become legally sanctioned and strongly enforced across the American South, had also become the reality on U.S. warships. The navy assigned blacks to positions that minimized their contact with the rest of the crew—as workers in the engine room, for instance, or as stewards— and had them live in separate sections of the ship. Even then white officers and enlisted men frequently complained about their presence, and fights between whites and blacks broke out on several ships. In addition, only whites held commissions as naval officers. The Naval Academy proved to be an unwelcoming place for black students. Three black midshipmen—appointed by Republican congressmen from South Carolina and Mississippi—entered the academy in the 1870s, but all three faced intense hostility from white midshipmen and instructors and resigned within a year. Annapolis would not graduate an African American student until 1949.[16]

Although the army offered blacks more opportunities than did the navy, it was not a refuge from prejudice and discrimination. During the Civil War the army had actively recruited African Americans, and 186,000 black soldiers had fought for the Union. Serving in segregated units, they performed well enough during the conflict to persuade many northern whites that they deserved a place in the postwar army. In 1866 Congress took the historic step of including black units in the regular army in peacetime, despite the fact that most army leaders were either unenthusiastic about the idea or strongly opposed to it. Congress set aside four of the reorganized army's forty-five infantry regiments and two of the ten cavalry regiments for blacks. In 1869, when Congress reduced the army to twenty-five regiments of infantry and ten of cavalry, it cut the number of black infantry regiments to two but let the two cavalry regiments remain. As had been the case during the war, white officers commanded the units.[17]

Black soldiers faced antagonism from whites both inside and outside the army. "Their advent astonished everyone," a white officer recalled of their addition to the regular forces after the war. "The frontiersmen looked upon them as a military caricature, the fruit of some political deal, unexplained and unreasonable. The officers detailed to serve with them were half ashamed to have it known. The white soldiers who came in contact with these recent slaves, now wearing the uniform of the regular army, felt insulted and injured." Tensions often ran high between black and white troops serving in the same garrison, and white townspeople usually protested when the army posted black soldiers near their communities. Members of black units believed, with good reason, that the army gave them the worst equipment and the worst assignments. Many white officers shunned opportunities to command black units and treated those who did so with scorn. Some officers made their contempt for black soldiers obvious. In 1867, for example, the commander of Fort Leavenworth, Kansas, assigned the troopers of a black cavalry regiment to a campsite on swampy ground and ordered them to stay fifteen yards apart from white soldiers when forming up on the parade ground.[18]

Despite such treatment, the black soldiers acquitted themselves well. The troops of the Ninth and Tenth Cavalry—the so-called Buffalo soldiers—established an impressive record in fighting Indians on the frontier. The white officers detailed to black units often became admirers of the toughness and devotion to duty of the soldiers under their command. The desertion rate for black soldiers was far below that of whites, suggesting that, even with the problems they encountered in the army, blacks saw the soldier's life as one that opened opportunities for honorable service and, within the enlisted ranks, advancement. As Secretary of War Proctor observed in 1889, "To the colored man the service offers a career; to the white man too often only a refuge." A former army surgeon, praising blacks as "brave and efficient soldiers," said of them in 1899, "You know they are always right behind you, they don't care what the danger is, so long as they have a white man for their leader."[19]

The notion that blacks were capable of following but not leading—something most army officers assumed to be true—made it difficult for blacks to cross the color line that separated them from the officer corps. In the late nineteenth and early twentieth centuries only a handful managed to do so. During the 1870s and 1880s a few members of Congress, trying to advance the cause of racial equality or seeking the support of black voters, or both, nominated twenty-five African Americans to West Point. Of that group, twelve passed the entrance examination and only three graduated from the academy. One of the three, Charles Young of the class of 1889, would be the last African American to graduate from West Point until 1936. The fact that few of the black cadets had received adequate schooling before entering West Point partly explained why so small a number graduated, but perhaps a more important reason for the low rate of success was the verbal harassment and social ostracism inflicted upon them by their white classmates.[20]

West Point's treatment of African Americans became a matter of national controversy in 1880, when a black cadet charged that he had been viciously attacked by a group of white students. Found bleeding and bound to his bed, Johnson C. Whittaker said that three white men had beaten him, slashed his face and an ear with knives, and then tied him up. The academy commandant, General John Schofield, immediately cast doubt on Whittaker's account. Opposed to racial integration and eager to protect the academy's reputation, Schofield and other officers suggested that Whittaker had injured himself in a pathetic bid for sympathy or perhaps as part of a plot to discredit the academy. A military court of inquiry and later a court-martial, no doubt influenced by Schofield's public pronouncements on the case, supported the conclusion that Whittaker had staged the incident. Many observers doubted Whittaker's guilt, however. Why would he mutilate himself, they asked, and how could he tie himself so tightly to the bed that those who found him had to cut the ropes to free him? The public uproar over the case led to political intervention. President Rutherford B. Hayes, determined to retain black support for Republican candidates in the 1880 election, ordered a review of the case and replaced Schofield with General Oliver O. Howard, former head of the Freedman's Bureau and an advocate of racial equality. Secretary of War Robert T. Lincoln overturned the ruling against Whittaker in 1882, but the academy dismissed the cadet for failing a course.[21]

The Spanish-American War provided both opportunities and frustrations for African American soldiers. Black units won praise for their service in Cuba and the Philippines—the Twenty-fourth Infantry and Tenth Cavalry, fighting beside Theodore Roosevelt's Rough Riders in the battle for Santiago, gained the most acclaim. In other respects, however, the war proved discouraging to black soldiers. Relations between white and black troops were often tense and at times degenerated into violence. Although the governors of several states had appointed a number of African Americans as officers in black volunteer units, higher-ranking white officers sometimes challenged their credentials and used qualification boards to drive them from the service. When the army sent the black regulars and black volunteers from the Northeast and Midwest to assembly camps in the South, the soldiers were angered by the rigid segregation and racial bigotry they encountered in the southern states. On occasion the soldiers resisted the unequal treatment. In Macon, Georgia, streetcar conductors shot and killed at least three black soldiers in a fight that broke out after the conductors had ordered the soldiers to leave the section of the streetcar reserved for whites.[22]

Overall, the Spanish-American War and its aftermath did little to improve the situation for blacks in the army. Although the regular army expanded in size in the years between 1899 and 1917, black soldiers made up a smaller portion of the enlisted force than in earlier years and were still relegated to the same four segregated regiments that had existed since the 1860s. The experience of a battalion of the black Twenty-fifth Infantry Regiment in Brownsville, Texas, in 1906 illustrated many of the problems that continued to afflict African Americans in the military. The army's plans to transfer three companies of the Twenty-fifth to Fort Brown in the Texas border town elicited protests from the state's political leaders. Secretary of War William

Howard Taft politely turned down the calls to halt the transfer, noting that white townspeople tended to complain whenever black troops were stationed near their communities but that the good behavior of the troops often quieted the objections.[23]

In the case of Brownsville, however, conflict between the soldiers and town inhabitants began immediately after the battalion's arrival at the fort in July 1906. The black troops, angry at the open hostility of the Brownsville residents toward them, became even more upset when local whites pistol-whipped one soldier and pushed another into the Rio Grande. On the night of August 13, 1906, a group of about a dozen men walked though the streets of Brownsville firing weapons. The shooters killed a bartender and wounded a police officer. A call to arms at the fort shortly after the gunfire began showed all the men and rifles present, but witnesses in the town claimed that black soldiers had done the shooting. Army investigators, assuming that at least some of the soldiers had been involved, demanded that members of the unit identify the culprits, but no names were forthcoming. Outraged at the incident and irritated at the lack of indictments, President Theodore Roosevelt ordered army leaders to discharge "without honor" any member of the battalion who refused to implicate the shooters. Still the men professed not to know, and the army discharged the 167 enlisted men who had been in the fort on the night of the incident.[24]

The discharges and the lack of due process that preceded them provoked an outpouring of protests from civil rights advocates. An investigation of the matter by the Senate Armed Services Committee resulted in a majority report that supported the army and the president, but a minority report highlighted the many inconsistencies in the testimonies of witnesses and the unfairness of the discharge. As some critics of the time noted, the army's handling of a similar case involving white soldiers suggested how race may have influenced the outcome of the Brownsville episode. In 1891 a mob of troops from Fort Walla Walla in Washington State broke into a local jail and lynched a man accused of shooting a soldier. When soldiers at the fort subsequently refused to admit guilt or identify the wrongdoers, the investigating officer suggested that the army discharge all of them. The army's acting judge advocate general rejected the idea, and a court-martial instead tried and convicted the fort's commander for negligence. The stark contrast in the way that the army treated the two groups of soldiers made apparent the lowly status of African Americans in the military in the early twentieth century. Blacks continued to enlist, but relief from institutional discrimination was still decades away.[25]

MILITARY OFFICERS AND THE POLITICS OF PROMOTION

Most officers came from a higher social class than the enlisted men they commanded. In the navy almost all officers were graduates of the Naval

Academy at Annapolis, and appointments to the academy typically went to the sons of politically well-connected families. A majority of the midshipmen had fathers whose occupations placed them in the ranks of the upper-middle class—attorney, businessman, government official, and banker were among the most common. Graduates of the Military Academy at West Point also tended to come from upper-middle class families, although they were less likely than their naval counterparts to be sons of wealthy and socially prominent parents. The army had a higher percentage of officers without an academy education than did the navy. In the late 1860s West Pointers represented only about 30 percent of army officers. Most of the rest had been Civil War volunteer officers who had received commissions in the regular army at the end of the war. Many of those former volunteers also came from the social elite—they often had obtained their original commissions in the state volunteer forces because of their political or social prominence. By the 1870s most new officers given commissions in the army were academy graduates, and by the 1890s West Pointers made up 60 percent of the officer corps.[26]

The army and navy permitted few enlisted men to rise to officer rank. The navy had promoted a limited number of enlisted men to officer rank in the 1860s but halted the practice in subsequent decades. The army gave its enlisted men a better chance of becoming an officer—in 1885 about one in four army officers had served in the enlisted ranks at one time. Still, officers as a group looked askance at the practice. As the *Army and Navy Journal* put it, most officers had "social objections" to giving officers' commissions to enlisted men, and "appointees from the ranks must necessarily contend against a powerful prejudice." Even the passage in 1892 of congressional legislation allowing enlisted men with at least two years of service to compete for commissions resulted in relatively few of them becoming officers.[27]

Whether academy educated or elevated from the enlisted ranks, most officers found much to condemn about the military's promotion policies. Officers desired promotion for obvious reasons—it signified professional accomplishment and brought an increase in status and pay. The problem was that promotion occurred with agonizing slowness in the years following the Civil War. The war had brought into the services a large number of relatively young officers, many of whom had held high rank in the volunteers. After the war the army and navy discharged many of these officers, but a substantial contingent remained. Receiving commissions as junior officers, they faced the prospect of a military career with few opportunities for advancement. Unless political leaders agreed to enlarge the armed services substantially—something that seemed unlikely until the 1890s—officers would move up only when the death or retirement of a superior officer created a vacancy.[28]

In the navy many officers complained about "the hump"—the large group of officers that had entered the Naval Academy during the Civil War—and its effect on the promotion prospects of those who followed them into the service. With promotions to positions below flag rank determined strictly by seniority, younger officers had no choice but to wait years at junior rank until members of the Civil War generation departed. Long periods spent at the same level, doing the same duties, left officers frustrated and, in some cases, unmotivated. "Individuality is crushed," said one officer of the time spent in a junior position, "no opportunity is given for the development of latent powers of command, and self-reliance dies a natural death."[29]

The root of the problem, in the opinion of some civilian observers, was an excess of officers. Secretary of the Navy William Chandler noted that the navy had over 1,800 officers on the rolls in 1882, far more than was necessary to staff the vessels that the navy had at the time. With Chandler's support, Congress passed legislation establishing a specified number of officers for each rank. The 1882 act required the navy to limit the commissions granted to members of the Naval Academy's graduating class to the number of vacancies in the officer corps; for the next several years only the top one-fourth of each class received commissions—the remainder received an honorable discharge upon graduation. Since the actual number of officers in the upper ranks exceeded the figure Congress had set, the act required the navy to limit promotions until the surplus had disappeared. In such circumstances, the law stated, an officer could be raised to a higher rank only when two vacancies existed at that level. Predictably, the act incensed younger officers. They denounced a system that, in the words of one critic, "required the death or retirement of 64 Commodores or 128 Rear Admirals to promote one Ensign." Junior officers mobilized against the act—some even hired lobbyists to work for its repeal. Recognizing that their prospects for advancement would remain grim unless Congress expanded the fleet, the young officers also began a campaign to build public support for a larger navy.[30]

Although efforts to repeal the 1882 act fell short, its opponents eventually succeeded in drawing attention to the problems surrounding promotion. In 1891 a board of officers recommended that the navy, in order to open opportunities for junior officers, force the retirement of captains who lacked the ability necessary for their promotion to flag rank. The idea, known as "plucking," became the subject of intense debate in the navy, with older officers usually opposed to it and younger officers viewing it with favor. In 1894, following a congressional committee's investigation of promotion practices, a member of Congress introduced legislation enabling the navy to remove inefficient officers. The bill drove the officer corps into two hostile camps, with both sides seeking to influence Congress. The opponents of this bill prevailed until 1899, when Congress approved a provision for "plucking" unpromising captains as part of the Naval Personnel Act. In the early twentieth century the rapid expansion of the navy—and with it the number of officer positions—made the promotion issue somewhat less contentious.

Many officers, however, continued to argue for changes that would make merit rather than seniority the main criterion for advancement. A major shift in that direction occurred in 1916 when Congress passed legislation that established screening boards for each rank to determine which officers were most qualified for promotion.[31]

Like their counterparts in the navy, army officers found much to dislike about the system of promotion. Seniority determined advancement in the army, but an additional frustration for junior officers was that promotions below the rank of major could occur only within a regiment. For example, a first lieutenant in the Fourth Cavalry could receive a promotion to captain only when the regiment had a vacancy at that rank. As a consequence, many officers languished for years waiting for a retirement or death to create an opening in their regiment. A study done in 1877 suggested that it would typically take a new second lieutenant thirty-three to thirty-seven years to reach the rank of colonel. Arthur MacArthur, father of World War II hero Douglas MacArthur and a capable officer, remained a captain for twenty-three years. He was not alone in his long wait—in 1889 a report stated that 110 officers had gone without a promotion for at least twenty years. General Oliver O. Howard expressed concern about the number of captains who had grown too old for extensive marching or drilling; indeed, in 1893 the average age of army captains was fifty.[32]

Officers sometimes sought to use political connections to accelerate their advancement. Many tried to secure an appointment to a staff bureau, where promotions occurred at a faster rate. Since a transfer from the line to a bureau required the approval of the Senate, officers usually needed the assistance of political patrons. Some officers lobbied civilian leaders to obtain an appointment to a bureau, prompting one general to complain that political and personal influence had "an undue share in these selections." Since promotion to the rank of brigadier general and higher required a presidential appointment and approval by the Senate, officers hoping to rise to those levels recognized the need for allies in the administration and in Congress. Critics accused President Rutherford Hayes of making promotions based on political influence when he appointed Colonels William B. Hazen and Nelson Miles to fill vacancies at the rank of brigadier general shortly before he left the White House in 1881. Both colonels had strong ties to President-elect James Garfield. Miles, who ranked only seventh among colonels in seniority, had the additional advantage of the support of an important relative by marriage, Secretary of the Treasury John Sherman. Nine years later, when the death of a major general opened a vacancy at that rank, Miles successfully mobilized a network of political allies to encourage President Benjamin Harrison to appoint him to the position.[33]

Reformers made slow progress in changing the system. In 1882 they convinced Congress to establish sixty-four as the mandatory age of retirement. Eight years later the reform-minded team of Secretary of War Redfield Proctor

7. Officers of the Seventh Cavalry Regiment, 1891. No issue caused more discontent among military officers in the late nineteenth century than the slow rate of promotion. In the small peacetime army, opportunities for advancement occurred only when officers at a higher rank retired or died. In the early 1890s the average age of an army captain was 50. LC-USZ62-11971, Library of Congress.

and Commanding General John Schofield persuaded Congress to enact legislation that opened opportunities somewhat by permitting the army to promote officers by seniority within their branch (i.e., infantry, artillery, and cavalry) rather than their regiment. The 1890 law also required examinations to ensure that all lieutenants and captains seeking promotion met basic physical and professional standards. The examinations were not overly rigorous and relatively few failed them, but Secretary Proctor believed that they pushed many officers toward greater professional development.[34]

The Spanish-American War necessitated a dramatic expansion of the army and, with it, the officer corps. In April 1898, Congress authorized both a larger regular force and the addition of volunteer regiments organized by the states. Army leaders hoped to avoid a repetition of the experience of the Civil War, when governors had often appointed men with excellent political credentials but little military experience or skill as commanders of the volunteer regiments. Congress deferred, however, to the demands of home-state politicians eager for patronage appointments and left the selection of officers of the volunteer regiments in the hands of the governors. As a concession to the reformers, the 1898 law permitted army and corps commanders to convene boards of review to examine volunteer officers and expel the incompetent.[35]

The law gave the president the authority to appoint volunteer generals and staff officers, and William McKinley, following the example of Abraham Lincoln during the Civil War, used that authority with political considerations in mind. McKinley took care to spread the appointments as evenly as possible among the states and made sure to name prominent Democrats as well as his fellow Republicans. In an effort to promote regional harmony, he even brought a number of former Confederate officers into the army as volunteer commanders. About half of the appointments to fill officer positions in the enlarged staff bureaus went to civilians, some of them the relatives of Republican politicians. McKinley's appointments were not purely political, however. He made military experience an important factor in the appointments, especially in the case of high-ranking officers. Two thirds of the generals he selected were promoted directly from the regular army, and most of the remaining generals were civilians who had previous experience in the regular army or the National Guard or had served as Civil War volunteers.[36]

The acquisition of a colonial empire following the victory over Spain and the outbreak of fighting between U.S. forces and Filipino nationalists created a continuing need for additional officers. In the expanded postwar army, many of those who received commissions were not West Point graduates. Some of the new commissions went to men who had served as officers in the volunteer regiments during the war and some to enlisted men promoted from the ranks. Regular army veterans griped about the new officers' lack of experience and ability, and some even referred to the non–West Pointers who had received commissions during the war as the "Crime of Ninety-eight." Many of the newcomers had talent, however, and brought energy and fresh ideas into an officer corps still dominated by Civil War veterans. Among the valuable additions were George C. Marshall, a graduate of Virginia Military Institute who became the leader of American armed forces during World War II, and Benjamin D. Foulois, an enlisted man elevated to the officer corps who became an innovator in the development of the military use of airpower.[37]

Theodore Roosevelt entered the presidency in 1901 determined to advance able and vigorous young officers to positions of leadership in the military. He disliked the seniority system and called upon Congress to scrap it in favor of a system based on merit. Resistance from senior military officers and Civil War veterans' organizations, however, kept Congress from undertaking such reform. In the meantime, Roosevelt showed his contempt for seniority in how he exercised the presidential authority to select officers for promotion to the rank of brigadier general and above. When vacancies occurred at the rank of brigadier general, he filled some of the openings with younger officers rather than promoting senior colonels to the positions. Several of the promotions propelled officers past hundreds of their seniors, much to the anger of many in the officer corps. Leonard Wood and John J. Pershing, both holding the rank of captain in the regular army, raced ahead of 509 and 862 senior officers respectively when Roosevelt named them as brigadier generals. The Senate grudgingly approved Roosevelt's nominations, in part because he sought to advance officers who, like Wood and Pershing, had undeniably strong records. Critics observed, however, that Roosevelt's abandonment of seniority opened the promotion system to political favoritism. Wood was a close friend of the president, they noted, and Pershing was the son-in-law of a powerful Republican senator, Francis Warren of Wyoming. Some advocates of reforming the promotion system praised Roosevelt for bringing merit into the process but argued that the responsibility for determining merit should rest with military professionals, not politicians.[38]

Another shift in promotion policies occurred during Woodrow Wilson's administration. Secretary of War Lindley Garrison, seeking to remove political influence as a factor in the selection of generals, instituted the change. The administration, he announced, would promote to general those officers chosen by the group best qualified to make the selection—the active general officers. In a bow to the tradition of seniority, Garrison stipulated that the generals must make their selection from among the army's colonels—there would be no more rocket-like ascents up through the ranks as in the cases of Wood and Pershing. The new policy did not completely eliminate political considerations from the process—the administration turned down some candidates for promotion who were closely aligned with the Republicans, and the Senate still had the authority to accept or reject the promotions. The administration and the Senate, however, usually went along with the selections made by the generals. That deference to the generals' judgment represented a victory for reformers, who, in seeking to develop the military as a profession, wanted to decrease the influence of partisan politics in military affairs and give the armed services greater autonomy over such matters as the management of personnel. Who better to judge the qualifications of practitioners in a field than fellow practitioners, asked advocates of military professionalism. At the same time, the new system satisfied another principle of professionalism by keeping the ultimate decision-making authority in the hands of civilian leaders.[39]

MILITARY PROFESSIONALISM

The idea of military officers as professionals requiring extensive training and a commitment to shared values and doctrines gained widespread acceptance in the United States in the late nineteenth century. Modern wars, supporters of professionalism believed, required military leaders able to mobilize and direct mass armies and to understand and employ new technologies. No longer could such leadership fall to amateurs relying on their innate abilities to command. Instead the armed forces needed officers well educated in the "military sciences"—the study of strategy, tactics, logistics, and other elements of warfare. Professional officers would share a common understanding of plans, theories, and even terminology so that they could function smoothly in a large and complex organization.[40]

The industrializing economies of Western Europe and the United States provided much of the impetus behind the rise of professionalism in the military and in other fields. The new economies encouraged specialized occupations, and that specialization led to the development of standards that would define the training necessary to pursue an occupation and the practices required to maintain good standing within it. In the late nineteenth and early twentieth centuries, doctors, lawyers, educators, and other occupational groups formed associations, promoted the value of their work to the public, devised criteria for admission to the profession, and established ethical guidelines for practitioners.[41]

The idea of professionalism gained greater support in the American military in part because of the uneven record of nonprofessional officers in the Civil War. The notorious wartime blunders of volunteer generals such as Benjamin Butler and Nathanial Banks—military neophytes given commands for political reasons—made some officers determined to exclude amateurs from the officer corps. The time had come, reformers said, to replace the volunteer commander—often brave but almost always deficient in military knowledge—with the professional officer—a highly educated, technically proficient specialist devoted to the military as a career and guided by well-defined procedures and ethical standards.[42]

An important tenet of professionalism was that the military existed to fight wars. Preparation for war, it followed, should be the military's principal focus in times of peace. That focus represented something of a new departure for the American military, which, in the absence of a threat from a foreign power, had busied itself with such tasks as Indian fighting, exploration, and showing the flag in ports overseas. The emphasis on preparing for future wars appealed to many officers; it gave them a clearer sense of purpose and helped diminish what one called "the desolate narrowness" of military life. The new emphasis on preparation for war proved especially useful to the army, which needed a rationale for its continued existence after the end of the Indian wars.[43]

Advocates of military professionalism formed associations designed to advance the cause. The U.S. Naval Institute, the Military Service Institution, and the National Guard Association of the United States, all founded in the 1870s, published journals and held meetings with the purpose of disseminating reform ideas and generating more public support for the military. To promote the continuing education of officers in the principles and techniques of command in warfare, proponents of professionalism succeeded in establishing schools that provided training to officers beyond that offered by the military academies. That success came despite the opposition of some civilian and military leaders, who dismissed the schools as overly theoretical or as an unnecessary expense. Rear Admiral Stephen B. Luce, convinced that officers needed education in the art of war in addition to technical instruction, persuaded Secretary of the Navy William Chandler to establish the Naval War College in Newport, Rhode Island, in 1884. The Naval War College survived the hostility of Chandler's successor, William C. Whitney, and with a faculty that included the influential naval historian Alfred Thayer Mahan, provided much of the strategic thought used to justify the rapid naval expansion of the late nineteenth and early twentieth centuries. In the army Commanding General William T. Sherman launched the School of Application for Infantry and Cavalry at Fort Leavenworth, Kansas, in 1881. By the early twentieth century the army's educational system had grown to include mandatory schools of instruction for officers on military posts, a network of special schools for line and staff officers, and, at the pinnacle of the system, the Army War College in Washington, D.C.[44]

The move toward greater professionalism had a paradoxical effect on civil-military relations. Advocates of professionalism such as William Sherman emphasized the principle of the military's subordination to civilian authority, and the frequent repetition of the principle in articles in professional journals helped to solidify support for it in the officer corps. At the same time, however, professionalism raised questions about the wisdom of automatically deferring to civilian leaders. In many fields—medicine and law as well as the military—professionalism led to the creation of a highly trained group of specialists who often resented decisions imposed upon them by those outside the profession. Many officers became certain that only they, as military professionals, possessed the expertise necessary to make sensible decisions on military issues. In many ways professionalism made it harder for officers to accept that civilian leaders—often ignorant about the military—would determine such important matters as the promotion of general officers, the armament on warships, or the disposition of troops.[45]

By 1917—the year the United States entered World War I—the American military had clearly changed dramatically since the days when the disgruntled cavalryman, William Jett, had suffered through his period of enlistment at Fort Huachuca in the 1880s. Changes in recruiting policies meant that the typical enlisted man in the army or navy was more likely to be white and native born than in earlier decades. The typical soldier or sailor received more training than his counterpart from Jett's time and, since the services provided him with better pay, food, and shelter, was less likely to desert. The typical officer of the early twentieth century was more likely than his nineteenth-century predecessors to have been educated at West Point or Annapolis. The establishment of professional schools in the services meant that he had greater opportunities to continue his education after receiving his commission, and with the enlargement of the armed forces and reforms in promotion policies, he had far better prospects for rising in rank during his military career.

The changes occurred largely because of the efforts of military reformers who believed that the realities of modern warfare required the creation of a better-trained enlisted force and a better-educated officer corps. Over time, reformers such as Stephen Luce in the navy and John Schofield in the army persuaded key civilian leaders of the desirability of such changes, and Congress eventually responded with the legislation necessary to implement many of them. The reforms signified a move toward greater professionalism in the military, and some civilians had misgivings about that development. The emphasis on training, experience, and expertise that characterized professionalism suggested a lesser role for the citizen soldier so cherished in the American imagination and a greater reliance on the standing army that Americans had traditionally viewed with suspicion. Civilian leaders were unlikely to accept the move toward professionalism unless they could be sure that a stronger and more professional military presented no threat to American liberties. Reformers provided this reassurance in part by making it clear that, in the American version of military professionalism, the principle of civilian control of the armed services would stand as one of the highest values.

4

"An Animated Machine": Military Subordination to Civil Authority

The principle of civilian control of the military met with no serious challenge in the United States during the late nineteenth and early twentieth centuries. With few exceptions, members of the military accepted that they fell under the authority of civilian superiors; these superiors made policies, the military merely implemented them. In their writings many officers described the military as an "instrument," a "servant," or a "machine" to be used at the discretion of the civilian government. General William T. Sherman imagined the army as "an animated machine, an instrument in the hands of the Executive for enforcing the law, and maintaining the honor and dignity of the nation." Although the military never achieved the absolute political neutrality suggested by those analogies, it generally obeyed the commands and attempted to carry out the policies of its civilian leaders.[1]

DIVORCING THE MILITARY FROM POLITICS

Military subordination to civilian authority required, according to the professional ethos taking root in the armed services, that members of the military scrupulously avoid involvement in partisan politics. The *Army and Navy Journal* referred to the abstention of officers from politics as one of the military's "unwritten but rigid" rules. Many of the advocates of that idea had absorbed it during their service before the Civil War, when the military began to emphasize political neutrality as an important element of its system of values. The experience of the military in the Civil War demonstrated to many officers the wisdom of eschewing political activity. As Ulysses Grant observed, generals who acted upon or even simply expressed their political opinions often fared poorly. "I had my own views," he recalled, "as decided as any man, but I never allowed them to influence me." Political bias "is fatal to a soldier," he said. Sherman, the army's commanding general from 1869 to 1883, held that "no Army officer should form or express an opinion" regarding party politics. Not all officers lived up to Sherman's stringent standard of neutrality, but few questioned its appropriateness. On a practical level, partisan activity by the military alienated political leaders in Congress and the executive branch, and the military could ill afford to create more enemies in those places. Partisan involvement also undercut the military's claim that it acted as an impartial servant of the public interest.[2]

Most officers on active duty followed the warnings to stay out of politics, but there were exceptions. Ulysses Grant captured the presidency in 1868 while still in uniform. Winfield Scott Hancock commanded the army's Department of the Atlantic when he ran for president in 1880, and Admiral George Dewey was the ranking officer in the navy during his brief and unsuccessful venture into presidential politics in 1900. More typically, though, soldiers who entered electoral politics had, like James Garfield and Rutherford Hayes, been volunteers rather than regulars and had left the military before becoming political candidates. Most active-duty officers also avoided open expressions of support for specific political candidates. General Oliver O. Howard, for instance, refrained from campaigning for the Republican candidates he favored until after his retirement in 1896. Winfield Hancock thought it inappropriate to campaign for the Democratic presidential candidate in 1868 even though he himself had sought the party's nomination that year. General Edward O. C. Ord caused a stir in military circles when he sent a congratulatory telegram to Hancock in the 1880 presidential election; interpreted as an endorsement of Hancock, the message hurt Ord's standing with the Republicans and their candidate, James Garfield. The principle of political neutrality did not prevent some officers from developing close ties to politicians, although the officers usually kept those connections discreet. Admiral Stephen Luce and General John M. Schofield were among the officers who exerted influence over public policy through their private correspondence with civilian leaders. A few officers—Generals Nelson Miles and Leonard Wood in particular—were more overt in their associations with prominent politicians and received much criticism as a result.[3]

Some officers argued that the military should abstain not only from partisan politics but also from participation in the making of policy. Sherman, for one, said that the army had "no voice in Congress, but accepts the laws as enacted" and declared that, as commanding general, he would not "condescend to importune members to obtain any special end, no matter how desirable." To the dismay of many of his fellow officers, Sherman repeatedly passed on opportunities to lobby Congress on the army's behalf. One of Sherman's successors as commanding general, John Schofield, expressed the prevailing view about the military's role when he said that officers should not "judge what ought to be the public policy of the government" and should

decline to go beyond explaining the military means available for implementing national policies. Admiral Dewey, hero of Manila Bay, was reluctant to
give his advice on such policy issues as the disposition of the Philippines following the victory over Spain in 1898. "Policy belongs to the cabinet," he
later declared, "that is, to the supreme civil authority, and must be decided
by that authority."[4]

In practice, however, officers often tried to shape the policies that affected
their branch of the service. Army officers made strenuous efforts to persuade
Congress to move the Indian Bureau from the Department of the Interior to
the War Department. Naval officers routinely lobbied Congress for more
ships and urged civilian leaders to secure overseas fueling stations. The military's influence in the formation of policy increased as the United States acquired foreign possessions and became more active in the Caribbean and
Central America. Still, civilian officials retained the dominant voice in policy
making. Sometimes these officials solicited the views of military officers,
sometimes they did not. Officers understood that civilian leaders would frequently call upon them to implement policies formed without advice from
the military.[5]

THE POLITICAL ENTANGLEMENTS OF RECONSTRUCTION

Reconstruction put the ideals of political neutrality to a severe test, and in
some respects it was a test that the army failed. The army's role in occupying
the southern states after the war and running the military governments created in the Reconstruction Act of 1867 put the service squarely in between
President Andrew Johnson and the Republican Congress in their battle over
Reconstruction policy. Johnson, an advocate of a swift reconciliation between North and South, clashed with the Republicans over what conditions
the rebellious southern states had to meet in order to be readmitted to the
Union. Johnson and the Republicans also disagreed over the issue of civil
rights for the former slaves, with Johnson opposed to the Republican efforts
to provide federal protection for those rights.

The army's responsibilities for governing and for supervising elections in
the southern states led almost inevitably to the increased politicizing of the
officer corps. Although many officers tried to be evenhanded in their dealings with the various political factions in the South, others became actively
involved in either promoting Republican state governments or working to
weaken them. Many conservative officers, who looked with disfavor on the
Radical Republicans' plan to remove the southern white elite from positions
of power and bring African Americans into the political system, found ways
to impede the Congressional Reconstruction program. John Schofield, commanding in Virginia, considered the constitution drafted by delegates to the
state's constitutional convention in 1868 too radical and refused to allow it
to go before the voters for ratification. The commander in Arkansas and

Mississippi, General Edward O. C. Ord, issued an order that called upon blacks to stick to their work rather than engage in discussions of political matters. General Lovell Rousseau, a friend and ally of President Johnson appointed to command in Louisiana in 1868, pressured the Republican governor to urge blacks to stay away from the polls on election day in order to prevent an outbreak of violence. Some officers cast aside any pretence of neutrality on Reconstruction by openly criticizing the policies of the Radical Republicans. In 1866 four regular army officers who had been generals during the war publicly denounced the Radicals' plans for the South. One of the officers, the famed cavalier George A. Custer, signaled his agreement with Johnson's policies by attending the National Union Convention that the president had organized to build support for his Reconstruction plan.[6]

Officers sympathetic to Congressional Reconstruction were no less willing to become politically engaged. Some openly expressed their support for the Republican program and Republican candidates. Nelson Miles, commanding in North Carolina, celebrated the victory of the Republican gubernatorial candidate with a fifteen-gun salute and in a speech hailed Grant's victory in the presidential election as a "triumph of patriotism over rebellion and secession." Some officers promoted Republican fortunes by using the authority that Congress had granted district commanders to remove uncooperative state and local officials. In Texas, Colonel Joseph Reynolds, after consulting with the Republican governor, removed over five hundred Democrats from office and replaced them with Republicans. A few officers leapt directly from the army into southern electoral politics. Lieutenant Colonel Adelbert Ames commanded the army's Fourth Military District when the Mississippi legislature elected him to represent the state in the U.S. Senate, and Colonel Reynolds commanded the Fifth District during the time of his failed bid for the Texas governorship in 1870.[7]

Whatever their position on Reconstruction, officers thought it important to show that their actions were in accord with policies established by their civilian superiors. So strongly held was the principle of subordination to civilian authority that no officer, it seemed, wanted to be accused of acting in defiance of it. Those who favored Congressional Reconstruction looked mainly to Congress and Secretary of War Edwin Stanton as the sources of authority; those opposed looked to President Johnson or to conservative state officials. General Oliver O. Howard, head of the Freedman's Bureau and a firm supporter of Radical policies, cited congressional authority in explaining to a subordinate officer the necessity of doing more to aid blacks in Mississippi. "The army cannot be a political machine," Howard wrote in response to the officer's assertion that he would not interfere in Mississippi politics, "yet Congress has given the work of reconstruction into its hands, and the law, like every other, must be executed by the army with energy and good faith."[8]

General-in-Chief Ulysses Grant tried to take care that his actions regarding Reconstruction fit into the framework of subordination to civilian authority. Having come to the conclusion by late 1866 that President Johnson's lenient policies would squander the gains produced by the Union victory, Grant turned to Congress for support. The Reconstruction Act of 1867 provided the authority he wanted for the army—in fact, Grant had a hand in drafting the legislation, and the press reported his support for it. He pointed to provisions of the act to defend district commanders like Philip Sheridan, who defied the president's policies by aggressively removing uncooperative state officials from their posts and preventing whites who had held public office under the Confederacy from registering to vote. When Johnson's assistant attorney general accused Daniel Sickles, commander of the Second Military District, of undermining civil authority by staying the action of a federal district court, Grant defended Sickles by citing the imperative of enforcing congressional laws. "My own views always have been that the military should be subordinate to Civil authorities as far as is consistent with safety," Grant informed Sickles, "unless such Courts were acting clearly in a way to defeat the Acts of Congress for the reconstruction of the 'Rebel states.' "[9]

In urging the district commanders to build public support in the South for the ratification of the Fourteenth Amendment, Grant defined the efforts to secure approval of the amendment not as political meddling by the military but as another case of the army simply seeking to carry out the will of Congress. Aware that the conservative Edward O. C. Ord might balk at taking a public stand on a question that was arguably political in nature, Grant attempted to recast the ratification issue as a nonpartisan one. "It is not proper that officers of the Army should take part in political matters," he wrote Ord. "But this is hardly to be classed as a party matter. It is one of National importance. All parties agree to the fact that we ought to be united."[10]

As ready as he was to promote an active role for the army in Reconstruction, Grant remained sensitive to charges that the military had overstepped its bounds. The appearance of partisanship on the part of the military, he realized, could upset the public in the North as well as the South. It also made sense for him, as a general with political ambitions, to avoid actions that his opponents could use to play upon Americans' traditional suspicion of standing armies. Grant's concerns may explain his opposition to congressional legislation that would have stripped President Johnson of his power to appoint district commanders in the South and given the authority to Grant as the general in chief. Once in the White House, Grant noted the cries of "bayonet rule" and "military despotism" that his opponents raised whenever he sent troops to restore order in the South. Grant's sensitivity to such rhetoric contributed to his growing reluctance to use military force to protect Republicans in the region from the violence and intimidation that Democrats were using to regain political power.[11]

Conservative officers who opposed Congressional Reconstruction also used the principle of military subordination to civil power to justify their actions. Winfield Scott Hancock, for example, won accolades from opponents of Congressional Reconstruction when, as commander in Louisiana and Texas, he issued an order containing a strong affirmation of civilian supremacy. President Johnson had dispatched Hancock to New Orleans in late 1867 to replace Sheridan, who had angered the president by removing conservatives from office in the two states. Hancock did not relish the assignment. "I am expected to exercise extreme military authority over those people," he informed his wife. The Radical Republicans, he predicted, would be disappointed in him. "I have not been educated to overthrow the civil authorities in time of peace." Upon taking command, Hancock published General Order No. 40, which included a statement of his conception of the correct relationship between civil and military authority. The order stated that when insurrection had ended and civil authorities were willing and able to fulfill their responsibilities, then "the military power should cease to lead and the civil administration resume its natural and rightful dominion." Few could object to such a statement of principle—the problem was how to determine whether civil authorities were indeed exercising their responsibilities. District commanders like Sheridan and Sickles pointed to the failures of state courts to treat blacks fairly as evidence that civilian officials had fallen short. Hancock took a more lenient view of the performance of conservative officeholders and restored many of the officials Sheridan had fired to their former positions.[12]

A key issue that divided army officers concerning Reconstruction, then, was not whether the military should defer to civil authority—all agreed that it should—but which source of civil authority was most significant. Supporters of Reconstruction stressed the importance of enforcing the acts of Congress; opponents emphasized the necessity of deferring to elected officials at the state and local level. Reconstruction also raised the issue of divided authority at the national level. The Constitution designated the president as commander in chief, but Congress provided appropriations for the military and passed laws that determined military policy. During Reconstruction, President Johnson and the Republican Congress disagreed emphatically over such matters as the removal of local officials, voter registration, and the use of military courts to try lawbreakers. The Reconstruction Acts limited Johnson's control over the army in the South, but he retained—and used—his power to appoint and remove district commanders. Army officers in the southern states had the challenge of trying to reconcile the often conflicting presidential and congressional directives. Many chose to act cautiously and declined to use the full range of powers provided by the Reconstruction Acts, an unsurprising response given the conservative temperament of much of the officer corps.

AN INSTRUMENT OF ORDER: THE ARMY'S RESPONSE
TO DOMESTIC DISTURBANCES

As was the case with Reconstruction, the army's role in putting down civil disorder generated debate about the nature of the military's subordination to civil authorities. Interventions by the regular army in the nationwide railroad strike of 1877, the anti-Chinese riots of the 1880s, the Pullman strike of 1894, and the labor strife in the northern Idaho mining district in the 1890s, raised questions about the degree to which federal troops were subject to the authority of state and local officials. Was it appropriate for the president to delegate his control over the troops to a governor or a mayor? Could a sheriff or a federal marshal call upon federal soldiers to help him enforce the laws? The issue of the military's neutrality also emerged during the interventions. Here the concern was not so much that the army had sided with a particular political faction—the main complaint directed against the army in Reconstruction—but that it consistently acted in favor of management over labor.

In the summer of 1877 the decision of several railroad companies to cut their workers' wages precipitated widespread strikes and violent protests in cities such as Pittsburgh, Philadelphia, Chicago, and Baltimore. When in some areas local law enforcement agencies and militia units seemed unwilling or unable to put down the protests, governors called upon President Rutherford B. Hayes to send in the regulars to restore order. He did so, and federal soldiers patrolled rail lines, guarded federal property, and, in the opinion of many observers, discouraged further eruptions of violence by their mere presence.[13]

The lines of command in the intervention were never entirely clear. Commanding General William Sherman, traveling through the West at the time, took little part in the operation. Secretary of War George McCrary and Adjutant General E. D. Townsend provided some direction, but much of the command responsibility fell to General Hancock, head of the Division of the Atlantic. President Hayes instructed Hancock and other commanders to report to the governors of those states requesting assistance and to act under their orders. Hancock obeyed, and governors such as John F. Hartranft of Pennsylvania directed the movement of many of the federal soldiers. Hancock, however, questioned the arrangement. Inserting the governors into the chain of command created confusion, he wrote to Secretary of War McCrary. It also left officers vulnerable to lawsuits claiming that they had acted without proper authority. The Hayes administration declined to change its course, but Hancock's position had support in the military. In 1885 Colonel Elwell S. Otis argued in an essay that the Constitution did not permit the president to place federal forces under a governor's command. The president, Otis wrote, "cannot transfer the control of [the military] in any degree to a party who is not subordinate to him in all respects."[14]

Another issue that arose during the 1877 strike concerned whether the army had been appropriately impartial in its dealings with the parties involved in the strike. Much of the press praised the army for its evenhandedness. According to editorial writers of the *Chicago Tribune*, the regular soldier had "no politics, no affiliations, no connections with trade unions or corporations" and "no sympathy with any class." The reality was somewhat different, at least as far as the officers were concerned. Coming mostly from middle-class backgrounds and belonging to a profession that valued hierarchy and order, officers usually identified with management far more than with labor. Many officers worked directly with railroad executives during the strike. Hancock, for instance, consulted with Thomas Scott of the Pennsylvania Railroad and generally acceded to his requests regarding the disposition of troops. Railroad officials, not army officers, made most of the decisions about where the soldiers should be posted. One colonel, angry that a railroad official had tried to force him to keep his troops in a particular town by denying him the use of a train to move the men, demanded to be relieved of his assignment "if I cannot act independent of" the railroad company. Hancock replaced him with a more cooperative commander.[15]

Another controversy that arose as a result of the railroad strike involved the use of federal soldiers as a posse comitatus. Under the common law, posse comitatus referred to the authority of law officers to call upon able-bodied men to assist in keeping the peace or in arresting suspected criminals. The authority to use soldiers as a posse comitatus rested in part on the Judiciary Act of 1789, which granted a federal marshal the power "to command all necessary assistance in the execution of his duty." During the 1877 strike, federal marshals and local sheriffs employed troops as posse members to protect property and accompany law officers making arrests and serving warrants. Even in the aftermath of the strike, the Hayes administration, at Governor Hartranft's insistence, kept regular army units in the restive coal-mining region of eastern Pennsylvania to provide support to local law enforcement officers. Federal soldiers played a similar role during Reconstruction, when federal marshals frequently called upon the troops for help. That assistance was especially important when the marshals attempted to arrest whites suspected of committing crimes against blacks.[16]

As white conservatives regained control of the southern states, they sought to use their growing political power to limit the army's role in domestic law enforcement. In 1877, with southern Democrats and their northern allies in the majority in the House of Representatives, the House Appropriations Committee attached to the army appropriation bill a rider that restricted the use of federal soldiers as a posse comitatus. Most of the debate over the measure centered on the army's actions during Reconstruction, with southern Democrats arguing that the army's participation in enforcing laws had violated states' rights and threatened liberty. A few northern Democrats also pointed to the army's recent actions in support of local law officers in Pennsylvania to warn that the practice had spread beyond the South. After much negotiating with the Republican Senate, which opposed the measure, congressional Democrats succeeded in securing passage of the Posse Comitatus Act in 1878. The act declared that "it shall not be lawful to employ any part of the Army of the United States as a posse comitatus, or otherwise, for the purpose of executing the laws, except in such cases and under such circumstances as such employment of said force may be expressly authorized by the Constitution or by Act of Congress."[17]

Passage of the act caused General Sherman to complain to his brother, Senator John Sherman of Ohio, that Congress had decided "that the Army must not be used to suppress labor riots. You had better overhaul all the muskets and pistols in the attic, for a time will come when every householder must defend with firearms his own castle." Sherman's hyperbole aside, he and other officers recognized that while the law did not preclude the involvement of federal troops in responding to strikes and riots—the president still had the authority to use them in certain circumstances—the regulars would no longer have the potential to serve as a reliable source of immediate aid to local law enforcement officers. As the act was interpreted, only when federal soldiers acted under the express orders of the president, transmitted through the regular chain of command, could they intervene in cases of civil unrest. The Posse Comitatus Act greatly reduced the possibility that the army might become a kind of national police force, a role that some officers had hoped it would assume.[18]

The government's response to an anti-Chinese riot in Rock Springs, Wyoming, illustrated the complications created by the Posse Comitatus Act and the absence of a settled federal policy for dealing with domestic disorder. In 1885 the governor of the Wyoming Territory asked that the local army commander provide soldiers to halt attacks by white miners on Chinese workers in Rock Springs who had refused to join a strike. The whites killed twenty of the Chinese and drove others into the hills near the town. The commander replied that he could not send troops without the president's authorization. President Grover Cleveland, however, was on a hunting and fishing trip in the Adirondacks of upstate New York and out of touch with the White House. While the Chinese who had sought refuge in the hills suffered from exposure and hunger, officials in Washington attempted to notify the president and considered various rationales for sending troops without his approval. The army's adjutant general took the initiative of ordering two companies of infantry to Rock Springs to ensure the passage of the U.S. mail, but since the soldiers were under orders not to act except to protect U.S. property they did little to help the beleaguered Chinese. Finally, five days after the governor had asked the commander for help, Cleveland returned to Washington and the next day signed an order authorizing troops to aid local authorities in maintaining order.[19]

When anti-Chinese violence broke out in Seattle in early 1886, President Cleveland was on hand to dispatch federal troops under General John Gibbon to the city with orders to "aid civil authorities in overcoming obstruction to the enforcement of the laws." Interpreting those instructions broadly, Gibbon persuaded the governor of Washington Territory to permit him to use the regulars to arrest the men suspected of organizing the riot. When the War Department questioned Gibbon's foray into domestic law enforcement, the general replied that governor's declaration of martial law and the unwillingness of local law officers to arrest leaders of the popular anti-Chinese movement made his actions both appropriate and necessary.[20]

The army's intervention in response to the widespread labor unrest of 1894 took place under a greater degree of control from Washington. Much of the unrest stemmed from the strike by employees of the Pullman Palace Car Company in protest of wage cuts. When members of the American Railway Union sympathetic to the strike refused to handle Pullman cars, rail traffic in much of the nation came to a halt. As the strike spread, crowds of discontented city dwellers, many of them unemployed, began to riot in Chicago and other cities. Unlike earlier episodes of unrest when presidents had sent federal troops at the request of state governors who claimed they could no longer keep order, in 1894 the governor of Illinois, the state most affected by the strike, had not called for help and planned to rely on the National Guard and police. The railroad companies appealed to the Cleveland administration, however, and Attorney General Richard Olney secured a federal court injunction against the strikers for interfering with the delivery of the U.S. mail. Federal marshals then asked for troops to provide them with support as they sought to arrest those who had violated the injunction. Cleveland gave the order, and eventually over 16,000 federal soldiers took part in the intervention.[21]

The army's commanding general, John Schofield, took an active role in directing the operation. Determined to stay within the bounds of the Posse Comitatus Act and to keep his forces under the command of the president and his subordinates, Schofield tried to prevent civil officials at the state and local levels from taking charge of the troops. "The commanding officers of the troops so employed are directly responsible to their military superiors," Schofield announced in an order. "Any unlawful or unauthorized act on their part would not be excusable on the ground of any order or request received by them from a marshal or any other civil officer." Despite requests from the Justice Department, Schofield firmly refused to allow his soldiers to serve in posses organized by federal marshals. Soldiers were not law officers, Schofield maintained, and should not make arrests or serve warrants. There were limits to Schofield's authority, however. As the strike spread and the violence increased, the War Department gave departmental commanders the authority to decide for themselves how to respond to the calls for assistance from the marshals. Some of those commanders were less scrupulous than Schofield in

8. "The Chicago Strikes—United States Cavalry in the Stock-Yards." The artist Frederic Remington reported on the Pullman Strike in Chicago in 1894 and had effusive praise for the regular army's handling of rioters. In an article for the July 21, 1894 issue of *Harper's Weekly*, he contrasted the disciplined and restrained soldiers with the impulsive and disrespectful rioters, whom he labeled a "malodorous crowd of anarchistic foreign trash." In illustrations accompanying the article, Remington emphasized the soldiers' effectiveness in restoring order. LC-USZ62-96502, Library of Congress.

making certain that their actions fell within the law. General Nelson Miles, for example, commanding the forces sent to Chicago, ignored Schofield's directives and allowed his soldiers to serve as posse members. Convinced that Chicago and perhaps the country teetered on the brink of revolution, the ambitious Miles involved himself in efforts to restore order throughout the city rather than focusing on the narrower task of providing support for the enforcement of a federal court injunction to open the rail lines.[22]

In the Pullman strike, as in previous cases of labor unrest, the army failed to take an impartial position between the disputing sides. Officers consulted frequently with railroad officials and usually granted their requests for troops to guard company property and provide escorts for trains carrying strikebreakers. Such cooperation seemed natural to many officers. To them, the railroad companies represented property and order, and civil authorities had sent the army to protect property and restore order. In addition, some officers, Generals Schofield and Miles foremost among them, had developed strong social and financial ties to railroad executives. On the other hand, officers tended to view with loathing the urban poor who participated in the riots. Even those officers who had a degree of sympathy for the striking workers agreed with the railroad managers that the strikers should not be able to prevent others from taking their jobs.[23]

The idea of the regulars as a necessary bulwark against the dangerous masses gave some officers a sense of purpose and raised hopes that Congress might approve a larger army at a time when, with the end of the Indian wars, the utility of the regular army to the nation was in question. Captain George F. Price spoke for many when he warned in an 1885 essay of the political influence of the "criminal and ignorant classes" and argued that the nation needed an "army of sufficient numbers ready to obey the summons of rightful authority" to keep the "vicious" masses in check. A decade later Lieutenant William Wallace made the case that, contrary to the complaints of many critics, the army did not favor capital when it intervened in strikes. Instead, Wallace wrote, the army simply worked to maintain the law and order that all decent citizens—even the workers—desired. Wallace described the army's role as a "power for good in the hands of the good."[24]

Commanding General Schofield shared the positive view of the army as a guardian of civil order as well as the feelings of contempt toward the rioters—he characterized them as "an enemy far more numerous and dangerous to the country than any savage enemy"—but he continued to have concerns about how to keep regular troops within the military chain of command during domestic disturbances. Following the Pullman strike, Schofield amended the army's regulations to make it clear that the president's authority to command the army could not be transferred to other civil officers. The regulations also emphasized that in cases of domestic disorder, troops were not to obey the orders of civilian law-enforcement officers to make arrests or guard prisoners. The new regulations, coupled with the earlier Posse Comitatus Act, placed civilian control over the federal military more securely in the hands of the president and his direct subordinates. Other civil officials such as governors, mayors, marshals, and sheriffs could no longer claim the authority to command federal forces, even in cases of emergency or when communication between the troops and their superiors in Washington had broken down.[25]

Old practices persisted, however, and Schofield's regulations had little effect on the next major intervention in a labor dispute by regular troops. In 1899, disputes between mining companies and their employees in the Coeur d'Alene region of northern Idaho had resulted in violence, and the governor, recognizing that local officials sympathized with the miners, declared martial law and called for federal troops to restore order. President McKinley obliged by sending a detachment of infantry commanded by General Henry C. Merriam. With his superiors in Washington focused on the war against insurgents in the Philippines, Merriam was free to act as he saw fit. The general publicly denounced the labor unions, endorsed a plan requiring state-issued work permits for mine employees, and worked closely with state authorities in their effort to smash the miners' union. In violation of Schofield's regulations, Merriam's troops assisted civil officials in arresting over a thousand suspected union members and guarded prisoners awaiting trial.[26]

Labor organizations charged soldiers in the Coeur d'Alene region with mistreating the arrested miners and accused the army of allowing itself to become a union-busting tool of the governor and the mine owners. Condemnations of the troops' actions prompted the House Military Affairs Committee to investigate the army's role in the strike. The committee, controlled by Republicans and therefore reluctant to criticize actions of the McKinley administration, exonerated the army of any wrongdoing. To the contention of the minority Democrats that General Merriam too readily carried out the anti-union policies of the governor, including policies of dubious legality, the majority replied that the president could delegate his authority over the military to anyone he chose, including the governor. That interpretation contradicted army regulations, which stated that troops could not be "directed to act under the orders of any civil officer" except the president.[27]

Continuing uncertainty about what the army could do in cases of civil disorder and who could legitimately command troops on those occasions caused many officers to act cautiously when confronted with domestic unrest. Waiting for orders from Washington seemed to be the safest thing to do. "As a rule," wrote General Charles B. Hall in 1908, "the action of regular troops when in the vicinity of any local disorder or disturbance, no matter how serious, and when not acting under the orders of the President, should be that of strict neutrality. 'Hands Off' should be our motto, unless we feel so sure of our position that we can risk in addition to official censure, civil action for damages, false arrest and imprisonment."[28]

That sense of restraint characterized the federal government's response to domestic disorder in the years between 1900 and the beginning of World War I. The regular army was seldom called upon to put down disturbances during that time, partly because civilian leaders in the states relied more often on local police and the National Guard, which had become better equipped and more reliable since the 1870s. On the few occasions when the state authorities did request help from the army, leaders in Washington took steps to limit its role. When President Theodore Roosevelt sent troops in response to a miners' strike in Nevada in 1907, he kept the soldiers firmly within the army's chain of command and had the secretary of war watch the situation carefully. President Woodrow Wilson did the same during the Colorado miners' strike of 1914. Both the Roosevelt and Wilson administrations communicated with union leaders as well as with managers and state officials. The regular troops were present to discourage violence, but their superiors forbade them from assisting with arrests, escorting strikebreakers, or guarding the property of mining companies. In the case of the Colorado strike, the neutrality of the regulars contrasted dramatically with pro-management activities of the Colorado National Guard, members of which had stirred national outrage by opening fire on a strikers' camp near Ludlow.[29]

The determination on the part of the White House and the War Department to supervise more closely the army's response to domestic disorder reflected two broader trends in American political life at the turn of the century—the move toward greater centralization of governmental authority, and the rise of a more active model of presidential leadership. The ability to keep tight control over the actions of federal troops in politically touchy situations such as labor disputes made sense from a pragmatic standpoint—it might prevent local commanders from taking steps that could alienate important constituencies—and also from a constitutional standpoint. To advocates of a strong presidency, the chief executive's power rested in part on his extensive authority as commander in chief. To relinquish some of that authority to state or local officials, or even to military commanders, was to diminish the president's potential for leadership.

AN INSTRUMENT OF ORDER BEYOND THE NATION'S BORDERS

The same considerations of pragmatism and principle affected the role presidents took in directing the armed forces in operations outside of the United States. As the nation grew in power and became more active in international affairs, presidents ordered troops and ships to points around the globe as instruments of the nation's foreign policy. The goal of most of these missions was to protect American interests in another country—usually in Central America or the Caribbean—by either safeguarding the government in power or assisting those who wished to overthrow it. A president had an obvious interest in seeing that the interventions he ordered went smoothly and accomplished the intended result. For that reason, presidents and the civilian heads of the departments most concerned with foreign relations—State, Navy, and War—took steps to ensure that they would exercise control over the operations. The military submitted to that supervision, although some officers complained that civilian leaders too often discounted the advice of commanders on the scene.

President McKinley demonstrated how a president could act as an assertive and vigilant commander in chief during the war with Spain in 1898. While McKinley left tactical decisions to his commanders, the strategic decisions were his alone, and he did not hesitate to go against the judgment of military subordinates on matters of policy. He decided at the beginning of the war to call up 125,000 volunteers in spite of Commanding General Nelson Miles's protests that the army could not supply such a large force. To the dismay of his admirals, who wanted to follow the established doctrine of gathering their ships into a single strike force, McKinley directed the navy to divide the Atlantic fleet so that ships would be available to protect the nation's eastern seaboard from attack by the Spanish, something that the navy considered a negligible threat.[30]

In May 1898, following the decisive American victory at Manila Bay, McKinley made decisions that dramatically altered existing plans. Over Miles's objections, the administration increased the number of soldiers being sent to occupy the Philippines from 5,000 to 20,000, a move that suggested a growing American interest in keeping the islands. Determined to end the war quickly, McKinley also cast aside an earlier plan to delay an invasion of Cuba until after a naval blockade had reduced Spanish forces there and ordered the army to prepare for an immediate attack on the island. "In all the movements of the army and navy the President's hand is seen," wrote one of his advisors. A member of his cabinet later remarked that McKinley "assumed a close personal direction, not only of the organization of the forces but of the general plan of operations. He was Commander-in-Chief not merely in name but in fact."[31]

McKinley's success in maintaining control over military operations came despite the fact that he commanded forces scattered from Puerto Rico to the Philippines without consistently reliable means of communicating with them. McKinley had established a "war room" in the White House containing, along with maps, numerous telephone and telegraph lines, but there were times when he had no way of knowing what his commanders were doing and they could not receive direction from him. After Commodore Dewey and his ships left Hong Kong with orders to capture or destroy the Spanish vessels in Manila Bay, for instance, McKinley could not contact him to modify the orders, nor could Dewey seek any clarification. The White House heard nothing from the commodore from the time of his departure on April 27 until notification of his victory arrived in Washington on May 7. Even closer at hand, in the waters off Cuba, administration officials were frequently out of touch with portions of the fleet.[32]

The difficulty of communicating over long distances, especially with ships at sea, meant that the practice had developed of allowing commanders on the spot some latitude in responding to a problem or a threat. Naval officers enjoyed substantial freedom of action when they sailed beyond American waters. Ship commanders overseas, it was understood, could act on their own initiative when American lives and property were in danger, and the navy had a long history of protecting merchants and missionaries abroad from angry mobs and hostile foreign governments without waiting for orders from Washington. Naval officers recognized that while the government trusted them to use their "good judgment" in such situations, their careers would suffer if their decisions resulted in embarrassment for the United States or disrupted the nation's foreign policy. Making those determinations was not easy, and some officers were reluctant to act until they had received instructions from their superiors.

The American response to the Boxer Rebellion in China provides an example of such reluctance. In 1900 members of the Society of the Harmonious Fists—to westerners, the Boxers—began to attack missionaries and Chinese Christians across northern China. In response, warships from eight nations, including the United States, gathered off the coast. Since the Boxers had surrounded the foreign legations in Peking and cut the telegraph wires leading out of the city, the ships could not communicate readily with their respective governments. When the other commanders of the hastily assembled fleet decided to attack Chinese forts guarding the coastline without waiting for the approval of their governments, the American commander, Admiral Louis Kempff, kept his sailors out of the fray. He had no orders to participate in the assault, he explained. Furthermore, he argued, such an attack would represent an act of war against a sovereign nation, something that he had no authority to carry out on his own initiative.[33]

President McKinley's decision to contribute U.S. soldiers and marines to the international expedition to relieve the besieged legation district required the administration to devise guidelines for the army and navy commanders on the scene, who would be out of direct communication with the outside world for some time. Secretary of War Elihu Root's instructions permitted the commanders to act "concurrently" with the forces of the other powers in order to protect American lives and interests yet told them to avoid "any joint action or undertaking with other powers tending to commit or limit this Government as to its future course of conduct." Secretary Root believed that such broad and rather vague guidelines were necessary for the commanders to accomplish their mission, and he understood that the administration would have to rely heavily on the discretion of the commanders. Fortunately for McKinley and Root, those commanders proved up to the task; U.S. forces aided in the rescue of the legations without lending direct support to the territorial ambitions of the other powers taking part in the intervention.[34]

The introduction of radio equipment on naval vessels beginning in the early twentieth century provided civilian leaders with a possible means of maintaining better control of the navy's far-flung ships. The navy had fifty-nine radio installations by 1904. In theory, radio communication would allow ship commanders to check with their superiors before acting. In practice, the early radios had limited range and proved unreliable, and commanders continued to have considerable autonomy. That autonomy sometimes posed a problem for civilian policymakers, especially as the navy increased in size and became more involved on the international stage. In the Caribbean and Central America in particular, the navy saw itself as the maritime equivalent of the policeman on the beat, ever watchful for threats to American interests.[35]

Like their nineteenth-century predecessors, naval officers of the early twentieth century were willing at times to, on their own initiative, steam their warships into seaports or to land contingents of marines in order to protect American citizens and property in foreign lands. Such interventions had the potential to upset the nation's diplomatic plans. Elihu Root, now serving as secretary of state, criticized a naval officer in 1907 for sending a landing party ashore to police a Honduran town invaded by Nicaraguan troops while Root was trying to negotiate a settlement between Honduras and Nicaragua. In 1906 another naval commander sent a battalion of marines into Cuba at the request of an American diplomat in Havana worried about a growing rebellion against the Cuban government. The marines landed without clearance from Washington, much to the irritation of President Roosevelt. A navy captain in Turkey in 1910 angered American diplomats there by failing to consult with them before taking his ship into Turkish ports and allegedly threatening local officials.[36]

As the State Department saw it, the larger and more active navy of the early twentieth century needed reminding that it was the tool and not the architect of American foreign policy. In 1908 Secretary of State Root's objections to a navy captain's interference in policy matters in Central America led the navy to order his ship to return to the United States. President William Howard Taft's secretary of state, Philander Knox, protested to the navy when an admiral, in Knox's view, stepped over the line by "exerting diplomatic pressure which had not been requested by this Department charged with the conduct of foreign relations." Another diplomat asserted that "the diplomacy of naval officers in Central America has become harmful to the carrying out of the State Department's policy in these countries." The presidents of the period—Roosevelt, Taft, and Wilson—agreed with the State Department that the navy should remain subordinate in the making of foreign policy and tended to back the diplomats who accused the navy of encroachment. Although some officers criticized the diplomats for neglecting to consult with them in making decisions that involved the use of naval power, the navy generally accepted its subordination.[37]

The issue of the navy's role in foreign policy came to the fore again in 1914, when Admiral Henry T. Mayo, commanding American ships offshore of Tampico, Mexico, demanded an elaborate apology from Mexican authorities for the arrest of some American sailors. Mexican soldiers had briefly detained a small group of American sailors who had come ashore at Tampico to purchase gasoline. Although the local Mexican commander quickly released the sailors and apologized for their arrest, Admiral Mayo, without first seeking authorization from Washington or even his immediate superior, insisted that Mexican officials produce a written apology, raise the American flag, fire a twenty-one-gun salute, or face retaliation. The Mexican government of President Victoriano Huerta refused to comply, and the Wilson administration had a crisis on its hands. Although normally defensive of the prerogatives of civilian officials in policymaking, President Wilson chose to support the admiral. The president, looking for opportunities to weaken the Huerta regime, ordered marines and sailors to seize the customs house at the important port of Vera Cruz and hold it until the Huerta government either backed down or, better yet, collapsed.[38]

Some in the Wilson administration found it disturbing that a single officer could, on his own, issue so sweeping an ultimatum. One advisor, Colonel Edward House, remarked that he had thought such authority had gone the way of the dueling code. Secretary of the Navy Josephus Daniels believed that officers should not make ultimatums to foreign officials without the president's approval. After waiting long enough so that it would not appear to be a rebuke of Admiral Mayo, Daniels amended the U.S. Navy Regulations so that no commander could issue an ultimatum "without first communicating with the Navy Department, except in extreme cases where such action is necessary to save life." The new regulation, which went into effect in 1916, reflected both the desire of the Wilson administration to uphold civilian supremacy in the making of foreign policy and the improvements in radio technology that made communication from ship to shore much easier.[39]

The American occupation of Vera Cruz that resulted from Mayo's ultimatum showed that President Wilson, like McKinley during the Spanish-American War, was determined to supervise military operations carefully and willing to disregard the recommendations of his commanders. The fact that the intervention met more resistance than anticipated may have spurred Wilson's interest in keeping a close eye on things. Facing armed opposition from Mexican soldiers and civilians, the commander, Admiral Frank Fletcher, decided that his forces should take the entire city rather than just the area around the customs house. After fighting that left dozens of Americans dead and wounded, Fletcher's forces gained control of Vera Cruz, which the admiral put under martial law. Responsibility for ruling the city then fell to General Frederick Funston, commander of the army troops sent as an occupation force.[40]

Wilson's policies regarding the occupation puzzled many officers. To General Funston and some of his fellow officers, a large-scale invasion of Mexico made more sense than simply keeping the troops in Vera Cruz to await some sort of response from Huerta. The occupation frustrated military planners, who had anticipated that a conflict with Mexico would result in an American offensive to capture the capital, Mexico City. Funston pressed for permission to push his troops toward Mexico City, but Wilson was determined to limit the intervention and wanted the military to avoid doing anything that might further upset the precarious diplomatic situation. At Wilson's request, Secretary of War Lindley Garrison issued numerous orders designed to keep Funston on a short leash. Garrison directed the general not to expand his lines outward from the city and warned him to avoid actions that could provoke fighting. Funston should do nothing, Garrison informed him, that the War Department had not authorized him to do. "The duty of the Army is to carry out a policy," said the secretary, "not to inaugurate one." Funston obeyed his orders, and the eight months of the occupation passed without major incident.[41]

Less than two years later, however, the army found itself in Mexico again, this time in pursuit of the rebel forces led by Pancho Villa. Villa's attack on the border town of Columbus, New Mexico, in March 1916 prompted Wilson to send an expedition into Mexico with orders to destroy, capture, or disperse the raiders. Although the Wilson administration believed that Mexican president Venustiano Carranza had consented to the expedition, it was anxious to prevent any missteps by American troops that could anger the Mexican government. Toward that end Wilson gave the command of the so-called Punitive Expedition to Brigadier General John J. Pershing, a man with a reputation for good judgment and obedience to civil authority. Pershing faced a daunting task—President Wilson expected him to pursue the Villistas aggressively and yet also gave him explicit orders to do nothing that might provoke a clash with the forces of Carranza's government.[42]

Pershing's command, which began with around 5,000 troops but eventually grew to almost 12,000, pushed hundreds of miles into Mexico, yet Villa eluded capture. Taken aback by the size and duration of the intervention, Carranza demanded that the Americans return across the border. Tension between the U.S. and Mexican troops rose, and in April a gun battle between a group of American soldiers and some Carrancistas in the town of Parral resulted in deaths on both sides. Pershing, furious over the incident, called upon his superiors to authorize some form of retaliation against Carranza's forces and even recommended that the army take over the state of Chihuahua as a prelude to a possible American occupation of all of Mexico. Pershing's message alarmed Wilson and his advisors; Secretary of War Newton Baker complained of Pershing's "failure to comprehend the delicate duty intrusted to him." Worried that the angry general might do something to precipitate more fighting, the administration ordered Pershing to draw back his forces and concentrate them along the rail lines. The goal now, it seemed, was less to capture Villa than to extract U.S. forces from Mexico without either losing honor or starting a war.[43]

The situation remained tense as American troops gradually pulled back. In June the commander of Mexican forces in Chihuahua announced that he would resist any movement by Americans other than northward toward the border. Without waiting for instructions from Washington, Pershing replied that he would move his troops as he deemed it necessary to fulfill his mission. To the press Pershing remarked, "I do not take orders except from my own government." Not long after that Pershing sent out a cavalry patrol to investigate a rumored massing of Carrancistas in a nearby town. Pershing had instructed the commander, Captain Charles T. Boyd, to avoid conflict with the Mexican troops. Boyd, however, impetuously ordered his command to attack a group of Mexican soldiers blocking his route near the town of Carrizal. The American cavalrymen were beaten back with considerable losses, with Captain Boyd among the dead. Early news stories reporting that the Mexicans had ambushed Boyd's troops caused outrage in the United States, and war with Mexico seemed likely. Fortunately, cooler heads prevailed. The Wilson administration rejected Pershing's call for retaliatory action against Carranza's forces. Eyewitness reports indicating that Captain Boyd, not the Mexicans, had been the aggressor in the fight dampened the war fever. The administration began to withdraw the expeditionary force out of Mexico, a task that was completed by February 1917.[44]

During the Punitive Expedition the Wilson administration succeeded, for the most part, in keeping the military campaign under the control of civilian officials. Given that the campaign took place deep within a foreign country and under extremely challenging circumstances, maintaining that control was no small achievement. Determined to prevent the expedition against Villa from escalating into a broader conflict, the administration placed numerous restrictions on how Pershing could use the forces under his command and carefully monitored his performance. Pershing disliked having to operate within such constraints, but he acquiesced to them. The only significant exception to this record of military compliance was Captain Boyd's ill-fated charge, undertaken in defiance of Pershing's orders. Although Wilson and his advisors did not appreciate Pershing's calls for retaliation following the battles between American troops and Carranza's forces, they admired his readiness to follow administration policies even when he opposed them. Pershing did indeed find much to dislike about those policies. "Having dashed into Mexico with the intention of eating the Mexicans raw, we turn back at the very first repulse," he complained to his father-in-law as the U.S. troops withdrew, "and are now sneaking home under cover like a whipped cur with his tail between his legs." He believed it the soldier's duty, however, to keep such sentiments private. As he explained to one of his aides, the future World War II commander George S. Patton, Jr.:

> When we enter the army, we do so with full knowledge that our first duty is toward the government, entirely regardless of our own views under any given circumstances. We are at liberty to express our personal views only when called upon to do so or else confidentially to our friends, but always confidentially and with the complete understanding that they are in no sense to govern our actions. [45]

PUBLIC EXPRESSION, LEGITIMATE AND OTHERWISE

Most officers seemed to be in accord with Pershing's view that members of the military should not make public their views on contentious issues.

Some, however, felt less hesitancy about declaring their opinions, at times to the distress of their civilian superiors. As the army's commanding general between 1895 and 1903, Nelson Miles often aired his disagreements with the policies set by civilian leaders. He publicly opposed two of the major policies of McKinley and Roosevelt administrations—the colonization of the Philippines and the creation of an army general staff. Miles's lack of discretion annoyed administration officials, but his popularity as a Civil War hero and Indian fighter made it difficult to rein him in. General Frederick Funston caused an uproar when, during a speaking tour of the United States following his capture of the Filipino nationalist leader Emilio Aguinaldo in 1901, he condemned critics of the Philippines War, declaring that those who accused the army of committing atrocities should hang for treason. Following a verbal attack by Funston on George Frisbee Hoar, the anti-imperialist senator from Massachusetts, President Roosevelt ordered the general to stop making public speeches. President Taft criticized Commander William Sims of the navy for remarks that, in the president's view, damaged American diplomatic efforts in Europe. In 1910 the commander had, in extemporaneous remarks made at a luncheon in London honoring the visiting U.S. fleet, voiced his opinion "that if ever the integrity of the British Empire should be seriously threatened by an external enemy, they might count upon the assistance of every man, every ship, and every dollar from their kinsmen across the seas." An irritated Taft, noting that the statement had riled the Germans as well as German Americans and Irish Americans, reprimanded Sims for exceeding the bounds of diplomatic propriety.[46]

Many officers believed that, while they should not speak out about such things as their political preferences, legislation unrelated to the military, or the foreign polices of an administration, they should be able to express publicly their opinions on matters within the sphere of their professional expertise—the design of warships, for instance, or the organization of the army. Officers often used public speeches and articles in the popular press to discuss what they perceived as the needs of the military, whether it be the creation of a general staff or the imposition of more rigorous training standards on the National Guard. But determining the line that separated the legitimate expression of professional opinion and the unacceptable expression of political views could be difficult. Much depended on whether the views that officers expressed meshed with polices of the current administration. The public advocacy by naval officers of a buildup of their service, for example, met with no objections from the Roosevelt administration, which favored expansion of the navy. During Woodrow Wilson's presidency, however, similar agitation for a larger army and navy by General Leonard Wood and Admiral Bradley Fiske brought rebukes from the White House because the officers called for spending beyond that sought by the administration.[47]

Distrustful of the military, Wilson thought that the line separating the armed services from politics should be a rigid one. General Hugh S. Scott, the army chief of staff during Wilson's first term, noted to a friend that the president "would resent my talking to him about any political matter; I have never done so on any occasion as I felt that any such attempt would get me a request to mind my own business." Wilson believed that military officers should not speak out on politics or policy issues and took steps to prevent it from happening. He seemed to have more difficulties with talkative officers than had Roosevelt and Taft, perhaps because so many in the military disapproved of the policies of his administration. At Wilson's request, Secretary of War Lindley Garrison searched military regulations for rules that prohibited officers from speaking publicly on controversial issues. Garrison found no such regulation, but maintained that the military had long accepted the idea that officers were not to voice their opinions regarding public policy. The secretary of war reported that he routinely sent letters of condemnation to officers who had publicly expressed their views on political questions.[48]

In the first year of his presidency, Wilson learned from press accounts that the annual dinner of the Washington, D.C. chapter of the Military Order of the Carabao, an association of veterans of the war in the Philippines that included many serving officers, had featured skits and songs ridiculing the administration. Incensed by the reports, Wilson asked his secretaries of the army and navy to investigate and recommend whether a court-martial would be appropriate for some of the participants. The secretaries suggested that reprimands would suffice. Wilson went along with the advice, but made clear his disdain for officers who did not show civilian leaders proper respect. "What are we to think of officers of the army and navy of the United States," he wrote the secretaries, "who think it 'fun' to bring their official superiors into ridicule and the policies of the government which they are sworn to serve with unquestioning loyalty into contempt?"[49]

While Wilson's standards for judging whether the military had "unquestioning loyalty" for civilian leaders may have been more stringent than those of his predecessors in office, few questioned his authority to reprimand officers for speaking out or his expectation that officers would adhere to the policies set by his administration without quibbling. The military's acceptance of its subordination to civilian authority was well established by the time he entered the White House. So too was the idea that the military's subordination required that it maintain political neutrality. Most members of the military understood that they should avoid involvement in partisan politics and abstain from making public pronouncement on controversial issues. The military also understood that—due to improvements in communication technology and the determination of civilian leaders to control military operations—individual commanders had lost some of the authority to act on their own initiative. If Admiral Mayo's blustering ultimatum to the Mexican officials in Tampico represented a last hurrah of the independent commander of old, the Wilson administration's tight supervision of General Pershing's expedition to capture Villa suggested the shape of things to come.

5

Civil-Military Relations and the Campaign for Military Reform

The rise of professionalism strengthened support in the military for two significant principles—first, that the armed services should be subordinate to civilian authority and, second, that a modern military should be led by a highly trained officer corps. Yet adherence to both principles created a dilemma for the military. Professionalism required that officers submit to the will of their civilian superiors, but it also emphasized that only officers trained in the profession possessed the specialized knowledge required to make good military decisions. If modern warfare and military operations were too complex for the nonprofessional to understand, some officers wondered, why must the armed forces yield to decisions made by civilian leaders lacking in military training and experience?

That question had no easy answers, but by the late nineteenth century some in the military came to believe that an innovation of the Prussian military—the general staff system—offered a way to allow the armed forces to benefit from the expertise of their best officers while still maintaining civilian supremacy. The creation of a general staff in the army and navy, they argued, would provide the means through which the military's top professionals could coordinate actions within the services, conduct long-term military planning, and provide expert advice to civilian leaders. Such a reform, proponents suggested, would reduce the conflicts that arose due to unclear lines of authority—here they had in mind the frequent quarrels that occurred between the secretary of war and the army's commanding general and, within the services, between line officers and the staff bureaus.

Unfortunately for the reformers, the general staff idea attracted strong opposition both inside and outside the military. Officers content with the status quo—particularly those in the bureaus—fought against the reform, as did civilians who perceived the general staff as a threat to civilian control of the military. Consequently, the reformers had only mixed success. Although Congress authorized the creation of a general staff for the army in 1903, the limited powers of the new staff, as well as continued resistance to it from within the army, undercut its effectiveness. The navy's General Board, created in 1900, offered a poor substitute for a general staff, and efforts to establish such a staff in the navy failed to overcome the opposition from the bureaus and their congressional allies. Nevertheless, both the army's general staff and the navy's General Board represented important steps toward improved planning and coordination in the military, and neither presented a serious challenge to civilian control.

COMMAND CONFUSION

The structure of command in the military in the late nineteenth century made conflict within the services almost impossible to avoid. In the War Department in particular, clashes between the secretary and the army's commanding general over issues of policy and prerogative occurred with discouraging frequency. Much of the conflict grew out of disputes over the authority of the secretary of war and the secretary of the navy in relation to the ranking officers of the two services. The commanding general and the admiral of the navy—appointed by the president but by tradition the highest ranking officers in their respective services—directed the line forces. The secretaries supervised the fiscal and administrative affairs of their departments. The division of responsibility appeared clear enough on paper, but in operation it produced confusion. In the words of General John Schofield, who served as both secretary of war and commanding general, the division led to "a fruitless controversy over the exact location of an undefined and undefinable line supposed to separate the military administration from the command in the army, or the functions of the Secretary of War from those of the commanding general."[1]

This divided system of control left many in the military dissatisfied. One problem, in their view, was that the system gave authority over the staff bureaus to the secretaries. The bureaus, headed by army or navy officers who supervised a workforce of civilian clerks, performed a number of essential functions. The army's administrative and technical bureaus had duties ranging from record keeping (the Adjutant General's Department) to the testing and procurement of weapons and ammunition (the Ordnance Department) to mapping and construction (the Corps of Engineers). The navy's bureaus included the Bureau of Construction and Repair and the Bureau of Equipment and Recruiting. Placing the bureaus under the control of the secretaries rather than the commanding general or the admiral of the navy meant that staff and line officers often acted without coordination and sometimes at cross purposes. The commanding general might order a company of infantry to a new location, for example, but he could not command the bureaus to provide that company with supplies and weapons once it arrived there. That authority rested with the secretary and the bureau chiefs.[2]

Line officers complained about the unwieldiness of the system. Requests for the simplest tasks, they noted, had to go through a bureaucratic labyrinth. One of the critics, Major General John Pope, described the convoluted process required to obtain permission to repair the roofs of supply buildings at Fort Yuma in the Arizona Territory. "[I]t would be absolutely necessary," he wrote, "before it could be done, to send estimates to department headquarters at Prescott, thence to division headquarters at San Francisco, thence to the General of the Army in St. Louis, thence to the Secretary of War, thence to the Quartermaster-General, thence back to the Secretary of War for his orders, and thence back by the same channel as it went, to Fort Yuma, which place it would reach, if lucky, probably six months after it left there, by which time it is to be presumed everything destructible would have been destroyed."[3]

The decades following the Civil War witnessed a nearly constant battle for power and influence between the secretary of war and the commanding general. Immediately after the war the efforts of Secretary of War Edwin Stanton to bring the staff bureaus under his control met with the determined opposition of General-in-Chief Ulysses S. Grant, who insisted that he have complete authority over the adjutant general's office, a vital cog in the army's administrative structure. Grant also argued that the commanding general should serve directly beneath the president without the secretary in an intermediary role. The commanding general, he said, should stand "between the President and the army in all official matters." Grant exerted his authority over the bureaus, and Congress gave the general more of what he wanted in the Command of the Army Act, passed as a provision of the army appropriation bill in March 1867. Aimed at preventing President Andrew Johnson from curbing the army's ability to carry out Reconstruction policies, the act stipulated that all orders to the army from the president or the secretary of war "shall be issued through the General of the Army." That procedure permitted Grant to stay fully informed about what civilian leaders were asking the army to do and gave him the opportunity to modify the orders. The act also prohibited the president from ordering the general in chief out of Washington or from removing him from office without the concurrence of the Senate. Although some observers saw the act as an unconstitutional restriction on the president's authority as commander in chief, it never faced a test in court and remained in effect until Congress repealed it in 1870.[4]

Grant's election as president in 1868 brought his wartime colleague William T. Sherman into the position of commanding general. With Grant's approval, the outgoing secretary of war, John Schofield, issued an order giving the commanding general direct control of the bureaus and requiring that all orders of the president and secretary of war be transmitted through the commanding general's office. To Sherman's dismay, the new secretary of war persuaded Grant to rescind the order soon after taking office. Secretary of War John A. Rawlins, who had served as Grant's chief aide during the war, established the old bifurcation of duties, with the secretary in charge of the bureaus and the commanding general directing military operations. Sherman asked for an explanation for the change, and Grant blamed Congress. Members of that body, he told Sherman, had insisted that Schofield's order be withdrawn because it violated laws and regulations regarding the bureaus. Republicans in Congress, and perhaps Rawlins and Grant as well, may also have been reluctant to let Sherman, known to be hostile to Congressional Reconstruction, exercise broad authority over the army.[5]

Secretary Rawlins died in September 1869, and under his successor, William W. Belknap, Sherman experienced a rapid erosion of his power and influence. Secretary Belknap issued orders, made appointments, and approved contracts without informing the commanding general. Sherman protested to the president, but Grant declined to act. The commanding general's position, Sherman said, had become a "sinecure." "Little by little the Secretary of War has regained the actual control of the Army," Sherman admitted in 1871. The secretary, Sherman complained, too often based decisions on political rather than military considerations. "Members of Congress daily appeal to the Secretary of War for the discharge of some solider on the application of a mother, or some young officer has to be dry-nursed, withdrawn from his company on the plains to be stationed near home. The Secretary of War, sometimes moved by private reasons, or more likely to oblige the member of Congress, grants the order, of which the commanding general knows nothing till he reads it in the newspapers." In 1874 Sherman sought to escape the embarrassment of his irrelevancy by moving his headquarters to St. Louis. To remain in Washington "as a kind of apologist" for the army, he said, was "beneath the dignity of my office and character." Sherman returned to Washington only after Belknap—caught selling the rights to sutlerships at army posts—resigned from office in 1876.[6]

A worrisome result of the secretary's ascendancy over the commanding general, as military reformers saw it, was the accompanying rise in the influence of the bureaus. The officers in charge of the bureaus developed close ties to the secretary of war, who often relied on them for advice, and with members of Congress, who valued the bureaus for the benefits they could provide constituents. A member of Congress might call upon the army's Bureau of Pensions and Records, for instance, to solve a problem regarding a constituent's military records, the Corps of Engineers to repair a river levy, or the navy's Bureau of Construction and Repair to award a contract to a business associate. Congress, in return, provided the bureaus with healthy appropriations and strong political protection.[7]

Appointments to the bureaus were permanent—officers who received a bureau assignment could spend the remainder of their military careers on such duty. For that reason, they identified closely with the bureau to which they had been posted. Staff officers recognized that their interests lay in running an efficient operation and in responding effectively to the requests of the secretary and of Congress. Keeping the line officers contented often became a secondary concern. With the bureaus focused narrowly on their own functions, both the army and the navy lacked an agency capable of taking a broader, service-wide view in planning for the long term. The bureaus produced fragmentation within the service, their critics said, and it was too much to expect that the secretary of the navy or the army—almost always someone without much military experience and likely to hold office for only a few years—could impose on the services the order and direction that they needed.[8]

THE GENERAL STAFF IDEA

A number of line officers found the situation unacceptable and pondered possible alternatives to the army's system of organization. In the 1870s two army colonels, Emory Upton and William Hazen, studied the Prussian military—recently victorious in wars against Austria and France—and concluded that an important element of its success was its general staff, a body able to make plans and provide coordination and direction for the entire army. Upton also suggested that the army rotate officers in and out of staff assignments, so that officers serving in the bureaus would not become partisans of their particular agency and would have a better understanding of the needs of troops in the field. Both Hazen and Upton published books that included praise for the Prussian system and suggestions for reforming the U.S. Army. Through their writings and personal contacts, the two officers influenced the thinking of reform advocates such as Sherman and Representative James Garfield of Ohio.[9]

An opportunity to reform the bureau system arose in 1878, when a joint committee of Congress investigated the army's organization and recommended significant changes. The committee, chaired by Senator Ambrose Burnside of Rhode Island, a former Civil War general, heard the testimony of Sherman and other army leaders before devising a reform measure—known as the Burnside bill—that included provisions reducing the size of the bureaus, requiring the army to rotate officers between line and bureau duty, and directing the bureaus to report to the commanding general. The bill also combined the departments of the adjutant general and the inspector general to create a general staff under the commanding general's control. Bureau officers—threatened by the reduction in positions and the rotation policy required by the bill and loath to lose the independence and influence they enjoyed under the secretary of war—quickly mobilized to oppose the legislation. Stationed in Washington and able to build on their close working relationship with members of Congress, bureau officers had an advantage over line officers in lobbying. With the army divided over the Burnside bill and Sherman unwilling to exert much effort on its behalf (he left on vacation at a crucial moment in the measure's legislative journey), Congress adjourned without passing it.[10]

In 1883 Sherman, having reached the age of retirement, stepped aside as commanding general for Philip Sheridan. Although Sherman had regained some authority for the office in the years following Secretary Belknap's resignation in 1876, he still lamented the commanding general's lack of power and influence. The position was not a true command, he explained to Sheridan, "but simple acquiescence in the system which has grown up . . . where the President commands, the Secretary of War commands, each Head of Bureau commands, and the real general is a mere figurehead." Believing that Sherman "threw up the sponge" on the question of his authority, Sheridan hoped to do better. An early test of his authority came when Sheridan, interpreting President Chester Arthur's order giving him command of the army to include the bureaus as well as the line, ordered a bureau chief out of Washington to conduct an inspection tour without first informing, let alone securing approval from, the secretary of war. Upon learning of the order, Secretary of War Robert Todd Lincoln, son of the martyred president, sent Sheridan a letter asserting that the general had overstepped his authority— the secretary of war, not the commanding general, controlled the bureaus. Thoroughly rebuffed, the general complied with Lincoln's directive.[11]

Sheridan's retreat had not ended, however. With the Democrats in power following Grover Cleveland's victory in the 1884 presidential election, Sheridan, a Republican, had few friends in the administration. The new secretary of war, William C. Endicott, made his intentions clear when he sent to each of the army's generals a copy of former secretary Lincoln's letter chastising Sheridan. Endicott later expanded his authority by insisting that Sheridan could not even order the movement of troops—something commanding generals had previously done routinely—without first obtaining the secretary's permission.[12]

John M. Schofield, appointed commanding general upon Sheridan's death in 1888, sought to redefine the position in a way that would increase its significance while allowing him to maintain a harmonious relationship with civilian leaders. A trusted subordinate of Grant and Sherman during the Civil War, Schofield had also served as secretary of war under President Andrew Johnson in 1868. He perceived that the commanding general stood little chance of prevailing in any contest for power with the secretary of war, partly because of the nation's tradition of civil supremacy and partly because the secretary was likely to be a political ally of the president. Rather than contend for authority, Schofield readily conceded his subordination to the secretary of war. As he conceived of his job, he served his civilian superiors as an advisor, facilitator, and conduit of information. He made sure that they stayed well informed about what was happening in the army (all of the orders he issued to officers of the line, for instance, went first to the secretary of war), and he worked to provide them with timely and well-considered advice on military matters. All that he asked in return was that orders from civilian leaders to troops of the line go through his office and that the bureau chiefs transmit orders to their subordinates in the field through the departmental commanders. Diplomatic, conscientious, and politically shrewd, Schofield provided a model for an effective chief of staff, a position that many military reformers wanted to create as a replacement for the commanding general.[13]

Schofield's model of military leadership, he noted shortly after his retirement, "worked well enough so long as I helped to work it." His replacement as commanding general had neither the ability nor the desire to keep the system functioning. Appointed to the position in 1895, Nelson Miles believed that the job of the commanding general was to command, not to advise. The commanding general had the authority to control the bureaus, Miles asserted, and the secretary should restrict himself to the purely administrative matters of the War Department. Schofield had demonstrated that the recipe for gaining influence as commanding general was to serve his civilian superiors as an efficient administrator and a provider of sound counsel and abundant information. Miles possessed an outstanding record as a field commander, but he was an indifferent administrator and too contentious and politically ambitious to become a trusted advisor.[14]

The many flaws in the army's command structure were exposed to the world during the war between the United States and Spain in 1898. The lack of advance planning, the absence of coordinated effort between the bureaus and the line, the unwillingness of the secretary of war and the commanding general to cooperate—all contributed to the army's less-than-impressive performance in the conflict. With Secretary of War Russell Alger overwhelmed by his department's responsibilities and Miles out of sync with the administration's war plans, President William McKinley turned to one of the bureau heads, Adjutant General Henry C. Corbin, to provide advice and manage the army's mobilization. The army thus had, in effect, three chiefs below the president—the secretary of war, the commanding general, and the adjutant general—and the three were frequently at odds with one another.[15]

VICTORIES FOR REFORM

The outcry that arose over the obvious organizational failures of the military during the war opened an opportunity for the reformers. The navy took the first steps toward an improved system of planning with the creation of the General Board in 1900. Established by Secretary of the Navy John D. Long, the General Board consisted of a group of senior line officers who were to provide advice to the secretary and coordinate the navy's ship-building and

9. President William McKinley and Admiral George Dewey, 1899. Admiral George Dewey, shown here with President William McKinley at ceremonies in his honor in 1899, won public acclaim for his decisive victory over the Spanish at Manila Bay in the Philippines. In 1900 Dewey became the first president of the navy's General Board. LC-USZ62-55743, Library of Congress.

war-planning efforts. The board was to form its recommendations by drawing upon the planning already being done in the Naval War College, the Office of Naval Intelligence, and the Bureau of Navigation. The appointment of George Dewey—the navy's leading hero and ranking admiral—as president of the board gave it immediate prestige and ensured that its work would receive attention.[16]

The establishment of the General Board gave proponents of reform a partial victory. For at least two decades prior to its creation, a number of naval officers had been pushing for an agency capable of providing planning and coordination for the entire service. The Naval War College and the Office of Naval Intelligence, both established in the 1880s, had fulfilled that purpose to some extent, but many officers agreed that a general staff would be better suited for the role. The general staff idea, however, failed to win the support of Secretary Long, who believed that a chief of staff would undercut the authority of his office by seeking to communicate directly with the president. The General Board, then, represented a compromise. It satisfied the advocates of professionalism by providing for a system of long-term planning and by giving high-ranking officers the responsibility for that task, but it posed little threat to the principle of civilian supremacy because it remained firmly under the secretary's control. It could advise, but it had no power to command. Its effectiveness in coordinating operations within the navy depended entirely on whether the secretary issued orders based on its recommendations.[17]

In the army the prospects for reform improved tremendously when President McKinley named Elihu Root to replace the discredited Russell Alger as secretary of war in 1899. A prominent corporate lawyer, Root embraced the managerial revolution then sweeping through business and government. "This is a time of organization," he announced. "Great results are produced only by that. . . . Effective and harmonious organization is the moving power of the world today." Although he recognized that his department fell far short of the "effective and harmonious" ideal he advocated, Root understood that an effort to rush reform measures through Congress would probably fall flat. The secretary instead set out to become familiar with his organization and to read what had already been written on the issue of military reform. The work of Emory Upton impressed him in particular, and he arranged for the posthumous publication of Upton's last manuscript, *The Military Policy of the United States*. Root's studies led him to the conclusion that what the army needed above all was a general staff—the "brain of the army," in the phrase of a contemporary British writer. Root saw the creation of a general staff as a way to help the army achieve the administrative efficiency he desired and to satisfy a central principle of military professionalism—that, as he put it, "the real object of having an Army is to provide for war."[18]

When Theodore Roosevelt became president following McKinley's assassination in 1901, Root gained a crucial partner in his push for a general staff. Like Root, Roosevelt had a keen interest in administrative reform. As lieutenant colonel of the Rough Riders during the Spanish-American War, the new president had also experienced firsthand the consequences of the army's inefficient planning. In his first message to Congress, Roosevelt endorsed the creation of an army general staff. Two months later Root sent the necessary legislation to the House and Senate Military Affairs Committees. The measure, drafted primarily by Root's chief advisor, Colonel William H. Carter, established a general staff responsible for coordinating planning, overseeing the bureaus, devising legislation and policies for the army, and advising the president and the secretary of war. The legislation abolished the commanding general's position and replaced it with a chief of staff, who, unlike the commanding general, would be limited to a four-year term of service. The bill also eliminated the powerful adjutant general's office, replacing it with a military secretary who would report to the general staff. In addition, it struck a blow at the entrenched political influence of the bureaus by requiring a rotation of officers between the bureaus and the line.[19]

Root promoted the bill as a means of improving the army's efficiency while at the same time enhancing civilian control over the military. The bill would end the old system of divided responsibility and put in its place a structure in which the army's leading officer—the chief of staff—would be directly subordinate to the secretary of war. The measure would allow for "civilian control to be exercised through a single military expert of high rank," Root later explained, "who is bound to use all his professional skill and knowledge in giving effect to the purposes and general directions of his civilian superior, or make way for another expert who will do so."[20]

The army as a whole did not rally behind the general staff bill. The measure had the support of the influential *Army and Navy Journal* and of such prominent generals as John Schofield, Henry Corbin, and Wesley Merritt, but relatively few officers spoke out in its favor. As expected, the bill drew strong opposition from most of the bureau heads and from the commanding general, Nelson Miles, whose arguments against the measure almost sank it. In testimony before the Senate Military Affairs Committee, Miles delivered a message designed to win the favor of Civil War veterans both inside and outside of Congress. He observed that the current system, the "fruit of the best thought by the most eminent patriots and ablest military men," had given the Union its victory in the war. "I trust," Miles said of the commanding general's position, "that the office which [Winfield] Scott and Sherman held with so much distinction will not be destroyed while any of their comrades and friends still survive." Seeking to remind Americans of the foreign roots of the general staff idea, Miles maintained that the bill would introduce into the government "a system proverbially adopted by monarchies. . . . It would seem to Germanize and Russianize the small army of the United States."[21]

Miles's objections went beyond emotional appeals to patriotism and tradition. He portrayed the general staff reform as threatening a major value of military professionalism—the necessity of maintaining a separation between the military and politics. Miles suggested that a general staff would end the military's standing as an apolitical institution. In place of the commanding general, invariably the army's senior officer, there would be the chief of staff, an officer appointed by the president perhaps on the basis of political affiliation or personal loyalty. Indeed, an administration might pack the entire general staff with loyalists. Officers who owed their positions on the staff to a presidential administration would be reluctant to differ with it, Miles said. As a result, civilian leaders "whose knowledge of affairs military may be meager or nil" would dominate the decision-making. General Arthur MacArthur, recently returned to the United States after having served as commander in the Philippines, echoed Miles's concerns. A general staff system would produce tumult in the army, MacArthur argued, because the staff would change every time a new administration came to power.[22]

The Root bill faced powerful opponents outside the army as well. The Grand Army of the Republic, the popular and politically potent organization of Union veterans, weighed in against the measure. Many Democrats, still wary of the regular army and therefore reluctant to back a bill that promised to make it more effective, vowed to vote against it. Critics of the Roosevelt administration warned that the measure would strengthen the president's control over the army, a development that could lead to military dictatorship. A Kentucky newspaper publisher predicted a "sentry box on each street corner" if the bill passed, and the *Atlanta Constitution* envisaged "warlord leadership." Swayed by Miles's testimony, Senator Joseph Hawley, a Civil War volunteer general and chairman of the Senate Military Affairs Committee, began to voice doubts about the bill, as did Republican senator Redfield Proctor, a former secretary of war. Noting the growing opposition, a newspaper supportive of the bill pronounced it a "cadaver."[23]

With the general staff bill nearly dead, the Roosevelt administration took steps to revive its chances for passage. In October 1902, Root dispatched General Miles on a lengthy tour to examine military conditions in the Philippines, China, and Europe, thereby removing the bill's most prominent opponent from the scene. Two months later President Roosevelt renewed his call for a general staff in a message to Congress. To placate the bureau chiefs and their friends in Congress, Root agreed to drop a provision that would consolidate the army's supply departments. He also accepted a change in the bill's language so that the chief of staff would have only "supervisory" and "coordinating" authority over the bureaus rather than the power to command them directly. The revised measure passed the House in January 1903. Senator Hawley appeared determined to bottle it up in the Senate Military Affairs Committee, but illness forced him to relinquish the chairmanship, and the bill passed the Senate. Roosevelt signed it into law in February 1903. As Root had promised Congress, the administration waited until after Miles had retired in August 1903 to put the new system into place.[24]

THE LIMITS OF REFORM

Once in operation, the general staff only partly satisfied the expectations of its supporters. Roosevelt and subsequent presidents appreciated that it gave them the ability to appoint as chief of staff generals congenial to the administration rather than having to put up with possibly unfriendly commanding generals who held the office because they outranked all other generals. When Roosevelt appointed General J. Franklin Bell as chief of staff, for example, he passed over the army's ranking general, the prickly Arthur MacArthur. The general staff did well in coordinating the intervention of 5,000 U.S. soldiers in Cuba in 1906, and the line officers commanding the troops in that episode seemed amenable to the general staff's supervision. The mobilization of regular troops along the Mexican border in 1911 went less well. Ordered by President William Howard Taft to assemble a "Maneuver Division" of 20,000 troops in Texas to provide field training for the soldiers and a possible intervention force should the upheaval caused by the revolution in Mexico threaten American interests, the army struggled to gather its scattered units. After three months, it had managed to put together a division containing only 13,000 troops.[25]

The ill-defined relationship between the general staff and the bureaus proved to be the greatest weakness of the system. Root's compromise giving the chief of staff supervisory rather than commanding authority over the bureaus meant that they retained much of their independence. The Roosevelt administration contributed to the problem by doing little to bolster the power of the chief of staff. The president and his secretaries of war rarely consulted with the men who served as chief during Roosevelt's time in office; one of the chiefs, J. Franklin Bell, was so poorly informed about the administration's policies that he first learned the White House was considering intervention in Cuba from articles in the press.[26]

The situation provided an opportunity for a capable and ambitious bureau veteran, General Fred C. Ainsworth. A medical doctor who had entered the army as a contract surgeon and then received a commission in the Medical Corps, Ainsworth had risen to become head of the Bureau of Records and Pensions. There he built a rock-solid relationship with members of Congress, who appreciated his smooth administration of the bureau and his ability to help them resolve constituents' problems regarding military pensions. Appointed to the new position of military secretary after the passage of the General Staff Act, Ainsworth continued to increase his influence by taking charge of routine administrative matters. He convinced Secretary of War William Howard Taft, eager to end the squabbling that arose between Ainsworth and the chief of staff over issues of authority, to give the military secretary complete control over the civil business of the bureaus. At Ainsworth's instigation, Congress reestablished the position of adjutant general, which the General Staff Act had eliminated, and approved a promotion for Ainsworth so that he could take the position. By 1907, when Ainsworth took office as adjutant general, it was obvious that the reformers had fallen short of their goals. The General Staff Act had failed both to rein in the bureaus and to centralize authority within the army under the chief of staff. Adjutant General Ainsworth, a man more concerned about bureaucratic efficiency than about long-term military planning, used his authority over the everyday affairs of army administration to become the dominant figure in the service.[27]

Ainsworth's ascendancy went largely unchallenged until General Leonard Wood became chief of staff in 1910. Like Ainsworth, Wood was a physician who had come into the army as a contract surgeon. His able performance as an administrator in Cuba and the Philippines, coupled with his close ties to civilian leaders such as Presidents McKinley and Roosevelt, helped him rise rapidly in rank. Determined to make the chief of staff the center of power within the army, Wood asserted his authority by, among other things, demanding that all orders from the War Department to the army go through his office. Ainsworth accused Wood of encroaching on the traditional responsibilities of the adjutant general. In the battle that ensued, both generals had important civilian supporters. Secretary of War Henry L. Stimson backed Wood, as did the still-influential former secretary, Elihu Root, now representing New York in the Senate. Ainsworth's key supporters came from Congress. Many members preferred Ainsworth's style of management, with its emphasis on patronage and civil projects, to Wood's, especially after Wood announced his desire to reduce the number of military posts around the country. Many members, Democrats in particular, also believed that the general staff represented a dangerous move toward militarism and rallied around Ainsworth as a defender of the old system.[28]

The climax of the Ainsworth-Wood battle came in 1912, after Wood and Stimson endorsed a plan to reform the War Department's procedures for managing personnel records. Viewing the recommendation as an intrusion into his area of expertise, Ainsworth responded with a lengthy memorandum condemning the proposal and denouncing its proponents as "uninformed" and "unmindful of consequences." Ainsworth's hotheaded reply challenged the authority of both the chief of staff and the secretary of war and left him open to charges of insubordination. With the support of President William Howard Taft, Stimson initiated court martial proceedings against Ainsworth, who chose to resign rather than go to trial. Congress, angered by the administration's treatment of Ainsworth and upset over the Wood-Stimson plan to close military posts, retaliated by including in the army appropriation bill of 1912 a provision to prevent Wood from continuing as chief of staff after March 1913. Persuaded by Stimson that the bill threatened the cause of military reform and interfered with the president's authority to choose the chief of staff, Taft vetoed the measure.[29]

In forcing Ainsworth out of the army, Wood and Stimson had won a victory that reinforced the authority of the chief of staff. The army became more inclined to look to the chief than to the bureau heads for leadership, a development that pleased the reformers. The episode also signaled a victory for the War Department and the White House in the long-standing battle with Congress over which branch—the executive or the legislative—would

10. General Leonard Wood. General Leonard Wood, shown here as military governor of Cuba in 1901, served as the army's chief of staff from 1910 to 1914. His determination to make the army more efficient by centralizing authority in the general staff brought him into conflict with the heads of the bureaus and their allies in Congress. LC-USZ62-121583, Library of Congress.

have the leading role in determining military policy. But Ainsworth's defeat marked only a small step, not a leap, in the direction of organizational reform. The bureaus retained much of their independence; only in 1918 did a chief of staff, General Peyton C. March, manage to bring the bureaus under his direct command. The general staff continued to formulate plans for possible wars, but its planning function often seemed disconnected from the army's day-to-day affairs. Furthermore, Congress showed itself to be skeptical about, if not openly hostile to, the reform project. Only a presidential veto had prevented Congress from ousting Wood as chief of staff, and the legislators succeeded in reducing the size of the general staff and limiting the length of time officers could serve on it.[30]

THE CAMPAIGN FOR A NAVAL GENERAL STAFF

Although reformers in the army met with difficulties in making the general staff system work, they at least had such a system in place. Reformers in the navy were not so fortunate. Attempts to win congressional approval of legislation creating a naval general staff consistently foundered. In 1904, the year after Congress passed Secretary of War Root's general staff plan for the army, Secretary of the Navy William H. Moody brought before Congress a bill establishing a general staff and a position of chief of naval operations to direct the staff and advise the secretary. Despite endorsements from President Roosevelt and Admiral Dewey, the bill failed to escape the House Naval Affairs Committee. An effort by reform proponents to slip into the 1906 naval appropriations bill a provision giving the chief of the Bureau of Navigation the duties of a chief of staff fell apart when Dewey, who thought the move too underhanded, protested. In 1908 reformers tried to use Senate hearings on deficiencies in battleship design as a forum to make the case for a general staff. When naval officers appearing as witnesses began speaking in favor of a general staff, however, Eugene Hale, chairman of the Senate Naval Affairs Committee, closed the hearings. No legislation to create a general staff would pass Congress, Hale declared, as long as he was a member.[31]

Supporters of a naval general staff faced many of the same obstacles that had nearly derailed the army general staff bill, including the fierce opposition of bureau officers who saw the general staff as a threat to their semiautonomous status and of the members of Congress who valued what the bureaus could do for them. Opponents also expressed concern, as they had in the case of the army bill, that a general staff would erode civilian authority over the navy. Supporters tried to allay such fears. Commander Bradley A. Fiske, writing in 1906, noted that a general staff "implies no surrender by the civil authorities of perfect control" over the military; "it simply implies abstention from interference with details, details which are purely technical. . . . The civil authorities lose no dignity by not interfering with matters that are purely technical, any more than an admiral does by not interfering with the internal administration of his flagship."[32]

Some members of Congress recognized that even if the general staff enhanced civilian control over the military as the reformers said it would, most of the increased civilian authority would belong to the executive branch, not to Congress. If it worked as the reformers intended, a general staff would give the chief executive an instrument for imposing his will upon the military, the bureaus as well as the line. Congress, on the other hand, stood to lose some of its influence if the bureaus, deprived of their independence, could no longer provide political favors in exchange for large congressional appropriations. The intensity of the congressional opposition, led by Senator Hale, may explain why Roosevelt declined to press aggressively for a general staff bill after Secretary Moody, the administration's leading promoter of the reform, left the Navy Department to become attorney general in 1904.[33]

Roosevelt's successor as president, William Howard Taft, supported the idea of a naval general staff, as did Taft's secretary of the navy, the capable and politically astute George von Lengerke Meyer. Meyer understood, though, that a bill to create a general staff was unlikely to pass Congress. Determined to reorganize his department, Meyer found an alternative route to accomplish what he wanted. With Taft's approval, he reorganized the Navy Department into four divisions—operations, personnel, inspections, and materiel—each led by line officers that he had appointed. These division heads, referred to as aides, helped coordinate activities within their areas and transmitted orders from the secretary to the bureaus and departments underneath them. Together they formed an unofficial "strategy board" that met periodically to advise the secretary. Under Meyer's plan, the aide for operations became a quasi chief of staff, responsible for overseeing war planning and movements of the fleet. Meyer's reorganization irritated the bureau chiefs, who now had to endure supervision by the aides. The new system also annoyed some members of Congress, who noted that Meyer had acted without congressional approval. The House Naval Affairs Committee seemed poised to move against the reorganization in 1910 until Admiral Dewey, still serving as chairman of the General Board, interceded with a letter to a committee member asking the group to give Meyer's plan "an unrestricted trial." Congress took no action, and the aide system remained in place.[34]

Another reform idea of the Taft years, the proposal for a "Council of National Defense" to help coordinate the nation's foreign and defense policies, had less success. The proposal, which emerged from the Naval War College in 1910, called for a council made up of three cabinet members—the secretaries of state, war, and the navy; four members of Congress—the chairmen of the military affairs and naval affairs committees in the House and the Senate; and two military men—the presidents of the army and navy war colleges. Later versions of the plan added the army chief of staff, the naval aide for operations, and the chairmen of the House and Senate foreign relations committees. Meetings of the council would provide opportunities for civilian officials to keep military leaders apprised of developments in national policies. The officers, in turn, could offer opinions about the military's capabilities.[35]

The idea presented a strikingly innovative way to improve communication and collaboration between branches of the national government, between branches of the armed services, and between civil and military leaders. The military could not make reasonable war plans, explained Commander F. K. Hill of the Naval War College, unless it had "a thorough knowledge of the diplomatic conditions with all foreign countries . . . and the diplomatic branch is the only one which can furnish correct knowledge of this." Some officers saw a more practical purpose to the council—its meetings would give the services a chance to impress upon key civilian leaders the urgency of their budgetary needs. Beyond the military, however, the proposal attracted little support. Secretary of State Philander Knox and the State Department, jealous of the department's primacy in the making of foreign policy, wanted nothing to do with the idea. Congress seemed equally unenthusiastic. Some members perceived the presence of military officers on the council as a threat to civilian supremacy—the officers, they warned, might dominate the council and thereby play an inappropriate role in policymaking. Congressman Richmond P. Hobson, an Alabama Democrat and former naval officer, introduced a measure to establish a Council of National Defense in 1910, but it had no chance of passage.[36]

The election of Woodrow Wilson in 1912 brought to the White House a Democratic administration distrustful of the military and disinclined to support the establishment of institutions that, like the Council of National Defense or a naval general staff, might increase the military's power. Wilson's secretary of the navy, Josephus Daniels, entered office determined to maintain civilian control over the navy. Daniels ran into difficulties almost immediately with officers who wanted to replace the aide system, which they found unsatisfactory, with a naval general staff. The problem with the aide system, argued reformers such as Admirals Bradley Fiske and William S. Sims, was that while the aides could provide advice to the secretary, they lacked the authority to command. The bureaus continued to operate independently, they said, with harmful consequences for the navy. Reformers pointed to problems in the design of some U.S. warships as an example of the results produced by the poorly coordinated bureau system. Admiral Fiske, serving as the aide for operations under Daniels, led the reformers' campaign for a general staff, a cause that took on greater urgency after the outbreak of war in Europe in 1914. Since the conflict might eventually involve the United States, Fiske believed, the navy needed strong leadership to prepare for war. As Fiske saw it, that leadership was unlikely to come from the civilian secretary, especially one as inexperienced in naval affairs as Daniels, formerly a North Carolina newspaper publisher. What the navy required, he said, was a general staff headed by a powerful chief of naval operations who had the authority to command both the line and the bureaus.[37]

As the naval reformers and their backers in Congress and in the press began to agitate for a general staff, Wilson and Daniels remained strongly opposed to the idea. That position became especially clear in early 1915 when Wilson instructed Daniels to reprimand Admiral Austin M. Knight after the admiral spoke in favor of a general staff in a public address in New York City. With the administration unsupportive, Fiske sought assistance from sympathizers in Congress, including Representative Hobson, sponsor of the National Defense Council bill. Hobson, an Annapolis graduate who won a medal and much positive press for his heroics at the battle of Santiago in 1898, met with Fiske and other officers to devise legislation establishing a chief of naval operations (CNO). Although the bill included language that showed deference to the principle of civilian control—it stated that the CNO would be under the secretary of the navy—it gave the chief extensive authority. The CNO, the bill said, "shall be responsible for the readiness of the Navy for war and be charged with its general direction." Aided by fifteen assistants, the chief would assume many of the duties then held by the General Board, the Naval War College, and the bureaus. Hobson introduced his proposal in 1915 as an amendment to the naval construction bill.[38]

Daniels immediately announced his opposition to the Hobson bill and suggested that he would resign should it pass. He worried that plan gave too much authority to one officer, creating a strong rival to the secretary for control of the navy. Daniels pointed out to Admiral Dewey that the measure would diminish the importance of the General Board, still chaired by Dewey, and persuaded the old war hero to speak out against it. Having damaged the bill's prospects for passage in its current form, Daniels negotiated some modifications to the measure. The original bill gave the chief of naval operations fifteen assistants and responsibility for the "general direction" of the navy. The compromise bill, passed by Congress in March 1915, established a chief of naval operations but provided no assistants and limited his authority to "the operations of the fleet," meaning that the bureaus would be largely beyond his control. The compromise bill also required that the CNO issue orders through the secretary of the navy.[39]

The result disappointed Fiske and his fellow reformers. Their conception of the chief of naval operations reflected the values of military professionalism—they had hoped for a CNO powerful enough to fend off political meddling, bring the self-serving bureaus to heel, and, acting on the advice of his staff of expert officers, build the navy into an efficient and battle-ready force. From the reformers' perspective, the compromise left the CNO too vulnerable to interference from the secretary above and the bureaus below. Still, the compromise bill was an important move forward in the campaign for organizational reform in the military. The authority of the chief of naval operations had substantial limitations, but the measure established a position from which a talented officer, working with the secretary, could provide the navy with some much needed direction and coordination.[40]

The army and navy entered the First World War in 1917 without a strong general staff system in place. To the frustration of the reformers, resistance within Congress and within the military to a highly centralized staff system on the European model proved difficult to overcome. In some respects, however, the reformers had made noteworthy progress in the two decades that had passed since the war with Spain in 1898. The efforts of officers such as Luce, Wood, and Fiske and of civilians such as Secretary of War Root and

Secretary of the Navy Meyer produced an improved process of military planning and a better system for providing military advice to civilian leaders. Perhaps most significantly, the reformers succeeded in ending the troublesome conflict between the commanding general and the secretary of war by eliminating the former position and replacing it with a chief of staff clearly subordinate to the secretary.

The fascination with organizational efficiency and professional expertise that characterized the military reformers reflected the interests of the broader progressive reform movement of the era. Like their civilian counterparts, the "progressives in uniform" sought to increase the power of the executive branch at the expense of the legislative, which they associated with inefficiency and a narrow devotion to local interests at the expense of the national interest. Also like the civilian progressives, the military reformers' emphasis on the importance of training and specialization caused them to disparage the non-expert, a development that led many in the military to resent the control that amateurs in Congress and the War and Navy Departments continued to exercise over military affairs.[41]

Military Disaffection and Challenges to Civil Authority

In 1874 William T. Sherman, commanding general of the army, announced that he was moving his headquarters from Washington, D.C., to St. Louis, Missouri. His disgust with Washington politics and the policies of Secretary of War William Belknap, he said privately, had become so great that he could not bear to stay in the capital. For the next nineteen months Sherman carried out his duties at a distance of over 800 miles from the nation's center of political power, thereby avoiding, in his words, "the mortification of being slighted by men in Washington who were using their temporary power for selfish ends." To a friend he wrote: "I thank God that I am not and never was a Courtier. The Court at Washington is as debasing as at Constantinople." Sherman returned to Washington following Secretary Belknap's resignation in 1876, but he retained his loathing for politics and his determination to remain aloof from them.[1]

In the years following the Civil War, many officers shared Sherman's hostility toward politics and his frustration with government policies. Civilian leaders, they believed, too often gave the military difficult tasks without providing the material support necessary to do them and too often interfered with the military's plans for getting them done. Believing themselves underpaid and underappreciated, officers griped continually about the stinginess of Congress in appropriating funds for the army and navy. They were appalled at the ignorance of most civilians on military matters and indignant when those civilians questioned how the military went about its job. Some officers became contemptuous of civilian leaders and the political system, and a few even questioned the wisdom of the military's subordination to civilian control.[2]

The resentful and sometimes disdainful attitude of many officers toward civilians led at times to troubled relations between the military and its civilian superiors. Yet the sense of estrangement from civil society that permeated the officer corps produced no lasting breach between the military and the civilian government. As frustrated as they were by politics and policies, officers generally accepted the military's subordination to civilian leaders. The relatively rare occasions when military officers challenged civilian superiors usually involved instances in which the lines of authority were unclear or, as in the cases of Generals Ulysses Grant, Nelson Miles, and Leonard Wood, the defiant officers had significant political support.

UNPLEASANT DUTIES

An important source of discontent for many in the military was the nature of the missions assigned to them by civilian leaders. With the exception of the Spanish-American War, the military's tasks between 1865 and 1917 provided few opportunities for martial glory. For the navy, peacetime duty meant mainly routine patrols and occasional visits to foreign ports. For the army, the campaigns against western Indians and insurgents in the Philippines offered little of the glamour associated with the Civil War, and some in the military cast doubt on whether service on the frontier or in the colonies was worthy of the soldier's calling. General Winfield Scott Hancock, one of the many Civil War heroes in the postwar army, called Indian fighting "of secondary importance," and the *Infantry Journal* complained that service in the new imperial holdings provided neither "important honor" nor "material reward."[3]

Members of the military sometimes had strong reservations about the policies they were expected to carry out, usually because they believed the policies to be injurious to their branch of the service or to the national interest. Many army officers, for instance, disagreed with Reconstruction policies that Congress had directed the army to implement. Often identifying with the "respectable" class of educated, well-to-do whites who were resisting Reconstruction measures, the officers favored a quick reconciliation between the North and South and opposed measures designed to help secure blacks the right to vote. George A. Custer announced his lack of sympathy for black voting rights in a letter to his in-laws: "As to trusting the negro of the Southern States with the most sacred and responsible privilege—the right of suffrage—I should as soon think of elevating an Indian Chief to the Popedom of Rome." The commander in Virginia, General John Schofield, doubted the legality of congressional measures to require black suffrage in the states and believed blacks unprepared to participate in the political system. General Edward O. C. Ord, commander in Arkansas and Mississippi, condemned the Reconstruction Acts and thought black suffrage a mistake.[4]

Whatever their views on Reconstruction, most army officers disliked duty in the postwar South. Congress had thrust them into the middle of a nasty political conflict, they believed, without clear guidelines or adequate resources.

Most officers saw themselves as representing the reasonable center trying to mediate between unreasonable extremes. Their attempts to be evenhanded seemed to bring only rebukes from the two opposing sides; Democrats attacked officers for enforcing Reconstruction measures while Republicans condemned them for not doing enough. General Ord expressed the sentiments of many in the army in a letter to Sherman: "I am in a breech between two exasperated and hostile elements who are being egged on to pitch in to each other by the knaves and fools of both sides."[5]

Officers serving in the West experienced a similar sense of frustration over the federal government's Indian policy. As was the case with Reconstruction, the government expected the army to accomplish a challenging task with a relative handful of troops, and here also the army had to try to follow the government's poorly defined and ever-shifting plans. Officers criticized the government for encouraging white settlement before it had dealt with potentially hostile tribes. They railed against what they perceived as the ineffective and sometimes corrupt administration of the reservations by agents of the Interior Department's Indian Bureau. Many officers considered the government's attempts to preserve peace by giving gifts to the tribes foolish. Above all, the army faulted the government's Indian policy for its inconsistency. At one moment the government seemed determined to resolve disputes with the tribes peacefully, yet at the next it called for aggressive military campaigns against them. Many in the army agreed with the editor of the *Army and Navy Journal* when he wrote of federal Indian policy, "We go to [the Indians] Janus-faced. One of our hands holds the rifle and the other the peace pipe, and we blaze away with both instruments at the same time."[6]

For all of the complaints about Indian policy, it was one of the few matters of national concern in the late nineteenth century upon which the army actually exercised some influence. Presidents, cabinet secretaries, and members of Congress listened to what generals had to say about Indian affairs. When in 1867 Congress established a peace commission to confer with leaders of the tribes of the Great Plains and make recommendations on Indian policies, three of its seven positions went to army officers. The opinions of frontier commanders such as Generals Philip Sheridan and George Crook frequently determined the government's course of action. The problem, from the army's perspective, was that it represented just one faction among many that were striving to shape the government's Indian policy. In the opinion of some officers, the other groups—frontier whites and eastern humanitarians in particular—had more political influence than the army and therefore more success in getting the policy they wanted.[7]

Many in the army developed a profound dislike for frontier whites, the very people that the government had sent the army west to protect. Whites often instigated conflict with the Indians, officers observed, by pushing onto tribal lands or attacking peaceful Indians. The editor of the *Army and Navy Journal* spoke for many in the military when he blamed "the unprincipled

11. Plenty Horses and soldiers at Pine Ridge, South Dakota, 1891. Two soldiers stand guard over Plenty Horses, under arrest for killing an army lieutenant following the Wounded Knee massacre in 1890. An Oglala Sioux, Plenty Horses had spent five years at the Carlisle Indian School in Pennsylvania before his return to the Pine Ridge Agency. Many in the army were frustrated by the federal government's Indian policies, which seemed to veer erratically between the humane treatment advocated by eastern "sentimentalists" and the punitive actions favored by many frontier whites. LC-USZ62-50458, Library of Congress.

greed, and the utter disregard of obligations" of frontier whites for convert-ing "so many well-disposed tribes into scalping, burning, ravishing fiends." In the army's view, settlers had unrealistic expectations about the level of protection that it could provide with so few troops in so vast a region. Sher-man grumbled that whites who lost a horse or some sheep called upon the army for help and complained to the press if the troops failed to scour the countryside on their behalf. Officers resented the pressure that politicians representing the settlers could bring to bear on the army. "These frontier people are wholly unscrupulous," a major wrote in 1879. "It is an outrage that we of the Army who have all the hardships to encounter should be made such catspaws of, mere tools of ambitious men who care only for their own interests, and cater to the public for popularity."[8]

Even more irritating to most officers were the "Friends of the Indian," eastern humanitarians who wanted to protect Indians from unfair govern-ment policies and to promote their assimilation into white society. Although some officers shared the reformers' faith in the possibility of "civilizing" the Indians, others expressed skepticism. The starry-eyed vision of assimilation promoted by the humanitarians, argued General Sheridan and other army leaders, kept the government from unleashing the army to conduct the kind of relentless campaign that would permanently pacify the frontier. In the dis-pute over whether the War Department or the Interior Department should control the reservations, the humanitarians' insistence on the army's moral unfitness to supervise the reservations both angered and insulted officers. Few went as far as Sheridan did in suggesting a tie between the reformers and the corrupt "Indian Ring" of bureau agents and suppliers, but many thought the Friends of the Indian ignorant and meddlesome.[9]

An even more vitriolic disagreement between officers and the humanitari-ans concerned how the army conducted its warfare against the Indians. Hu-manitarians denounced the army for methods that resulted in the deaths of Indian women and children; the practice of launching dawn attacks on In-dian villages in the wintertime attracted particular criticism. Army officers responded to the censure with anger. How could the humanitarians, they asked, safe in their comfortable homes in the East, understand the realities of Indian warfare? Distinguishing between friendly and hostile Indians was at times impossible, argued Sherman, and "to get the rascals, we are forced to include all." The *Army and Navy Journal* disparaged the "eastern sentimen-talists" who protested "with plaintive howls about the barbarity of the sol-diers, as instanced in the shooting of some squaw in the confusion of a daylight attack or the failure to take alive some savage whose hands are reeking with the blood of women and children."[10]

In the years following the Spanish-American War, some officers found as-pects of the nation's foreign and colonial policies objectionable. While many in the army and navy were delighted with the government's new colonial possessions and supportive of the military interventions in Central America and the Caribbean, others privately questioned the nation's new international role. In the case of the Philippines, some officers sympathized with the Filipinos' aspirations for independence and privately expressed doubts that the distant islands were worth the trouble of quelling the insurgency and then providing the defenses necessary to protect the colony from other powers. In the case of the Caribbean and Central America, some wondered whether the United States should be so quick to dispatch ships and troops to unruly nations. The interventions received criticism from officers who looked with distaste upon some of the governments that the United States sought to protect in the region and who argued that the increasingly frequent incursions by the United States distracted the services from their central purpose of preparing for war.[11]

AMBIGUOUS MISSIONS

In both Reconstruction and the Indian wars the army had to forge ahead even when federal policies were poorly defined or in flux. Major shifts in policy, as occurred with the passage of congressional legislation establishing military rule in the South in 1867 or with the announcement of President Grant's Peace Policy regarding the Indians in 1869, left officers uncertain about what was expected of them. In the case of Reconstruction the conflicting interpretations of the army's authority that emerged from the White House, the War Department, and Congress compounded the confusion. The Reconstruction Acts were notoriously vague about the extent of the army's powers, and uncertainty about the military's role increased once the southern states had established civil governments and had been readmitted to the Union. Those states no longer had military governments, but Republican governors frequently called on U.S. troops to protect their regimes and their supporters. Military officers in the South had difficulty determining when they had the authority to do so.[12]

Understandably, local commanders sought direction from their superiors, but the superiors often preferred to leave matters to the discretion of the officer on the scene. In 1872, for example, the commander of federal forces in Louisiana received little guidance from Washington about whether he had the authority to send troops into New Orleans to prevent a possible outbreak of violence or if he could send them only after such an outbreak had occurred. President Grant acknowledged the uncertainties inherent in Reconstruction duty when, in defending the use of federal troops to quell violence in Louisiana in 1874, he observed that "the Army is not composed of lawyers, capable of judging at a moment's notice of just how far they can go in the maintenance of law and order," nor could the army "give specific instructions for all possible contingencies that might arise."[13]

A similar haziness about goals and responsibilities hindered the army at the beginning of the war against Spain in 1898. The McKinley administration gave the army little indication about how it would be used in the conflict, leaving it ill prepared when the president decided to send an invasion force to Cuba in the early months of the war. The army and navy forces sent to occupy Manila following Commodore George Dewey's victory over the Spanish at Manila Bay spent many months without a clear indication from the administration about what the United States intended to do with the Philippines, a lack of guidance that complicated the officers' dealings with Emilio Aguinaldo and other Filipino nationalists.[14]

The absence of a clearly defined mission also frustrated soldiers sent to Mexico in pursuit of Pancho Villa in 1916 following Villa's raid on the border town of Columbus, New Mexico. Initially the purpose of the Punitive Expedition was reasonably clear—General John J. Pershing and his command were to enter Mexico with the goal of breaking up Villa's band of outlaws. The expedition did much to disrupt the band, but Villa remained at large. When the government of President Venustiano Carranza protested the American incursion and fighting broke out between U.S. and Mexican soldiers, the nature of the mission changed. With the search for Villa all but abandoned, American troops spent seven months occupying portions of northern Mexico while the Wilson administration negotiated with the Mexican government over the issue of border security. For the men of the Punitive Expedition, stopped from pursuing Villa and under strict orders to avoid clashes with Carranza's forces, the administration's course of action in Mexico seemed confused and increasingly pointless.[15]

CIVILIAN INTERFERENCE

Also irritating to officers were the occasions when civilian officials interfered with the military's efforts to carry out its duties. The rising professionalism of the officer corps made it difficult for some officers to tolerate what they perceived as the intrusion of civilians into military matters. Officers increasingly saw themselves as members of a professional group, admittance to which required extensive training and mastery of a specialized body of knowledge. They believed that the education and training they received—and by the 1880s both the army and navy had established schools of instruction so that officers could continue their education beyond the service academies—gave them the expertise necessary to make sound military decisions. The more that officers viewed themselves as members of a distinct vocational group with special training and a common set of values, the more likely they were to question military decisions made by those outside of the profession. Commander Bradley A. Fiske of the navy, writing in 1906, articulated that point of view when he argued that unless civilian leaders possessed "absolute mastery" of military principles, they should leave the decisions on "purely" military matters to the trained officers of the services.[16]

Certainly most of the men who served as secretary of war and secretary of the navy fell far short of the standard of "absolute mastery" advocated by Fiske. While some of the secretaries won the confidence of the service they supervised—Secretary of the Navy Benjamin Tracy and Secretary of War Elihu Root were examples—officers assumed that political ties, not knowledge or ability, explained the appointments of most of them. Secretary of the Navy Richard W. Thompson's reported comment on his first tour of a navy ship—"Why, the durned thing's hollow"—may have been apocryphal, but it reflected how little the Iowa politician knew about the navy when he took office in 1877. The scandals that surrounded two members of President Grant's cabinet, Secretary of the Navy George M. Robeson and Secretary of War William Belknap, also lowered the reputation of civilian leaders. Robeson, a New Jersey lawyer, had managed to amass over $300,000 in his bank account during his years as secretary of the navy despite a salary of only $8,000 a year. Evidence suggested that he had received payments from a company supplying food to the navy. Belknap resigned after a congressional inquiry uncovered his practice of taking bribes from businessmen in exchange for granting concessions to run trading posts at army forts. Secretary of War Russell Alger, blasted by both the press and many officers for his inept handling of the army's mobilization in the war with Spain in 1898, seemed to epitomize the political appointee whose unfamiliarity with military practices and policies proved a hindrance. "We never had a civilian Secretary of War," complained an army officer in 1906, "who understood the foundation principles of army organization, the science of command, the relations between officers and men necessary to discipline."[17]

On the frontier, the policies of civilian officials sometimes imposed limitations on actions that the army thought necessary to pacify the Indian tribes resisting white expansion. Under President Grant's Peace Policy, for example, the Indian Bureau barred the army from entering reservations in search of Indian raiders, much to the annoyance of many officers. The army's dealings with the Department of the Interior over how to respond to a conflict between Ute Indians and the government in 1879 illustrated how the actions of civilian officials could frustrate the military. In this case the army acceded to the request of Secretary of the Interior Carl Schurz that it hold off in attacking Utes who had killed some soldiers and Indian Bureau employees at the White River Agency in Colorado. Schurz used the opportunity to reach a peaceful settlement with the Utes, but the army officers in command of the 3,000 troops gathered for the attack found the delay irksome. Colonel Wesley Merritt expressed his exasperation at "being equipped for a campaign by one arm of the government and halted in its execution by another arm of the same government." General Sheridan noted that the Indian Bureau had called the army to the reservation, but "now we are left in the heart of the mountains with our hands tied and the danger of being snowed in staring us in the face. I am not easily discouraged, but it looks as though we had been pretty badly sold out in this business." The peaceful resolution of the incident reduced the army's aggravation somewhat, but the episode contributed to the army's perception that it too often had its "hands tied" by civilians.[18]

The issue of civilian interference also emerged during the Spanish-American War and its aftermath. Naval officers objected when the McKinley administration, responding to the cries for protection from East Coast newspapers and politicians, divided the American fleet so that a portion of it remained close to home to safeguard coastal cities from a Spanish attack. The decision violated the strongly held strategic principle that a naval force, to be effective, must be concentrated; Alfred Thayer Mahan had made that point repeatedly in his popular writings on naval history. One officer called the decision "the badge of democracy, the sop to quaking laymen whose knowledge of strategy derived solely from their terror of a sudden attack by [Spanish Admiral] Cervera."[19]

In the campaign against Filipino nationalists, army officers complained that the Philippine Commission, a group sent by President McKinley to establish civil government in the colony, hampered their efforts to defeat the insurgency. McKinley appointed the five civilian members of the commission in 1900 and named as its chairman Ohio judge William Howard Taft. The president intended the commission to work with the military to create civil governments in areas that the army had pacified. In a move that almost ensured that a clash between the military and the civilian commission would occur, the McKinley administration set up a governing structure in which the commanding general in the islands would act as chief executive while the commission acted as a legislature with the power to approve laws and appropriate funds. From the perspective of General Arthur MacArthur, commander in the Philippines, the commission soon overstepped its authority and hindered the anti-insurgency campaign in a number of ways. The commission was too hasty, MacArthur and other officers thought, in declaring areas pacified and therefore ready for civil rather than military government. MacArthur protested when the commission began appointing military officers to positions in the civil government without his permission. Many soldiers thought that the commission, with its program of promoting "benevolent assimilation" through civic improvement projects, treated the Filipinos with a naïve kindness that undercut the sterner measures they believed necessary to defeat the insurgency. The commission's "soft mollycoddling of treacherous natives" only encouraged resistance, according to General Adna Chaffee, MacArthur's successor as commander in the Philippines.[20]

Soldiers in the Philippines also bristled at what they saw as the dangerous meddling in the war against the insurgents by anti-imperialists in the United States. The anti-imperialists' ardent opposition to the McKinley administration's decision to annex the Philippines, some officers said, emboldened the Filipinos to resist American control. Officers reported that the insurgents were hopeful that their continued resistance would result in the victory of the anti-imperialist William Jennings Bryan in the presidential election of 1900, and that Bryan would then approve a political settlement leading to independence for the Philippines. General Frederick Funston informed a Republican congressional candidate that he possessed documents captured from the insurgents that included "instructions transmitted by [nationalist leader Emilio] Aguinaldo to his subordinates to keep up the fight hoping that it may bring about the defeat of McKinley." The notion that the words of Bryan and other critics of the war were inspiring the insurgents to carry on the fight angered many soldiers. "I wish Bryan and his friends would come over here and talk to the soldiers," wrote a private. "I would like nothing better than to string them up." Even some of the soldiers who had doubts about the government's policy in the Philippines expressed disapproval of the critics at home. One lieutenant, writing to his wife, confessed that he thought annexation of the Philippines a mistake but believed that public condemnations of the policy should not come until after the war had ended—"before then no one ought to attack."[21]

THE "SLIMY OIL" OF POLITICS

What many officers found especially galling about the intrusions of political leaders into military matters was that politics, not concern for the national interest, seemed to drive many of their decisions. The fact that political considerations determined so many aspects of military policy, from the awarding of supply contracts to the promotion of admirals and generals, disturbed many in the military. The disdain that members of the officer corps felt toward politicians and the political system was not new, but it seemed to grow in strength in the late nineteenth and early twentieth centuries.

The professional ideal that the military should keep itself separate from politics contributed to the military's contempt for the political system. Admonished to shun political activity and told that such activity would demean them, officers not surprisingly came to see politics as something disreputable and even harmful. "If any convictions . . . were acquired by the cadet," one officer said of education at West Point, "they were generally of contempt for mere politicians and their dishonest principles of action." A sense of professional frustration also fed the antipathy that many officers had for the political system. Most of the complaints that officers had about their chosen field—the low pay, the lack of influence, and the unbearably slow rate of promotion—resulted from policies established by the nation's political leaders. Those leaders, not surprisingly, bore the brunt of the officers' resentment.[22]

Perhaps more than any other civilian institution, Congress drew the ire of the military. Congress had such great power over the armed services—it determined their appropriations, set pay rates, approved promotions, and established military policies—yet members of Congress often seemed unconcerned about the military, and some members showed strong antagonism toward it. Officers were well aware of the repeated attempts to cut the size of the army and reduce the pay for officers in the 1870s and of the many congressional speeches warning of the dangers of a standing army and denouncing the service academies and the "aristocratic" officer corps. "In the debates they insult us to our teeth," wrote Sherman of Congress in 1877. Officers recognized that, given the public's apathy regarding the military, congressional critics were unlikely to suffer politically for their attacks on the armed services. "No man's position in Congress depends on his attitude towards the army," an officer noted in 1899.[23]

Officers appreciated that some members of Congress supported the military and were knowledgeable about it—Congressman James Garfield of Ohio and Senator Henry Cabot Lodge of Massachusetts, for instance, were valued friends of the army and the navy respectively. In general, however, officers were dismayed by the combination of partisanship and ignorance of the military that they found in Congress. One army officer expressed that dismay in pungent terms in an article published in 1906: "[L]egislation for the army comes out of the hopper greased with the slimy oil of political spoils and party expediency unredeemed by the salt of honest, manly independence and belief as to the right and justice of the cause and the needs of the country."[24]

The pessimistic view of political leaders grew stronger as officers watched the rapid buildup of European armies and navies and the striking successes of the German military against France in 1870 and the Japanese against Russia in 1905. As the great powers added to their strength and adopted many of the German innovations in military organization, the irritation U.S. officers felt over the apparent indifference of many civilian leaders intensified. Articles bewailing the nation's unreadiness for modern war and its disregard of the armed services filled the military journals. The United States had "no army except in name," lamented one officer, "a natural result of the past and present lack of any military policy."[25]

Most officers accepted the political system, even with its defects, as simply part of the environment in which the military existed. As others saw it, however, the partisanship and ignorance that prevailed in the government raised the question of whether civilian control of the military served the nation well. Colonel Emory Upton, the influential advocate of military reform, criticized the way civilian officials exercised authority over the military and argued that the army and navy should have greater autonomy in deciding how to accomplish the tasks given to them. "Battles are not lost alone on the field," he wrote in 1880. "They may be lost beneath the Dome of the Capitol, they may be lost in the Cabinet, or they may be lost in the private office of the Secretary of War." Secretaries of war, he said, should focus solely on administrative tasks and not take a role in directing military operations. He turned to the Civil War in particular to support his contention. Under the direct supervision of Secretary of War Edwin Stanton, he said, the army failed miserably; giving army commanders the independence to act as they thought necessary would have brought the war to a close much more quickly. Even the president, Upton contended, should resist the temptation to take an active role in directing the military and instead defer to the judgment of military commanders.[26]

Upton's gloomy appraisal of civilian leadership found a receptive audience in the military and strengthened the cynical attitude many officers had toward the political system. Lieutenant Colonel James S. Pettit, for example, echoed many of Upton's points in an essay published in 1906 by the Military Service Institution of the United States, a voluntary organization of regular officers created to spread ideas within the military and promote the military's interests. Pettit's piece won a prize in an essay contest on the topic of how democratic political institutions affected the military. The effects, he argued, were not positive. The American system of government had failed to produce a consistent and well-thought-out policy for its military. Much of the blame for this he placed on Congress. "Members [of Congress] are more interested in the public works in their districts than in army appropriations," he wrote. "As a rule their knowledge of military affairs is limited, and their interest small. When war comes the army represents so many appointments to be secured from either the President or the governors." Civilian control of the military in a democracy meant that the preferences of the public at large determined military policy. Under the democratic system, the prejudice of Americans against large standing armies and in favor of militias became governmental policies, leading Pettit to the pessimistic conclusion that it was "impossible to organize and discipline an effective army from the point of view of military experts."[27]

THE MILITARY LOOKS AT CIVIL SOCIETY

For some in the military, the problem was not simply the political system but the society that sustained it. A number of officers, discouraged by the lack of public support for the military policies they desired, developed a highly negative view of American society. As they saw it, since political leaders responded to public opinion, the public bore a good share of the responsibility for the civil government's neglect of the military. There may have been some reciprocity of sentiment at work—members of the military disparaged a society that seemed to disparage them. What could there be to admire, some officers wondered, about the values of civilians who were apathetic about the military or even hostile to it? Some officers seemed offended that the public did not accord the military more respect. "The trouble has been," wrote an army captain in 1899, "that the people out of the army do not take enough interest in the army; do not regard it as concerning them or affecting them, when it should be the nation's pride as something vital to its welfare." Another army officer, writing in 1906, asserted that civilians had "an unreasonable feeling against the sight of the uniform of the service." Perhaps someday, he hoped, the uniform "will receive everywhere in our land the respect and consideration that it truly merits."[28]

Many of the officers who criticized American society focused on what they perceived as the wide gap between the values of civilians and those of the military. They contrasted the soldier's discipline with the civilian's self-indulgence, the military's self-sacrifice with civilian greed, and the orderliness of military life with the clamor and contentiousness of the civilian world. Some officers worried that the nation's prosperity had created a complacent and pleasure-seeking society unwilling to make the sacrifices necessary to support an adequate military. Captain Alfred Thayer Mahan warned that society's "worship of comfort, wealth, and general softness" could lead to an erosion of the martial virtues. Mahan's naval colleague, Stephen B. Luce, complained of the "tendency to 'softness'" that he identified as "a grave symptom of national decadence." Perceiving themselves as men of honor devoted to duty, officers looked with distaste at a society that celebrated self-seeking and material gain. The idea of military officers as inheritors of chivalric values, expressed in such places as Captain Charles King's novels of the Indian-fighting army and articles in the *Army and Navy Journal*, added to their sense of standing apart from—and perhaps above—the rest of society.[29]

Military critics of civilian society argued that the laxity of modern American life made it difficult for the military to transform recruits into disciplined fighting men. "We are ruled by an arbitrary and irresponsible popular opinion," stated the editor of the *Army and Navy Journal*, "which . . . treats military service as inconsequential and renders it well-nigh impossible to maintain that vigorous discipline which is indispensable to an effective army." According to the author Richard Stockton, an army supporter, desertions occurred not because of harsh conditions in the military but because a permissive American society had not prepared its young men to endure such conditions. The blame for desertion, Stockton wrote in 1915, "lies neither in undue severity nor unfairness in the service, but to the fact that the modern American youth is brought up without restraint, without discipline, without training."[30]

In the view of some officers, the excessive individualism of American society had a damaging effect on the military. That strong sense of individualism, they believed, explained why many young men shunned service in the military—they feared losing their individual identities in an institution that demanded subordination. An army captain in 1913 fretted over the "martial retrogression" that he believed had occurred in the United States since the Civil War. The war, he said, had caused Americans to "press back our individualism into its confines of common sense before it ran amuck." Since then, however, "modern business life" had encouraged overindulgence and produced widespread contempt for the military. Evidence of the decline, asserted the captain, could be seen during the war with Spain, an effort characterized by "braggadocio, waste, confusion . . . impatience, disobedience, and disorder."[31]

While many officers shared the perception that American society was in a sorry state, they held no common view on what could be done about it. Some imagined the military coming to society's rescue. If civilian leaders enlarged the armed forces substantially or made military service obligatory, they reasoned, more young American men would acquire the military virtues of self-discipline and self-sacrifice. General Nelson Miles envisioned the army as "one great school of patriotism" capable of turning young American men into better citizens. Other officers recognized that bringing about a significant change in American culture was a task far beyond the ability of the military to accomplish. Instead, they maintained, the military had to find ways to adapt to the society that surrounded it without compromising its effectiveness. These officers understood that efforts to improve the armed forces would require them to accept civilian control of the military, work within the flawed political system, and persuade an indifferent public of the military's importance.[32]

CHALLENGES TO CIVIL AUTHORITY

Very few members of the military directly challenged the authority of their civilian superiors between 1865 and 1917. So deeply engrained was the habit of obedience and the principle of civilian supremacy that it is unlikely that most officers even contemplated such defiance. The army's actions during Reconstruction appeared, at first glance, to be an exception to the rule. In Reconstruction, after all, military commanders removed state governors from office, overturned state laws, and carried out policies contrary to those desired by President Andrew Johnson—hardly, it seemed, the performance of a military reluctant to encroach upon civilian authority. Yet in each case officers were acting in accordance with the Reconstruction Acts passed by Congress in 1867 and in that sense remained subordinate to civilian control.

The officer who stepped closest to the line of insubordination during Reconstruction was General in Chief Ulysses Grant. Grant sided openly with the Republicans in Congress against the Reconstruction policies of his commander in chief, President Johnson, and at times worked actively to undercut those policies. Grant's actions angered Johnson, but the general's popularity with the public made it politically hazardous for the White House to rein him in. Initially supportive of Johnson's plans for Reconstruction, Grant came to believe by late 1866 that the president's policies would effectively nullify the Union victory in the Civil War by restoring the former rebels to power in the South and leaving the freed slaves unprotected. Johnson sensed Grant's growing estrangement and began to doubt that he could trust the general to carry out his orders. Hoping to replace Grant at least temporarily with William Sherman—thought to be more sympathetic to the administration's policies—Johnson asked Grant to accompany the new American minister to Mexico on a diplomatic mission to Mexico City. Grant at first accepted the assignment, but he soon realized the president's intentions and withdrew his acceptance.[33]

Johnson persisted with his plan. At a cabinet meeting that included Grant, Johnson asked Secretary of State William Seward whether he had drawn up the instructions for Grant's mission. Grant announced that he had already declined to go. The president then turned to the attorney general and asked whether Grant had any grounds for refusing a presidential order. Interrupting the attorney general's response, Grant stated that while he was subject to the president's commands in military matters, the president was asking him to undertake a diplomatic assignment, something he had the right to turn down. "No power on earth can compel me to it," Grant declared. Faced with such determination, Johnson dropped the subject. Grant had prevailed, but his grounds for refusing the order were somewhat dubious. Johnson had called upon him to accompany the American minister to Mexico, not to undertake a diplomatic mission of his own. Johnson backed down because he recognized that Grant's status as the main architect of the Union victory in the Civil War made him tremendously popular—firing or reprimanding the general for disobeying the order would create a political firestorm, and Grant knew that Johnson would not risk it.[34]

Secure in his post, Grant continued to have concerns about the effects of Johnson's policies. He found particularly upsetting the president's efforts to close down the military courts that army commanders in the South had established to provide an alternative system of justice for blacks and white Unionists who were unlikely to receive fair treatment in the local courts. Quietly, but not covertly, the general began to work against Johnson's program. In meetings with southern political leaders, Grant urged them to press for the ratification of the Fourteenth Amendment in their states despite the fact that Johnson had called for the amendment's rejection. Grant then cooperated with Republicans in Congress to devise Reconstruction legislation that the president opposed. Passed over Johnson's veto, the Reconstruction Act of March 1867 divided the South into five military districts headed by army generals.[35]

The Johnson administration and some of the district commanders— General Philip Sheridan in particular—were soon embroiled in a controversy over whether the Reconstruction Act had empowered the commanders to remove uncooperative state officials from office and to determine the eligibility of officials who had held public office under the Confederacy to register to vote. When Attorney General Henry Stanbery issued an opinion containing a restrictive view of the commanders' powers regarding removal and voter registration, Sheridan publicly announced his disagreement and predicted that it would encourage greater resistance to Congressional Reconstruction from white conservatives in the South. A member of Johnson's cabinet labeled Sheridan's criticisms "impudent and disrespectful if not disobedient." Acting more circumspectly than Sheridan, Grant privately advised the district commanders to delay complying with the opinion until Congress could clarify its intent. Congress did so in July 1867, passing legislation that repudiated Stanbery's narrow reading of the act and gave the commanders expansive powers to remove officials and determine voter eligibility. In order to prevent Stanbery or other administration officials from interfering, the act also stated that the commanders were not obliged to follow "any opinion of any civil officer of the United States."[36]

Grant favored going beyond even that significant restriction on the Johnson administration's authority. He advocated including a provision in the act that would prohibit the president from removing the district commanders. Congress disregarded the advice, and Johnson retained a powerful lever with which he could influence the course of Reconstruction. By the end of the year he had replaced the three commanders most sympathetic to Congressional Reconstruction—Sheridan, Daniel Sickles, and John Pope—with more conservative officers. Unfortunately for Johnson, he could not so easily dispense with Grant. His appointment of Grant as the interim secretary of war in 1867 failed to pull the general onto the administration team, and Grant captured the Republican nomination and then the presidency the next year while still serving, at least in theory, under Johnson. Grant's success in defying President Johnson depended on three things—his popularity with the public, his strong base of support in Congress, and his talent for keeping disagreements with the president from escalating into open warfare. His opposition to the president's program became widely known, but he avoided making the kind of public denunciation of administration policies that would have required a public response from the White House and perhaps a presidential rebuke.[37]

Like Grant, Nelson Miles enjoyed substantial popular and political support during the time he served as the army's commanding general. Unlike Grant, he had little interest in keeping his disputes with the president out of the headlines. Miles held the commanding general's position between 1895 and 1903, and during that period he irritated officials of both the McKinley and Roosevelt administrations with his pronouncements condemning their policies. Forthright, arrogant, and ambitious to reach the presidency himself, Miles angered McKinley's secretary of war, Russell Alger, when he ignored an order to inspect army camps in Georgia and Alabama during the Spanish-American War in 1898. Someone in the War Department, perhaps Alger, noted on a copy of the secretary's instructions, "Order not obeyed, Gen. Miles saying he was in the habit of issuing his own orders." After the

12. General Nelson A. Miles at Tampa, Florida, 1898. General Nelson Miles (pictured at right in the dark suit), confers with an officer during the mobilization of forces for the expedition to Cuba early in the Spanish-American War. As the army's commanding general, Miles opposed many of the policies of the McKinley and Roosevelt administrations, and he often made his opposition known to the public. LC-USZ62-122405, Library of Congress.

war, Miles added to Alger's anger by passing documents to the press in an effort to place on the secretary the blame for allowing the disease-ridden troops of the army's Fifth Corps to languish in Cuba rather than sending them back to the United States. Miles completed his break with the administration by alleging in public hearings that the army's commissary department had supplied bad beef to the troops during the war.[38]

Miles continued to court controversy under Roosevelt. The president and his secretary of war, Elihu Root, suspected that Miles was leaking War Department documents about the army's actions in the Philippines to the anti-imperialist press. When in 1901 Miles publicly criticized the decision of a naval court of inquiry regarding a dispute between two admirals, Roosevelt, infuriated by this breach of military propriety, dressed Miles down during a White House reception. Miles should be "reprimanded severely," the president wrote to the secretary of war. Secretary Root did so. "You are in error," he informed Miles, "if you suppose that you have the same right as any other citizen to express publicly an opinion regarding official questions pending in the course of military discipline." Miles protested the reprimand. Members of the military, he said, "do not cease to be citizens." In 1902 the general's assertions that U.S. soldiers had committed atrocities in the Philippines and his outspoken opposition to Root's proposal for the creation of an army general staff left Roosevelt fuming. "To my mind his actions can bear only the construction that his desire is purely to gratify his selfish ambition, his vanity, or his spite," Roosevelt wrote. The president wanted badly to oust Miles from his position, but such an action presented political risks. Miles, the old Civil War hero and Indian fighter, had many admirers. Removing him might stir a backlash against the administration and generate enough sympathy for Miles to make him a contender for the presidency in 1904. The administration followed the more prudent course of putting up with Miles in the post until his retirement in 1903.[39]

THE WILSON ADMINISTRATION AND ITS MILITARY CRITICS

The policies of President Woodrow Wilson generated more discontent in the military than had those of any president since Johnson, but only a few high-ranking officers openly challenged the authority of his administration. Wilson readily used the instruments at his disposal—the power to reprimand and the power to make appointments—to keep most of the malcontents in the military in line. Members of the military cast a skeptical eye on the Wilson administration from the start. As a Democrat, Wilson belonged to a party that had traditionally been more critical of the regular military and less inclined to spend money on it. Officers became even more uneasy when Wilson appointed two men with anti-imperialist leanings, William Jennings Bryan and Josephus Daniels, to his cabinet as secretary of state and secretary of the navy. Both men, committed to egalitarianism and suspicious of concentrated power, regarded the officer corps as a privileged elite, and both believed that the military would encroach upon civilian authority if not watched carefully. Bryan, whose past denunciations of militarism had long made him an object of scorn for many officers, incurred more of the military's wrath when he visited an army post in Texas and announced that he failed to understand how men could prefer service in the armed forces to a "respectable civilian profession."[40]

Josephus Daniels's policies as secretary of the navy reflected both his suspicions of the officer class and his desire to uplift the enlisted men. Daniels distressed many officers by banning liquor from navy vessels and facilities (it had been denied to enlisted men since 1899, so the order affected mainly officers). Admiral Bradley Fiske, the aide for naval operations, warned that officers, deprived of their beer and wine, might turn to whiskey and cocaine! Daniels's programs to improve the lives of enlisted men by providing such things as shipboard laundries and classrooms—he envisioned the navy as "a great university"—prompted many officers to complain that the secretary's coddling of the sailors would undermine discipline. Officers shook their heads over the story that Daniels, touring a battleship in the company of an admiral, had chatted amiably with some stokers in the boiler room and chastised the admiral for not doing the same. "Do you think that you are too good to shake the hand of a sailor?" he allegedly asked the officer.[41]

Suspicious of the pretensions and ambitions of military officers, Wilson and many of his advisors were sensitive to signs of disrespect for civilian authority. Wilson ordered reprimands for officers who participated in a meeting of the Military Order of the Carabao, an association of veterans of the war in the Philippines, at which skits mocking Secretary Bryan were performed. Wilson also reacted strongly against what he perceived as the attempt of a group of officers to push the policy they preferred on the administration during a dispute between the United States and Japan in 1913. The dispute arose when the California legislature passed a series of laws designed to prohibit Chinese and Japanese residents from owning land in the state. In May 1913 the Japanese government formally protested the legislation. The sternly worded protest spurred the navy's General Board and the army's general staff into action. Already concerned about the possibility of a Japanese attack on American possessions in the Pacific, the military planners considered ways to shore up the defenses.[42]

The Joint Army-Navy Board, a group made up of representatives of the General Board and the general staff that had been established in 1903 to improve coordination between the services, developed recommendations that called for, among other things, the movement of three cruisers to the Philippines to provide additional protection for the islands. Secretary Daniels, worried that moving the warships would provoke the Japanese, declined to approve the recommendation regarding the navy but agreed to take the matter to the White House. In discussing the issue with his civilian advisors, Wilson received conflicting advice. Secretary of War Lindley Garrison argued that the administration should defer to the military's expertise and go along with the recommendations. When in a cabinet meeting Garrison, speaking in favor of the navy's plan, suggested that the opinions of the civilian secretaries on military matters had little value, Secretary of State Bryan replied heatedly that "army and navy officers could not be trusted to say what we should or should not do" unless the United States was actually at war. Wilson sided with Bryan and Daniels and ruled against the ship movement.[43]

The following day, to Daniels's annoyance, Admiral Fiske arrived at the secretary's office bearing another memorandum from the Joint Board calling for the movement of ships in the Pacific. Daniels told Fiske that the president had made his decision, but the admiral insisted that the memorandum go to the White House. Daniels also received questions from a reporter about the Joint Board's proposal, an indication to the secretary that Fiske or others in the navy had leaked the plan to the press. Told of the continuing agitation over the issue, Wilson responded angrily. Daniels reported Wilson as saying, "When a policy has been settled by the Administration and when it is communicated to the Joint Board, they have no right to be trying to force a different course, and I wish you would say to them that if this should occur again, there will be no General or Joint Boards. They will be abolished." Wilson directed the Joint Board to hold no more meetings until he had asked it to do so. The Joint Board's memorandum may not have represented the serious threat to civilian authority that Wilson and Daniels imagined it to be. The Joint Board had composed the memorandum without knowing that Wilson had made a decision, and Fiske may have been acting on his own in continuing to advocate for the ship movement. Still, Wilson perceived Fiske's action as a challenge emanating from a wider group of "Navy and Army gentlemen," as he put it, who disliked his decision and hoped to pressure him into reversing it. Wilson responded to the challenge with an emphatic assertion of presidential authority.[44]

The advent of war in Europe in 1914 increased tensions between the Wilson administration and the military. Many in the military were critical of the administration for failing to support the policies and spending increases that they believed necessary to prepare the nation for war. A sizable number of military officers, businessmen, and political leaders joined together in a loose coalition that became known as the preparedness movement. Centered in organizations such as the Navy and Army Leagues and led by such well-known figures as Senator Henry Cabot Lodge and former president Theodore Roosevelt, the movement sought either to persuade or compel the administration to do more to build up the nation's military forces. Wilson resented the pressure, but in late 1914 he had officers such as General Hugh S. Scott, the army's chief of staff, and Admiral Frank F. Fletcher, commander of the Atlantic fleet, on hand to reassure Congress and the public that the nation's defense forces were perfectly adequate. The public seemed to agree with Wilson's point of view, and the preparedness advocates failed at first to generate a broad base of popular support for their cause.[45]

Frustrated by the Wilson administration's stand, a few active-duty officers sought to take the preparedness message directly to Congress or to groups of influential civilians. Admiral Bradley Fiske riled administration officials when he met with members of Congress to speak on what he saw as navy's unreadiness for war. In doing so he not only delivered a message that contradicted the administration's, he also broke with established practice that only officers sent by the War or Navy Departments, or those formally invited by Congress or one of its committees, should go to Capitol Hill to give their views. Fiske further alienated the administration by working behind the scenes with several members of Congress to produce legislation to create a powerful chief of naval operations, something that Secretary Daniels opposed. Exasperated by Fiske's maneuvers, Daniels finally directed him to stay silent on matters of policy. "You cannot write or talk any more," Daniels told Fiske, "you can't even say that two and two make four."[46]

Fiske experienced a rapid loss of influence as a result of his activities. Daniels ordered him to take the command of the Naval War College in Newport, Rhode Island, thereby separating the admiral from his allies in Congress. After Congress created a chief of naval operations in 1915, Daniels sought to fill the position with an officer of, in his words, "practical judgment who believed in the American system," and not an officer with a "consuming passion . . . to confer all power on the head of Operations." As Daniels saw it, that formulation excluded Fiske, who as aide for operations had a reasonable expectation of receiving the post. Daniels instead selected Admiral William S. Benson, an officer who, though an advocate of preparedness, had refrained from making public criticisms of the administration's naval policies. By the time that the administration itself took up the preparedness cause in the middle of 1915, Fiske was no longer in a position to help guide the naval buildup that he had championed for so long.[47]

The strongest challenge to the administration's military policies came from the army's leading promoter of preparedness, General Leonard Wood. Wood's close ties to Republican leaders such as Theodore Roosevelt and Henry Cabot Lodge and his reputation as a successful colonial administrator gave him more political protection than Fiske or other preparedness advocates possessed. From his position as commander of the Department of the East, Wood used speeches and writings to warn that the United States was ill prepared for war with a major power. In December 1914, a week after President Wilson had announced to Congress his determination to stay out of the European war and his belief that the United States should continue to rely on citizen soldiers rather than a standing army, Wood made a speech to a group of businessmen in New York in which he deprecated the nation's readiness for war. He also censured the "fake humanitarians who recommend that we shall turn the youth of this country into the battlefield unprepared" as the "unconscious slayers of their people."[48]

Wood may not have considered Wilson one of the "fake humanitarians" guilty of murdering the young, but some chose to read the speech that way. Wilson learned of the remarks and asked Secretary of War Lindley Garrison to reprimand Wood for his imprudent words. Garrison did so, although rather mildly. The War Department also issued a general order directing army officers to not give out "for publication any interview, statement, discussion, or article on the military situation in the United States or abroad, as expression of their views on this subject is prejudicial to the best interest of the service."[49]

The rebuke did not stop Wood from speaking on the preparedness issue—

he merely took greater care to avoid direct criticism of the administration and to keep his remarks out of the press. He gave speeches to audiences of, in his phrase, "the better class of men—men in law, business, and finance." He permitted a newly formed pro-preparedness group, the American Legion, to establish its offices in a building at the departmental headquarters on Governor's Island, New York, and detailed an aide to assist the organization. The Wilson administration, keeping a wary eye on the general, ordered the Legion offices off government property and criticized Wood for his role in its operation. The administration had no objection to Wood's work in establishing a military training camp for young business and professional men at Plattsburg Barracks, New York, in 1915, but the general's decision to invite former president Roosevelt to address the trainees was another matter. A fierce critic of the administration, Roosevelt used the visit to Plattsburg to condemn Wilson's response to the sinking of the passenger ship *Lusitania* by a German submarine. The episode brought Wood another reprimand—his third—from Secretary of War Garrison. "It is difficult to conceive," the secretary wrote to Wood, "of anything which could have a more detrimental effect upon the real value of the [the Plattsburg camp] than such an incident."[50]

The reprimands failed to silence Wood. Even after Wilson endorsed preparedness and called for an increase of the army and navy in July 1915, Wood continued to make speeches maintaining that the nation's preparations for war were insufficient. He also began to test the political waters by meeting with a group of Republican leaders and allowing supporters to promote him as a possible candidate for the Republican nomination for president in 1916. Wood's venture into politics angered the White House. The administration made no official comment, but one anonymous presidential advisor denounced Wood for his "pernicious political activity" while on active duty. Wilson considered initiating disciplinary action against Wood for violating the earlier War Department order banning officers from making public statements on the "military situation in the United States," but his advisors convinced him not to follow that course. Wood had too many influential supporters, they argued, and the Republicans would try to turn any punishment of the general into a political issue in the 1916 presidential elections.[51]

Although a fellow officer advised Wood to "put yourself in the right attitude toward these people who are running the government," the general, perhaps with an eye toward building up an issue that could carry him to the White House in 1920, carried on with his criticism of the administration. In a hearing before the House Military Affairs Committee in January 1917, he delivered his harshest blast yet against the administration's military policies. The United States, he said, was "practically as unprepared as when the great war began." Again the administration chose not to discipline Wood, but he did face consequences for his outspokenness. In March 1917, shortly before Wilson asked for a declaration of war on Germany, the War Department divided Wood's Department of the East into three smaller departments and assigned Wood to command the least important of the three, the Southeastern Department. The administration later exiled Wood to a command at Camp Funston, Kansas, where he spent most of the war.[52]

Bradley Fiske and Leonard Wood both believed that the goal of improving preparedness justified the means of challenging the authority of their civilian superiors. Officers unwilling to speak out against the civilian secretary on vital issues because of anxiety about their careers, Fiske declared in 1915, were "unworthy of the uniform we wear." Many of their fellow officers agreed with the preparedness message that Wood and Fiske offered—the two men gave voice to the frustration that many in the military felt over what they perceived as the civilian government's disgraceful neglect of the armed forces and its misunderstanding of the realities of modern war. Nevertheless, most chose not to follow Fiske's path of working with sympathetic members of Congress against the administration's policies, or Wood's path of making public his disagreement with the administration. Most officers, despite their frequent complaints about the ignorance, indifference, and ineptitude of civilians regarding military matters, accepted the principle that the American system of civil-military relations required them to carry out the policies put in place by the civilian government, even those policies they considered wrongheaded. Established by the Constitution and reinforced by both long tradition and professional training, the principle of civilian supremacy endured even during the early years of the Wilson administration, a time when the gap between civilian leaders and the military on matters of policy had rarely been wider.[53]

During the late nineteenth and early twentieth centuries, defiance of civilian authority came primarily from a few powerful individuals within the military, not from the military as an institution. Generals Grant, Miles, and Wood and, to a lesser extent, Admiral Fiske enjoyed the high rank, public popularity, and strong political support that made it possible for them to challenge openly their commanders in chief without destroying their military careers. Of those four, only Grant benefited from his stand against the president—his work against Johnson's Reconstruction policies persuaded Republican leaders that he shared their political values and would be a good choice to carry the party's banner in the 1868 presidential election. Miles, Wood, and Fiske, in contrast, discovered that their public criticisms of civilian superiors resulted in their increased marginalization within the government. Defiance of civilian leaders, it seemed, came at a price.

Documents

1. MILITARY RULE IN THE SOUTH, 1867

In the aftermath of the Civil War, President Andrew Johnson battled with Congress over what should be done with the states of the defeated Confederacy. The Republican-controlled Congress, concerned that Johnson's lenient Reconstruction policies would permit the establishment of state governments in the South dominated by former Confederates and hostile to the rights of the former slaves, seized the initiative from the president by passing the Military Reconstruction Act in March 1867. The act gave the army the daunting task of governing ten southern states until those states had ratified constitutions that met with the approval of Congress. Under the act, the ten states were divided into five military districts, each commanded by an army general. The commanders had tremendous authority. They could overturn state laws, for example, and remove civilian officials from their positions in the provisional state governments if the officials refused to cooperate with the military government. The commanders were responsible for the registration of eligible voters and the organization of elections for delegates to state constitutional conventions. Congress also authorized the commanders to use their powers to ensure that the black population could participate in the political process and that blacks received equal treatment under the law. As explained in Chapters 1 and 4, Reconstruction duty placed the army in the middle of a heated political controversy. It also put army officers in the often awkward position of governing civilians. The document below, excerpted from the

"Digest of Orders of the Military Commanders," provides an indication of the commanders' extensive authority. The document contains General Winfield Scott Hancock's controversial order of November 1867 (discussed in Chapter 4), in which he announced his intention not to interfere with the actions of local government officials.

Digest of Orders of the Military Commanders, and General Action under the Reconstruction Acts

First Military District—Virginia

1867, March 15—General Schofield prohibited whipping or maiming of the person as a punishment for any crime, misdemeanor, or offence. An order was issued, same day, disbanding and prohibiting any further organization of the militia forces of the State. . . .

May 28—Where civil authorities fail to give adequate protection to all persons in their right of person and property, it was announced that military commissioners would be appointed; trials by the civil courts in all cases where there is satisfactory reason to believe that justice will be done. . . .

December 2—General O. O. Howard instructs General O. Brown, of Freedman's Bureau, to allow no man to suffer for food, and to assist to a home and employment those who he ascertains may have been, or may be, discharged for having voted as they pleased. . . .

Second Military District—North and South Carolina

1867, April 18—General Sickles issued an order that, it having become apparent that justice to freedmen cannot be obtained in the civil Courts of Edgefield and Barnwell districts, a provost court be established, with jurisdiction of any case to which a person of color is a party, except murder, arson, and rape.

April 20—No sentence of such court, affecting the liberty of any person, to be executed till approved by the commanding general. . . .

August 17—The finding of a court-martial confirmed, fining the captain of a steamer $250 for refusing a person a first-class ticket on account of color. . . .

October 16—An election ordered in South Carolina, November 19 and 20, for or against a "convention," and for delegates to constitute the Convention. Violence, or threats of violence, or of discharge from employment, or other oppressive agencies against the free exercise of the right of suffrage, prohibited. All bar-rooms, saloons, etc, ordered closed from 6 on the evening of November 18 to 6 on the morning of November 21. Military interference, unless "necessary to repel the armed enemies of the United States or to keep the peace at the polls," prohibited. . . .

Third Military District—Georgia, Alabama, and Florida

1867, April 4—General Pope issued an order directing post commanders to report acts of local or State authorities or tribunals which discriminate against persons on account of race, color, or political opinion. . . .

August 2—No civil court will entertain any action against officers or soldiers, or others, for acts performed in accordance with the orders of the military authorities. All such suits now pending to be dismissed.

August 12—Ordered, that all advertisements or other official publications under State or municipal authority shall be made in such newspapers only as have not opposed and do not oppose reconstruction under acts of Congress, nor attempt to obstruct the civil officers appointed by the military authorities. . . .

Fourth Military District—Mississippi and Arkansas

April 15—No elections to be held for any purpose, till a registration of voters be made. Freedmen urged not to neglect their business to engage in political discussions, but to continue to provide for themselves and families, lest "a famine may come and they have no food." Due notice will be given of the times and places for registration. . . .

May 13—Instructions to registering officers directed the exclusion of all persons who held an office under the General Government prior to the war, and who afterwards engaged in or gave aid and comfort to the rebellion. . . .

June 17—A poll-tax having been imposed upon freedmen by the county boards of police in Mississippi . . . it being, so far as it discriminates against freedmen, manifestly contrary to the civil rights act, all civil officers are forbidden to collect it. . . .

December 12—Whenever a citizen is arrested by the military, he will be at once furnished with a written copy of the charges. Writs of *habeas corpus* by the United States courts will be in all cases obeyed and respected by all officers of the military service in this command. . . .

December 17—All freedmen who are able will be required to earn their support during the coming year. Those who can, but will not work, will be liable to arrest as vagrants. . . .

Fifth Military District—Louisiana and Texas

March 23—No elections will be held till the reconstruction laws shall have been complied with. . . .

June 3—The order appointing a new board of levee commissioners suspended, under President Johnson's directions. J. Madison Wells, having made himself an impediment to the faithful execution of the reconstruction act, was removed as Governor of Louisiana, and Thomas J. Durant appointed thereto. . . .

July 30—J. W. Throckmorton, Governor of Texas, removed as an impediment to reconstruction, and E. M. Pease appointed. . . .

August 22—General Griffin issued an order, at Galveston, that all distinctions on account of color, race, or previous condition, by railroads, or other chartered companies, that are common carriers, are forbidden in the district of Texas. . . .

November 29—General Winfield S. Hancock assumed command. He issued this order:

II. The general commanding is gratified to learn that peace and quiet reign in this department. It will be his purpose to preserve this condition of things. As a means to this great end, he regards the maintenance of the civil authorities in the faithful execution of the laws as the most efficient, under existing circumstances.

In war it is indispensable to repel force by force, and overthrow and destroy opposition to lawful authority. But when insurrectionary force has been overthrown and peace established, and civil authorities are ready and willing to perform their duties, the military power should cease to lead, and the civil administration resume its natural and rightful dominion. . . .

Source: Edward McPherson, *The Political History of the United States of America during the Period of Reconstruction* (Washington, DC: Philip and Solomons, 1871), 316–25.

2. A CONGRESSMAN CALLS FOR A REDUCTION IN NAVAL SPENDING, 1870

The U.S. Navy underwent a dramatic reduction in size in the years following the Civil War. Between 1865 and 1870 the wartime fleet of over 600 ships shrank to a few dozen vessels. After spending extravagantly on the war, Congress was in a mood to economize, and both the navy and the army experienced large cuts in their appropriations. The officer corps of the army and navy became a favorite target of the economizers. The war left the navy with a larger number of officers and, as Congressman George W. Morgan noted in the speech reproduced below, many of them had high rank but few responsibilities. In the 1870s Morgan and other critics of military spending frequently introduced legislation to restrict officers' pay or to reduce the number of officers in the armed services. In passage below, excerpted from Morgan's speech of May 17, 1870, the congressman criticized the naval appropriation bill under consideration by the House of Representatives for not reducing the number of naval officers. The navy had become "top-heavy," Morgan complained, with far more officers than were necessary. Like many critics of the military in the late nineteenth century, Morgan condemned the expanded officer corps not only because of its expense but also because of its potential to damage democratic institutions. The awarding of such high ranks as admiral and commodore, he warned, could lead to the creation of an American aristocracy.

George W. Morgan had once been a high-ranking officer himself, although as a volunteer rather than a professional. After fighting in the Texas revolution in the 1830s, Morgan attended West Point for several years before low grades forced his resignation. He became a lawyer in Ohio and commanded a regiment of volunteers from that state during the Mexican War. In the Civil War he held the rank of brigadier general and commanded a division. In poor health and opposed to the Lincoln administration's policies against slavery, he resigned his commission in 1863. Elected to Congress as a Democrat in 1866, Morgan represented his Ohio district in the House until 1873.[1]

Speech of the Hon. G. W. Morgan, of Ohio, in the House of Representatives, May 17, 1870

I confess that until this Congress assembled, I was wholly ignorant of the condition of our Navy, and the abuses which had grown up under the eyes of Congress, without Congress being aware of the fact. And now, as a representative of the people, on behalf of the people, I stand here today to expose and denounce these abuses, and I call upon the members of this House to apply the remedy and correct them.

Mr. Chairman, in 1860 the highest officer in the American Navy was a captain; today he is an Admiral. In 1861 we had no admirals; today, in all, we have thirty. In 1861 we had no commodores; today, in all, we have seventy-eight. . . . In fact, sir, our fleets are top-heavy, and the Navy itself is like a gallant vessel running before a high wind with every sail set, but without a pound of ballast.

We have six fleets and thirty admirals! Six fleets and seventy-eight commodores! And at this moment there are in the capital of the Republic on some assigned duty ten admirals and nine commodores. Our six fleets are composed of thirty-eight vessels. For every vessel we have more than two commodores, but only three are at sea; and for all we have thirty admirals! I speak of the total number, including those on what is called the active list and those on what is called the retired list, which has sprung up within a few years. I speak with the authority of the Secretary of the Navy in a report to the Senate of the United States, when I speak of the number of admirals and commodores who are on assigned duty in the city of Washington. Nor is it in the city of Washington alone that naval officers are thus grouped together. We find them dotted down in clusters along the coast and in the interior of the land. At a place in Illinois, on the Ohio River, called Mound City, they have nine naval officers on what is called, I presume, shore duty!

Now, sir, you will observe that in this process—so highly commended by the gentleman from Maine [Mr. Hale]—aristocratic titles have been introduced into our Navy, and for the first time in the history of our Government we have the rank of admirals. And without any spirit of unkindness, without any wish to do injustice to the Navy, let me ask, what did this navy do with thirty admirals and seventy-eight commodores beyond our own shores during the war? Our commerce was destroyed and swept from the ocean, while we had a Navy commanded by admirals and commodores. As for the pluck of the Navy, we all know and appreciate its courage; but that its usefulness has diminished as the titles of its officers have been increased is too true. . . .

Sir, I have no hostility to the American Navy; I desire only to correct the abuses connected with its administration. In my early boyhood my heart was fired by reading of the immortal deeds of our naval heroes. . . . But when I came to examine the corruption and abuses which have grown up, I shrank back with astonishment, and became satisfied that they could only be corrected by the application of the caustic and the knife, and if they are not corrected by Congress the overburdened taxpayers of the country will take the matter in hand themselves. . . .

Now, Mr. Chairman, I desire to do the Committee on Appropriations full justice. I wish to do injustice to no one. The Navy Department asked, as salaries, allowances, and traveling expenses for officers, the sum of $5,000,000. The Committee on Appropriations have reported only $4,000,000, cutting down the amount asked for $1,000,000. If the committee have a sincere desire to correct these abuses their conduct will be applauded by the country; but the people will not be satisfied with finely gilded words; they want economy and reform. The appropriation asked for by the committee is too much by more than eight hundred thousand dollars, and to that extent it should be reduced. . . .

We are told by gentlemen who stand here in defense of these abuses that the pay of naval officers was small, and that therefore the Secretary of the Navy was justified in increasing it. I hold in my hand the Naval Register for 1860, which shows that at that time the highest salary paid to any naval officer was $4,500. We find by the Naval Register for 1861 that they advanced a little. Their approaches on the Treasury were skillfully made, and we find that in 1861 the highest pay of an officer, that of an officer commanding a squadron, had been increased from $4,500 to $5,000. We advance now to 1862, and then, for the first time in our history, we find in our statutes the title of "admiral." You have been lately told by a distinguished citizen who holds a high position, the General of the Army, for whose genius as a general and whose gallantry as a soldier I entertain sincere admiration—you were told by that General in a letter . . . that England did more for its generals than the United States. I believe that had General Sherman been an Englishman instead of an American he would have been made a duke. It would have been in accordance with the spirit of monarchical institutions. England has a monarch. I thank Almighty God that the United States have not yet.

Sir, it has become fashionable to hold up the monarchies of Europe as models for our imitation. The gentleman from Maine [Mr. Hale] has referred to the vast navies of England and France; but he forgot to tell us that France keeps a standing army of one million men to keep the people down. And it behooves the people of America to beware how they follow in the footsteps of monarchies, lest the day be not distant when large armies will be maintained to keep them down.

These titles of rear admiral, vice admiral, and admiral are but progressive steps toward the titles which England conferred upon Wellington, first of marquis and then of duke. I say such titles are hostile to the spirit of our free institutions, and unless corrected by the people they establish a precedent which sooner or later will undermine the columns of the grand edifice built by our fathers, and it will crumble in ruins over our heads.

Source: United States Congress, *Appendix to the Congressional Globe*, 41st Cong., 2nd sess., May 17, 1870, 349–53.

3. CONGRESSMAN GARFIELD ON THE PROBLEMS FACING THE ARMY, 1878

By the late 1870s Ohio Republican James A. Garfield had established himself as one of the leading authorities on military matters in the U.S. House of Representatives and one of the regular army's most steadfast defenders. Garfield had served as a volunteer general during the Civil War and had developed close ties to a number of officers who were interested in modernizing the army, including William T. Sherman, Emory Upton, and William Hazen. In early 1878 Garfield wrote a two-part article for *The North American Review* in which he discussed his chief concerns about the army as it then existed. Many of his observations, especially those regarding the need to limit the authority of the secretary of war and the staff bureaus, reflected the concerns of reformers such as Upton. Shortly after the article below appeared, Garfield and some congressional allies succeeded in creating a joint committee to consider "the establishment of a sound military system for the United States." The joint committee produced legislation to place the staff bureaus under the control of the commanding general and to create a rudimentary "general staff," but the bill went down to defeat in 1879. In the following year Garfield, a "dark horse candidate," secured the

Republican nomination for president and was elected as the nation's twentieth chief executive. Shot by a deranged office-seeker, he died of his wounds in September 1881, having served as president for less than a year.

James A. Garfield, "The Army of the United States, Part II"

The officers and friends of the army are neither unmindful of its defects of organization nor of the mistakes which have been made in its administration. They have criticized both, with a freedom and vigor which does credit alike to their independence and intelligence. But these criticisms have disclosed such differences of opinion, that Congress has frequently been more confused than aided by the multitude of counselors.

There are, however, a few vital questions which should not be omitted from even a brief discussion of the army. Prominent among these is the relation of the army proper to the Department of War and to the political administration of the Government. . . . We shall endeavor to state briefly a few of the leading topics in controversy, and suggest some possible improvements.

I. The Secretary of War and the Army

The Constitution makes the President commander-in-chief of the army and navy. In addition to his great civil functions, he is, as Hamilton aptly phrased it, the first general and admiral of the nation. . . . The Secretary of War is a civil officer; one of the constitutional advisers of the President, his civil executive to direct and control military affairs, and conduct army administration for the President. . . . [I]t is worthy of note that our most eminent Secretaries of War have been civilians, who brought to the duties of the office great political and legal experience, and other high qualities of statesmanship. . . .

The necessities of the [Civil War] compelled the Government, for the time being, as a matter of practice, to restore unity to the army by making commanders of corps and departments responsible to one military head, and placing both the line and the staff under due subordination to the commanders of armies in things strictly military, and to the general orders of the Secretary of War in all matters of administration. But these reforms were not embodied in the laws; and, on the return of peace, the old, vicious system was revived. The staff officers in the War Department became, virtually, the staff of the Secretary of War, and received orders directly from him. . . .

But reform had been made difficult by long habit and by the fact that Congress, from time to time, had passed special acts prescribing special duties to the Secretary of War, which seemed to warrant his continued usurpation of the functions of military command. When General Grant became

President, he promptly undertook the restoration of the older and better practice, by directing that all orders to the army should be communicated through the commanding general. But he had appointed, as Secretary of War, a distinguished soldier who had served on his staff during the war [John A. Rawlins]; and it was hardly possible that the old relation should be changed. In a short time the new order of things was revoked, and the Secretary of War became again virtually the military head of the army. The general who should have been military commander, next in rank to the President, was made almost as powerless as a clerk, and wholly useless as a commander. Unwilling to remain in Washington with only the shadow of his rightful authority, General Sherman obtained permission to fix his headquarters at St. Louis, where he wielded less actual authority than a captain in command of a frontier post. . . .

It should be remembered, to the honor of Secretaries [Alphonso B.] Taft, [J. D.] Cameron and [George W.] McCrary, that the General of the Army was restored and has been maintained in his rightful authority. They possessed sufficient largeness of mind to deny themselves the gratification of commanding the army. This, however, was, on their part, a policy of wise discretion and patriotic self-restraint. Their practice should be made law. The functions of the Secretary of War should be defined and limited; and Congress itself should respect the discipline of the army by addressing its laws, not as now, to the chiefs of bureaux and staff departments, but to the President or to the Secretary of War.

II. The Staff

Whatever may be the merits of the controversy between the staff and line of the army (and it is an old one, not only here but in other countries), the importance of a trained staff can hardly be overstated. . . .

An effective army staff is, of necessity, a work of years. It cannot be created in an emergency, and sent at once to the field, ready for efficient work. Without thoroughly well-organized staff and supply departments, made efficient by long-previous training, an army is foredoomed to dogs and vultures. No expenditure at the moment, however lavish, can supply these wants or avert this doom. . . .

Any military legislation, therefore, which destroys the staff, puts out the eyes of the army, impairs its intelligence and fatally cripples its strength. The staff of our army rendered efficient and distinguished service during the late war, and is still an honorable, intelligent, and effective body of public servants. But its functions have been distorted by the usurpations of the Secretaries of War.

The generals of the army, the commanders of military divisions, districts and posts, complain, with reason, that they are deprived of that authority over officers of the staff which proper subordination and the efficiency of the service demand. And this arises, in large measure, from the extent to which the numerous details of authority and service have been centralized in the War Department and in the several staff departments. . . .

As matters are now conducted, an officer who may be required to defend our sea-coast fortifications in war may see them built of worthless brick and mortar; mounted with guns of useless calibre and badly placed; and yet not be able to offer a suggestion or apprise the Government of the defective work and useless expenditure he daily witnesses. All of this arises from breaking away from the established usages of other armies, simply to gratify our natural love of personal independence, which is as strong in the army as in civil life.

No commander can perform his duties with intelligence and success unless he can also command the means of arming, clothing, feeding and transporting his troops. The complaints of the younger officers of the line are not without foundation. A majority of them are assigned to duty on the frontiers, at posts remote from civilization, while a majority of the staff serve in Washington, or at cities within easy reach of the centres of military authority, where they frequently receive the honors and favors of the service in undue proportion. . . .

IV. Congress and the Army

It is evident that during the last three years there has been manifested in Congress a growing spirit of unfriendliness, if not of positive hostility, toward the army. . . .

At the present session one of the smaller appropriation bills, which usually passes without opposition, was made the occasion of a fierce and bitter attack upon the Military Academy, an institution which, for seventy-five years, has been the fountain of military honor, has given to our soldiers a thorough and liberal culture, and has filled the army with the spirit of national patriotism. A republic, however free, requires the service of a certain number of men whose ambition is higher than mere private gain, whose lives are inseparable from the life of the nation, and whose honors and emoluments depend absolutely upon the honor and prosperity of the Government, and who can advance themselves only by serving their country.

To educate a body of young men to this standard of duty is the primary object of the Military Academy. Yet, when the bill for its support came before the House, it was violently assailed, and its passage was long delayed. Attempts were made to cut down the pay of professors; to prevent the completion of the hospital; to reduce the number of cadets by preventing the filling of vacancies; and to cut down forty-five per cent the pay and allowances of cadets, now barely sufficient for their support.

Mr. Aiken, a representative from South Carolina, denounced the institution as an incubus upon the country, and declared himself ready to vote to put West Point up to the highest bidder, or to give it away. . . .

Not content with crippling our present organization and reducing its force below the limit of efficiency and safety, the House Committee on Military Affairs have reported a bill for a large reduction of the pay of those who may continue in the service. The rank and pay of the general and lieutenant-general were created, not as a permanent part of our peace establishment, but as marks of national gratitude and honor for great and distinguished service in the late war. Further to reduce the pay of these officers is an attempt to belittle their services and stint the gratitude of the nation. The proposed reduction of the pay of company officers would render it almost impossible for a poor man to serve in any of those grades. . . . Should this bill become a law, it would be better, so far as pay is concerned, to be a doorkeeper in the House of Representatives than a senior captain of infantry; better to be the locksmith of the House than a second-lieutenant of the line!

The friends of good government and fair dealing will not be slow to condemn these repeated assaults upon the honor and usefulness of the army.

Source: James A. Garfield, "The Army of the United States, Part II," *The North American Review* 126 (May 1878): 443–65.

4. THE ARMY AND THE BUREAU OF INDIAN AFFAIRS, 1879

During the late nineteenth century, the federal government assigned responsibility for dealing with the Indian tribes to two agencies— the Interior Department's Bureau of Indian Affairs and the army. Responsible for the Indians living within reservation boundaries, the Indian Bureau provided food and other supplies to the Indians and supervised the efforts of religious and educational institutions to bring about the Indians' assimilation into white society. To the army fell the responsibility for Indians outside of the reservations. Its task was, whether by force or diplomacy, to persuade the Indians to move onto the reservations and to stay there. As discussed in Chapter 2, many army officers believed that the system of divided responsibility led to confusion and conflict. They also complained that the Indian Bureau did its work poorly. The corruption and incompetence of Bureau agents, the officers contended, caused many Indians to leave the reservations. When that happened, the army had to go after them, and violent clashes often resulted. Critics of the Indian Bureau urged Congress to transfer the Bureau from the Interior Department to the War Department, which could then appoint army officers to serve as agents on the reservations. The writer James Joseph Talbot presented the main arguments for the transfer in an article published in 1878 in *The United Service: A Quarterly Review of Military and Naval Affairs*. Talbot's article emphasized the corruption problems that had plagued the Bureau and made the case that army officers, more honest by nature than the typical civilian agent and more experienced in dealing with Indians, were best suited to govern the reservations.

_____

James Joseph Talbot, "The Indian Question"

So much has been said and written upon the interminable "Indian Question," that it would seem like an imposition upon public patience to add another line to the volumes now accumulated upon the subject. But, as the proposed transfer of the Indian Bureau to the control of the War Department has recently aroused a new interest in the question—accompanied by not a little high-pressure official, as well as popular, feeling—and as it is only by general discussion that such an important matter can ever be definitely and satisfactorily settled, the circumstances will probably justify me in contributing to the literature upon the subject. . . .

Possessing, as the result of some years of travel and close observation in the Far West, an intimate and wide personal knowledge of the nature of the Indians, of the character of the Indian country, of the general management of the Indian agencies, of the peculiarities of Indian campaigning, of the military in general, and of the conditions of military life at the Western posts, it may be granted that I am fairly qualified to express an opinion upon those points. As I am not in the service of either the War or Interior Department, it is but justice for the reader to assume that that opinion will be an impartial one, unaffected by any considerations of favor or position, and seeking only to establish impregnable facts, learned, not from newspaper reports or doubtful hearsay, but from personal observation.

In considering the policy or the impolicy of the proposed transfer, the first question to be asked is: Is the Interior Department capable of an honest and efficient management of the Indians? Judging it from its management in the past, by which standard alone we are authorized to pass judgment upon it, the answer is a most decided NO. In this connection it is as idle as it is illogical to discuss what that Department *may* do in the future; we can fairly argue only upon what it has done in the past, when it had power and opportunities of which it availed itself only to pervert them to the worst possible ends. It would be purposeless to rehearse here the frauds, deceptions, and impositions which have been practiced in the Indian service. They are already painfully familiar to all who read. During the past fifteen years the country has been startled and shocked by an almost unbroken series of revelations of Indian frauds and mismanagement, which have been a disgrace to our civilization, and which, it is no exaggeration, to say, are without parallel in the history of the world's government. . . .

An Indian agent has not merely to dole out certain amounts of food and clothing at certain times, and make an honest return thereof to the government; any school-boy could do that. He has, in addition, to assume the general executive management of the Indian, to decide many questions of policy, to settle many knotty points of dispute, and to exercise a large discretion in the government of the restless and peculiarly sensitive ones under his control. To do this wisely and successfully, avoiding all cause of complaint and trouble, requires an intimate knowledge of the nature, wants, habits, and customs of the Indians. So far as this essential requirement is concerned, an ordinary white man is about as well qualified to govern an Indian agency as an Indian is to govern one of our cities. Yet the glaring impropriety (to use a very mild term) of sending men out as agents who, however gifted and well qualified they might be for other and even higher positions, are as incapable of managing the Indians as of managing the Hottentots, never seems to occur to those who advocate the continuance of the present system, with all its evils. If we would have an efficient management of the Indian service we must have efficient agents—not Utopian theorists, whose only ideas of the Indians are derived from books of fiction and from the wooden Pompeys standing in front of cigar-stores, but men of sound, practical views, who have had more or less experience among the Indians, and have a personal knowledge of their necessities and idiosyncrasies, and who, with this knowledge and experience, are qualified to manage them wisely and well.

Having thus explained why the Interior Department cannot manage the Indian service honestly and efficiently, it might be well to explain why I believe that the War Department can manage it so.

In the first place, it may be said that, while there may be, as there have been, cases of irregularity and fraud perpetrated by army officers, such cases are extremely rare, and whenever they have been discovered they have been followed by the swift and relentless punishment of the guilty ones. Such a record in the past is the strongest possible guarantee that could be offered in the future. Therefore, if we would have honest Indian agents, why not appoint army officers as such? In them we would have a double assurance of fidelity. First, they would be under the close surveillance of their superior and brother officers, to whom they would be directly responsible, and who would keep a jealous watch over every movement, lest they should bring disgrace upon the army by committing any improper acts, so that there would be little opportunity for officers to commit such acts even if they were so disposed. Second, they cannot afford to be dishonest. An army officer enjoys his position for life, independent of changes in the administration and of fluctuations in his political or personal influence. He cannot, therefore, entertain the sentiments of the civil agent, who, enjoying his position for but a short time, takes advantage of the opportunity to help himself, feeling that, even if detected, his greatest punishment will be removal for an office which he would soon lose in the ordinary course of events. Not so with the officer. Detection of wrong in his case would mean, not quiet removal from his agentship, leaving him to resume his former life among his former friends, but it would mean a court-martial, sentence and dismissal, not only from the agentship, but probably from the army, leaving him a ruined man, despised by his late companions and avoided by the world, for the story of his crime has been heralded forth and no one will have aught to do with the wretched criminal. . . . [Officers] have everything to lose, while they have little to gain in any fraud which they could commit, so that even the few who might be disposed to take the risk, hesitate when they think of the possible consequences. It is for this reason that the army and navy officers, as a class, are more honest than other men. The great majority of them are so as a matter of professional education and life-long principle, while the rest of them are so as a matter of personal interest; they cannot be otherwise and remain officers, because all faithless ones are summarily court-martialed out of the service as soon as they are discovered. Under such circumstances, if army officers would not make honest Indian agents, no class of men on earth would. . . .

[An] objection is, that army officers are not qualified to, or will not, give the moral, mental, and industrial instruction necessary for evangelization and civilization of the Indians, which instruction is the grand aim of the present system. Before answering this objection it might be asked, Are the present agents qualified for the task; or do they perform it? In view of what has already been said in the preceding pages, it might be just as well not to say anything about the "moral" instruction which the agents have given or still give. The spectacle of an Indian agent undertaking the role of a "moral instructor" would be too much for a wicked world to gaze upon. I draw the veil. Upon the other points, a remark made by [Secretary of the Interior Carl] Schurz before the Congressional committee . . . may be quoted, to the effect that "not one army officer in a thousand would like to teach Indian children to read and write, or Indian men to sow and reap." Does Mr. Schurz mean to intimate by this that the civil agents teach, or like to teach, the Indians these things? If he does, I can tell him very flatly, from a personal knowledge of the subject which is much more extensive than his, that they do not; and it is not at all creditable to him that he should attempt to make so cheap a point in the controversy. I admit that army officers would not like to personally teach Indian children and men, just as the civil agents neither teach, nor like to teach, them—simply because they are not employed, *and are not supposed to act*, as teachers—and it must be confessed that the dislike is a natural one, which most men would be apt to entertain. . . . [italics in original]

A third objection to the proposed transfer is the statement that the army would manage the Indians by mere brute force, keeping them in humiliating subjugation, and making no effort to Christianize them or to teach them the industrial arts. Secretary Schurz says that such would be the result of army management, "for the simple reason that it is their business to keep the peace and prevent troublesome tribes from getting into mischief." Precisely; and the country at large will be very apt to exclaim that that is just what we want—peace and the prevention of further trouble, after which, Christianity and the industrial arts can be hopefully taught when the Indians are in a more favorable frame of mind and physical condition to receive them. In considering this subject, one paramount fact must be kept prominently in view: the fact that the Indians, like all barbarous people, are naturally wild and warlike, and must be treated accordingly. With them, a settled habitation is exceedingly irksome; peace is an inglorious waste of time; and industrial employment is the occupation of women. Such are the facts, and it is useless to argue against them. We cannot change the nature of such a people so completely, in one year or ten years, as to convert them from a nomadic, barbarous tribe to a settled, civilized community, and any attempt of overzealous theorists to do it will end only in disappointment, if not in disaster. Any one conversant with the history of such attempts in the past can cite may instances, some of them very amusing, in support of this statement. The Indians may be bribed by presents of cattle, wagons, and houses to settle down quietly for a short time, but the restraints of the new life are soon thrown off and the freedom of the old resumed. Force is the only argument the Indian will heed, and it is therefore necessary to maintain a display of force in order to preserve his submission. The Interior Department has not such force; the War Department has.

Source: James Joseph Talbot, "The Indian Question," *The United Service: A Quarterly Review of Military and Naval Affairs* 1 (January 1879): 141–52.

5. "REPRESENTATION THAT DOES NOT REPRESENT": A MILITARY PERSPECTIVE ON POLITICS, 1883

The *Army and Navy Journal*, a weekly newspaper devoted to publishing news about the services and commentary on military affairs, often contained editorials critical of the political system in the United States and the tendency of politicians to neglect the armed services. The journal's denunciations of the system's failings both reflected and helped shape the opinions of its principal readers— officers of the army and navy. The editorial reproduced below included an argument commonly made not only in the journal's pages but also in the writings of many officers—that the nation's civilian leaders lacked sufficient knowledge of, or interest in, military matters. The editorial's scathing observations about harm done to the military by frontier whites and eastern "sentimentalists" would have found an appreciative audience among army officers, especially those stationed in the West. The editorial writer's contention that the policies of the civilian government posed a greater danger to the navy than to the army would soon need revision; by the end of the 1880s the navy was enjoying a substantial increase in appropriations and a revitalized ship-building program while, with the end of the Indians wars, the army had greater reason to worry about its future.

Army and Navy Journal, "Representation that Does Not Represent"

. . . [I]t is a mere matter of luck if some man who has served his country and knows something of the needs of the Services happens to be in Congress. The Army had a willing and intelligent advocate in General [Henry] Slocum, for example, and a prominent senator has shown undeniable zeal in certain directions, such as wishing to give bounties to the extent of some hundred millions or so, to men who have been already treated with the wasteful liberality that characterizes American legislation, where every million voted out of the Treasury brings its return in the shape of political support. But intelligent and thoughtful discussion, such as grows out of the presence of numerous officers of high rank and long service in the English Parliament, is almost unknown in our legislation. A democratic atmosphere is not congenial to the profession of arms, and the spirit of the age is unfriendly.

There are two prominent political types in this country, the Scylla and Charybdis of legislation, who obstinately obstruct military and naval progress: these are the backwoods' statesman and the eastern sentimentalist—the one pachydermatous, narrow, illiterate, possessing some grains of boisterous common sense, cordially detesting reformers and instinctively distrusting all acquirements beyond the scope of a "deestrict" school; the other thin skinned, scholarly, thinking himself fastidious, in reality fretful, upright, wrong-headed, visionary.

Such politicians represent communities to whom questions of commerce and international relations are meaningless and unreal as the discussion of the genuineness of the Shapira Manuscripts. What difference does it make to them that at this moment we can barely put four worthless vessels in Chinese waters, where we have great interests? What appreciation have they of the fact that there, owing to English and French jealousies, we might, if decently provided with the only power that is recognized in troubled times, maintain a strong neutrality and do much toward keeping two great nations from each other's throats? What is it to them that decrepit states like Spain, and petty republics like Chili, know that they can say "bah" to us with tolerable impunity? All this does not affect the price of hogs and has not half the possibilities of a wild-cat railroad, and until water will rise about its own level it is chimerical to expect the representative to represent anything higher or better than the mean average of his constituents.

The sentimentalist has generally liberal views upon international subjects; not always practical, for the constitution of his mind tends to idealism. He is readily captivated by . . . phrases like "the brotherhood of nations," and looks on complacently while the refuse of Europe is emptied upon our shores, until our race characteristics are in danger of disappearing in a hodge podge of nationalities, and he is totally unable to distinguish between the screech of the hoodlum and a thoughtful and temperate protest against the demoralization attendant upon Chinese invasion. Naturally, he looks not unkindly on the Navy as something possessing a flavor of Webster's fine sentence about the "gorgeous ensign of the republic now known and honored throughout the whole earth," and will do something for it when he can abstract his mind from the engrossing question of how some savage, who has roasted sundry teamsters and brained divers babies, can be best protected against harsh treatment.

It is curious to see how the backwood's statesman and the philanthropist play into each other's hands where the Army is concerned. We leave the cheese-paring economist of the central Western States out of the question entirely. He is simply a commonplace exponent of narrowness, one of the caterers to agricultural isolation. The true frontier representative is not hostile to the Army, as a rule, though now and then you find him echoing the spite against officers, inspired by vulgarity which they think democratic, of some Arizona or Oregon paper, or repeating the bombast about the experienced volunteer, the Indian exterminator, usually a truculent braggart, brave only in the glory of unlimited buckskin patches. But he encourages, if he does not organize and direct, the unprincipled greed, and the utter disregard of obligations that have converted so many well-disposed tribes into scalping, burning, ravishing fiends, and then when the Army proceeds to the thankless task of hunting these fiends down, the philanthropist comes to the front with plaintive howls about the barbarity of the soldiers, as instanced in the shooting of some squaw in the confusion of a daylight attack or the failure to take alive some savage whose hands are reeking with the blood of women and children.

What is the remedy? Representation either in Congress or out. Representation in Congress is hopeless, in view of the fact that every year diminishes the number of men who have had the experience of a great war, and of the unwritten but rigid rule that officers must abstain from politics. For representation out of Congress we must look to the press, which still expresses the most courageous and honest thoughts of the country; and the press is doing noble work in this crisis. Such presentations of the necessity for an efficient Navy, such revelations of its decrepitude and such appeals for its reconstruction, one would suppose could not fail to move even a country lawyer. The question of the Navy is the engrossing one; the Army is merely hampered and badgered; the very existence of the Navy is in danger. Happily or unhappily events are hastening some solution of the question: happily if our legislators are roused to a recognition of the demands and needs of

American interests, unhappily if false economy and narrow localism are allowed to extinguish the spirit which fired Decatur and the enthusiasm which nurtured Farragut.

Source: "Representation that Does Not Represent," *Army and Navy Journal* 21 (October 6, 1883): 191.

6. SENATOR LOGAN PRAISES THE CITIZEN SOLDIER AND DENOUNCES WEST POINT, 1887

Raised on tales of the minutemen's stand against the British regulars in the Revolutionary War and proud of the volunteers who had fought so valiantly during the Civil War, many Americans in the late nineteenth century considered the establishment of a larger, professional army neither necessary nor desirable. No politician expressed the reservations Americans had about the professional military more effectively than John A. Logan of Illinois. From the time of his election to the House of Representatives in 1866 to his death in 1886, Logan often paid tribute to the role that citizens serving in militias or as national volunteers during wartime had played in the nation's military past. Although he acknowledged the importance of military training, he believed that excellence in military leadership was more a matter of inspiration than preparation. The Military Academy at West Point became the chief target of his criticism; the academy, he argued, instilled elitist attitudes in many of its students and graduated too many young men who either left the army at the first opportunity or stayed in and performed poorly as military leaders. Logan's animus against West Point was partly personal. During the Civil War, General William T. Sherman, a West Point graduate, had replaced Logan as commander of the Army of the Tennessee with another West Pointer despite Logan's distinguished record as a volunteer officer. Logan's resentment of what he perceived as the prejudice of the professional officer against the volunteer came through clearly in his book, *The Volunteer Soldier in America*, published posthumously in 1887.

John A. Logan, *The Volunteer Soldier in America*

The American volunteer, so far as mere physical strength, strong endurance, and iron courage are concerned, may not be a better "Greek" than he who fought the battles of Sparta and Athens twenty-five centuries ago, but there are circumstances connected with the modern American that have made him the most invincible of soldiers. What are these circumstances? They belong strictly to his Americanism.

Briefly stated, it may be said that he is an integral part of the government and country for which he fights. He is a citizen of the freest government that the world has yet seen. There is no avenue of life closed to him; no possibility denied him. From a private station he may pass to high political position. In his humblest and most obscure capacity his voice is as potent as is that of the richest and most prominent citizen. Today poor in purse, half a dozen years may not elapse until industry and enterprise bring him honest fortune. Whether poor or rich, the beneficent laws of his country give him personal guarantees not enjoyed in any other land. However poor, or however rich, he has a personal and direct interest in the government. He belongs to it; he is part of it. He helps to make its laws, to elect its officials, to direct its affairs. . . .

The circumstances stated give the soldier of America a purely distinctive character. He follows the banner of no potentate as hireling, dependent, vassal, or menial. He is a free man, fighting for home, family, country, and the government of which he is a factor. His arm is raised for a principle, for right, for justice. The immense difference between the man who is a soldier through such considerations, and him who is one by mere occupation or by force, need not be dwelt upon. . . .

. . . In broad terms, then, it may be said that *the tendency of our present military and naval system of education is to create a body of men in a republican country, the very nature of the circumstances under which the body is created and maintained implying the same feature of class-distinction, or of aristocracy, that distinguishes the similar bodies of men in purely aristocratic or monarchical countries* [italics in original].

. . . The young men of these national institutions are prepared for their career by an education which, in the points of liberality and general application, can be secured at but few of the collegiate institutions of America. With this education they are started upon a career promising much honor and great glory, and which, as frequently stated, practically covers a life-tenure irrespective of any civil or political authority whatever. Further than this, they are the defenders of the Government—the firm rock upon which the nation rests. Why should not such conditions result, especially in the absence of the strength of mind, possessed by a Grant, a Sherman, a Sheridan, and by many others, in the gradual growth of a feeling of superiority over the commoner conditions of men? Let the advocates of the system say what they will, this is the legitimate, and it is the practical effect. The American army or navy officer, if worthy in private character, has a ready *entrée* into every grade of society at home and abroad. It makes no difference if in his school days he belonged to the class whose parents were in "indigent circumstances," . . . his reception into any society whatever is assured by the honorable class-position which he occupies. Therefore, notwithstanding the exceptions which may be freely adduced to the contrary, the tendency to the creation and growth of the caste or aristocratic feeling exists as a veritable and incontrovertible fact, and it may be deduced in general terms that it was through the feeling of aristocracy engendered in the Southern people as part of their domestic system, added to by the education and tendencies of the West Point system, that such men as Lee and his *confreres* found it so easy to glide from the defense of their country to an open war upon its life. The tendency, then, is there; the circumstances warrant it, and it requires strong republicanism to resist it.

The army and navy are, numerically, so infinitesimal, as compared with the fifty odd million common people, that the military power is wholly swallowed up, so far as any dangerous possibility is concerned. In the present disposition of things, the evil is wholly theoretical, not practical. But, unquestionably, the system of a privileged class, holding a life-tenure of office, is foreign to the constitution and best interests of the republic. . . .

Strangely enough the military interest of the governing classes of our country has always centered in the small body of men—a mere national police force—called the "regular" army of the United States. Since the effective establishment of the Academy at West Point this institution has been constituted the special repository of the entire military establishment. Instead of its functions being limited to imparting an education in the science and art of war to such pupils as may be sent there for the purpose of receiving it, the institution, arrogating to itself the sole military knowledge of a people military by natural impulse and by the general habits and surroundings of their life, has for years past taken possession of the military interests of the Government and has conducted those interests as the sole property of the select circle which by the decrees of West Point has been constituted the only true exponent of the art of war upon the American continent.

Now this may seem a harsh statement, and by some it may be deemed an ill-natured one. The author sincerely wishes that the facts were not such as to compel it, but there is no volunteer soldier in our country who does not know that they are. The matter now under consideration is one of great importance to our country; and it is the duty of every citizen to become familiar with the question embraced in it, as this question, soon or late, must be met and solved by our people.

The assertion just made that the West Point influence had become the dominating power of our military interests does not need much argument for its support, as a superficial investigation of the facts will be amply sufficient to demonstrate its truth. This influence, in virtue of our military system, by which expert military knowledge of the country is confined by the Government to the small number of individuals whose names constitute the official roster of the United States army, has usurped the military organization of the country to an extent not realized by a superficial observer. Giving the institution personality, it may be said that West Point has pushed itself to the head of the various executive bureaus of the War Department. . . . Its officers, with some recent exceptions, fill the whole army, and while it has not as yet taken the Cabinet portfolio of the War Department, it practically directs that department, as, because of the circumstances that the War Secretary is generally a civilian, the actual administration of the office falls upon the military advisers of the Government. But the West Point goes farther than this, and by means of its potent and extended influence it manages to control to a very large extent the military legislation of Congress.

The effect of this preeminence has been, and still is, to prevent any development of the volunteer service. Regarding no man as a competent soldier who does not pass the sacred portals of West Point, an *ex-cathedra* ban is pronounced by the institution against the volunteer officer, who is then registered as an empyric in the profession of arms.

Source: John A. Logan, *The Volunteer Soldier in America* (Chicago: R. S. Peale and Company, 1887), 90–91, 118–19, 406, 421–22, 464, 580–82.

7. THE ARMY AND THE PRESERVATION OF LAW AND ORDER, 1895

On a number of occasions in the late nineteenth century, presidents employed the regular army to help restore civil order. In most cases, the presidents dispatched the troops in response to the requests of state governors who claimed that local law enforcement agencies and state militia forces were unable to quell the unrest. The federal troops generally won praise for their discipline and restraint in carrying out the interventions, especially during the nationwide railroad strike of 1877. Many observers compared the regulars favorably with the National Guard, some units of which proved unreliable in the 1877 strike. In the Pullman strike of 1894, President Grover Cleveland's decision to use federal troops to enforce a court injunction against leaders of the American Railway Union broke up the strike, much to the delight of Americans hostile to the labor movement. Some commentators, alarmed by the increasing frequency and violence of the labor upheaval, wanted the regulars to play a more prominent role in preserving law and order. One of those commentators, George W. Baird, noted in the article reproduced below the factors that made the National Guard—or state troops, as he called them—less than satisfactory as protectors of the social order. Baird also argued for a change in the laws so that regular army troops could be used in enforcing state as well as federal laws. Those changes were not forthcoming. Many army officers had little interest in making strike duty a major responsibility of their service, and the long-standing American suspicion of standing armies limited popular support for the idea. Congress kept the Posse

Comitatus Act—an 1878 law that placed restrictions on the role of U.S. soldiers in domestic law enforcement—on the books (see the discussion of the act in Chapter 4).

George W. Baird, "The Army as Guardian of the Peace"

Americans of the older stock, who can recall the events of forty, or more, years, need to make an effort of the will and to take a second look at current events to become fully aware of the condition of the America of today. It is not my purpose to dwell upon the change, or to indulge in prophecy as to what it may lead to, but to take a view of the actual facts, and to make them the basis of a brief suggestion of something to be done.

Our military system, National and State, retains still the impress of the ideas of that earlier time, before the reign of the irresponsible walking delegate began, when in large areas of our country there were no formidable lawbreakers—when boys grew to manhood without once seeing a soldier, a marshal, a sheriff, or even a constable, in the exercise of his authority. At that time the little army—though even then larger relatively than the army of today—availed for all National purposes; State organizations, where they existed, rarely had any duty to perform that required the exercise of force; and membership in organized companies was easily compatible with the most exacting private occupation. How greatly these conditions have changed is at once obvious on stating them.

Concurrently with this change—in some sense cause, and in some sense part of it—industrial changes have gone on, methods of business have become complex, its various branches interdependent in an increased degree, men have come to be the adjuncts of machinery, margins of profit have narrowed, and competition has become closer, so that the employer of labor is asked to make a great sacrifice when he is asked to have his employees mustered into the State troops, and the employee is asked to imperil his living as well as his life by rendering service in the militia.

From causes that need not be recited, the need of an armed force to keep the peace and to afford protection to property has increased in urgency, the calls for such a force have increased in frequency, and its use has been required for gradually lengthening periods just when, from causes in part pointed out, it has become increasingly difficult to maintain it in the form now prescribed.

The question, then, that confronts the American people, who are at once practical and liberty-loving, is how to keep the peace, protect their property, and preserve their liberties without unnecessary sacrifice of their business.

The efficiency and the devotion to duty of the State organizations have had conspicuous illustration in recent years in several of the States, and it cannot be doubted that those qualities are characteristic of those forces as a rule, although in some well-known instances the orders of governors, acting in their capacity of commanders-in-chief, have been emphatically disobeyed. But the question does not turn upon that issue; it is rather whether the specializing which characterizes every other form of activity, professional, and industrial, shall be applied to that most fundamental of all occupations, keeping the peace. But if this duty is to devolve mainly upon professional soldiers, it must needs be, under the third clause of Section 10 of our Constitution, that they be the soldiers of the nation, since "no State shall . . . keep troops . . . in times of peace." It is quite probable that a large fraction of our people would prefer that this duty should devolve upon the national force. They would prefer to pay, if necessary, the slight additional tax which would leave them at liberty to conduct their business enterprises secure both from violence and from the need of defending themselves against it. . . .

An additional source of disquietude has been recently pointed out by the *Army and Navy Journal*. It appears that in New York, and doubtless in other States also, the existence of the militia is contingent upon act of legislature, not being secured by the Constitution. The possibility of serious danger and of immense loss growing out of that fact is too obvious to require mention. All the conditions named point to an enlarged use of the National forces, and the cordial response to the recent action of the President—a truly national response, that disregarded party and sectional lines, and was made even more emphatic by the source and nature of the very slight opposing sentiment—affords basis of confidence both that those forces will be available, and that they will he rightly employed.

The teaching of this situation of affairs for the army is plainly that it shall continue to be at its best, and make that best, for the future, superior to that of the past if possible; also, that it shall be, above all things else, a loyal American army.

This accords with its best traditions, and Congress, by adopting the wise suggestion of Captain Philip Reade, U.S.A., has given emphasis as well as approval to this requirement in the law of August 1, 1894, which provides that only citizens of the United States, and those who have made legal declaration of their intention to become such, can be enlisted.

The demeanor, discipline, and services of the National forces have recently commended themselves to the cordial approval of all good citizens: even some of the less good have been compelled to accord unwilling praise. The army's part, then, is easily discerned, and not very difficult of achievement.

The modifications of law which would enable it to play its part in the best way for the public weal will be less easily arrived at. In dealing with a real but undeclared public enemy, as was recently the case in Chicago, the army has a qualified mandate. A large "if" intervenes between it and the attainment of its object—the restoration of peace and order—and conscientious men, the breath of whose nostrils is loyalty and obedience to the law, cannot employ to the full extent the power intrusted to them so long as that "if" qualifies the mandate which they are executing.

A man in the midst of conflagrations started by a murderous mob that crowds upon him, hurling vile epithets and missiles at him, is not favorably placed to discern between the violators of Federal law and the violators of State law or city ordinance. To him they all look much alike as, patiently submitting to insults, he grasps his rifle and scans their furious faces but obediently awaits the word of command.

Indeed their impartial contempt for all laws is forcibly expressed by their yell of "To hell with the Government."

Title LXIX of the Revised Statutes on Insurrection was recently found to be ample authority to secure the execution of the laws of the United States; if, as has recently been the case in several States, security and peace, menaced by violators of State laws, can only be maintained by the retention of armed men in camp for weeks or months, it is clear that either the Constitution must be amended so as to permit the States to "keep troops," or the law must be modified so as to enable Federal troops to keep the peace.

In common with their fellow-citizens generally army men hope that wise legislation affecting industrial matters—if it comes—and the strenuous and persistent application of the forces of our Christian civilization to the ignorant and the misinformed, will avail to diminish greatly the forces that menace our peace and mar our fair fame. They share with them also the fixed determination that the nation they stand pledged to maintain shall not succumb to lawlessness, however speciously, that lawlessness may use—and abuse—the sacred words, "liberty" and "rights."

Source: George W. Baird, "The Army as Guardian of the Peace," *The Century* 49 (April 1895): 958–59.

8. CARL SCHURZ DENOUNCES MILITARISM, 1899

From the perspective of the American military, the Spanish-American War of 1898 brought, for the most part, positive changes. Victories in battle—especially the navy's dramatic triumphs at Manila Bay and Santiago—enhanced the prestige of the armed services, and the acquisition by the United States of the former Spanish colonies of Puerto Rico, Guam, and the Philippines gave the army and navy new responsibilities and a stronger rationale for increased military appropriations. While many Americans took delight in the victory and the military's expanded role, others looked upon those developments with misgiving. Critics of the war and of the new empire—known as the anti-imperialists—endeavored to persuade the public that the more aggressive foreign and military policy being charted by President William McKinley imperiled American political institutions. One of the most prominent of the critics, Carl

Schurz, argued strenuously against the enlarged military that McKinley's policies necessitated. In a speech delivered in April 1899, Schurz warned that an expanded military would squander the nation's wealth, undermine its liberties, and draw it into foreign conflicts. Schurz's speech, excerpted below, won praise, but most political leaders disagreed with his sentiments. Congress provided the armed services with larger and larger appropriations and supported a major military campaign against Filipino nationalists.

A native of Prussia, Carl Schurz arrived in the United States as a refugee from the failed European uprisings of 1848. He fought for the Union as a volunteer general during the Civil War, represented Missouri in the U.S. Senate between 1869 and 1875, served as secretary of the interior under President Rutherford B. Hayes, and enjoyed renown as an orator and writer until his death in 1906.[2]

Carl Schurz, "Militarism and Democracy": An address
before the American Academy of Political and Social Sciences
at Philadelphia, April 7, 1899

The subject of "Militarism and Democracy," which has been assigned to me for discussion, is at the present moment of peculiar interest. We are apt to speak boastfully of the progressive civilization characterizing this age. While the very foundation of all civilization consists in the dispensation of justice by peaceable methods between nations as well as individuals, instead of the rule of brute force, it is a singular fact that at the close of this much-vaunted nineteenth century we behold the nations of the world vying with each other in increasing their armaments on land and sea, exhausting all the resources of inventive genius and spending the treasure produced by human labor with unprecedented lavishness to develop means of destruction for the defense of their possessions, or the satisfaction of national ambitions, or the settlement of international differences, on a scale never before known.

Thus the very advances in the sciences and the arts which constitute one part of our modern civilization are pressed into the service of efforts to perfect the engineries of death, devastation and oppression, which are to make brute force in our days more and more terrible and destructive, and to render the weak more and more helpless as against the strong. It looks as if the most civilized Powers, although constantly speaking of peace, were preparing for a gigantic killing-and-demolishing match such as the most barbarous ages have hardly ever witnessed, and this at the expense of incalculable sacrifice to their people. . . .

In a monarchy a standing armed force is a thing congruous with the nature of the government, and it is the more so, the more the monarchy is of the absolute type. The standing army in such a monarchy may be said to be the enlarged bodyguard of the monarch. The monarch represents an authority not springing from the periodically expressed consent of the people, and relying for the maintenance of that authority, if occasion requires, upon the employment of force, even against the popular will. An army is an organization of men subject to the command of a superior will, the origin or the purpose of which it is assumed to have no right to question. The standing army is in this sense, therefore, according to its nature and spirit an essentially monarchical institution. . . .

It is for reasons like this that the true democratic spirit has always been jealously opposed to the maintenance of large standing armies. It has always insisted that the organizations of armed forces that may be necessary for the enforcement of the laws and the keeping of order at home, or for the defense of the integrity or honor of the state in foreign warfare, should remain as much as possible identified with the people themselves—should be, in fact, of the people in their origin, their interests, their sympathies, as well as in the character and aspirations of those commanding them; and that if a standing army as a permanent institution be indeed indispensable for certain necessary objects, it should, in point of numerical strength, be confined to the narrowest practicable limits.

That democratic spirit has therefore always demanded that the armed force should be composed principally of the militia, the citizen soldiery, or, in the extraordinary emergencies, of volunteers called out from the ranks of the people, to serve as soldiers for certain well-defined and stated purposes, and then, those stated purposes being accomplished, to return to their civic pursuits. . . . All this rests upon the leading principle that the soldiers of a democracy as well as those commanding them should, while temporarily submitting to military discipline, remain in all essential respects active citizens without any interests, or sympathies or aspirations in any manner or degree different from those of the general citizenship. . . .

[T]he policy of this Republic was in entire harmony with that democratic instinct which abhors large standing armaments, and our position among the nations of the world was singularly favorable to the maintenance of that policy. None of those anxieties arising from the possible hostility of powerful neighbors, which keep European nations in a heavily armed state, existed here. Absolutely nothing to alarm us. . . .

There seems to be, then, in all these respects not only no necessity, but no valid reasons for our turning away from the old democratic policy and embarking in that course the pursuit of which costs European nations so dearly, and which they justify only on the ground that the constantly threatening dangers of their situation actually force them to follow it. On the contrary these would seem to be overwhelming reason for doing everything to preserve our happy exemption from such dangers and necessities, as a blessing so exceptionally great that the American people could not be too grateful for it. . . .

We are not a very economical people. We are apt to become lavish and wasteful upon the slightest provocation. Even a little war will cost us much. Whether the little war with Spain, which was practically over in three months, has cost us less or more than $500,000,000 may still be a matter of doubt. I speak here only of the cost in money, The cost in blood and misery I leave you to think of.

That, if the new policy be persisted in, our naval establishment also will have to be much enlarged, is generally admitted. How much—who can tell? Certainly, we can not tell. For it will not depend upon us how many new battleships, and armored or unarmored cruisers, and light draft vessels, and torpedo boats, and destroyers we shall want. It will depend upon the naval armaments our rivals and possible enemies have on the field of competition. Until recently, when we were proud, not of possessing large armaments, but of not needing any, it has afforded us much occasion for compassionate amusement to observe the almost hysterical nervousness into which old world Governments were thrown when one of them began the building of new warships by which the proportion of power on the seas might be disturbed. Already we begin to feel that nervousness in our bones, and we cannot tell how many and what kind of warships we shall be obliged to have in order to maintain what is so vauntingly called our new position among the Powers of the world. . . .

Taking it all in all, assuming our standing Army not to exceed 100,000 men, but a large part of it to be engaged in the tropics, and our Navy to be gradually enlarged to the strength which it "must have" in order to enable this Republic to play the part of a colonial Power, we are sure to have, including our pension roll, an annual expenditure for army and navy purposes not only far exceeding that of any European Power, but not falling very much short of the two-fifths of the expenses for the same purposes of all the six great Powers of Europe together—that is not far from $400,000,000 a year. By honest and strenuous effort we have paid off the bulk of the heavy National debt left by the civil war, and we have been very proud of that achievement. We are now in the way of running up a new National debt, of which, if we go on with the new policy, nobody can foretell to what figures it will rise. . . .

But even in such a country and among such a people it is possible to demoralize the Constitutional system and to infuse a dangerous element of arbitrary power into the government without making it a monarchy in form and name. One of the most necessary conservative agencies in a democratic republic is general respect for constitutional principles, and faithful observance of constitutional forms; and nothing is more apt to undermine that respect and to foster disregard of those forms than warlike excitements, which at the same time give to the armed forces an importance and a prestige which they otherwise would not possess. . . .

History shows that military glory is the most unwholesome food that democracies can feed upon. War withdraws, more than anything else, the popular attention from those problems and interests which are, in the long run, of the greatest consequence. It produces a strange moral and political color-blindness. It creates false ideals of patriotism and civic virtue. . . .

We should, in the first place, restrict our standing armaments to the narrowest practicable limits; and those limits will be very narrow, if this democracy does not suffer itself to be carried away by the ambition of doing things which, as history has amply shown, a democracy cannot do without seriously endangering its vital principles and institutions. There is no doubt that a regular standing army is a more efficient fighting machine, especially at the beginning of a war, than citizen soldiery. But our experience has been that, in the peculiar position we occupy among the nations of the world, we need not have any war unless, without any compelling necessity, we choose to have it. It would be most unwise to shape our whole policy with a view to the constant imminence of war, there being no such imminence, unless we ourselves choose to create it. We should have as our main armed force, and as the natural armed force of a democratic republic, the citizen soldiery, to be called out for specific purposes in extraordinary emergencies. . . . We should have a Navy strong enough to do our share in the police of the seas, but not a navy rivaling those of the great naval Powers, for, as our history has conclusively taught us, we shall not need it if we keep out of quarrels which do not concern us, and cultivate peace and good will with other nations—a disposition which the rest of the world will be glad to reciprocate. In this way we shall avoid the burdens and evil influences of militarism, and give even our pension roll at last a chance to decrease.

Following a policy essentially different from this we may have our fill of military glory and conquest, but with them other things which in the course of time will make the American people ruefully remember how free and great and happy they once were with less military glory and with no outlying dominions and subject populations.

Source: Frederic Bancroft, ed., *Speeches, Correspondence and Political Papers of Carl Schurz*, Vol. 6 (New York: G. P. Putnam's Sons, 1913): 48–76.

9. SECRETARY OF WAR ELIHU ROOT DEFENDS THE REGULAR ARMY, 1903

Elihu Root, secretary of war from 1899 to 1903, accomplished a great deal during his time in office. He launched the Army War College, guided the establishment of military governments in the colonies that came into American possession as a result of the Spanish-American War, and persuaded Congress to pass important legislation regarding the military, including the bill creating an army general staff. As the speech below indicated, he also became a dedicated advocate of the service he headed. The speech revealed something of the pessimistic view of human nature that led Root to call upon the country to support a stronger professional military—aggressor nations would always prey upon the weak, he suggested, and the United States needed to build a larger and more effective military to keep from becoming a victim. Influenced by the writings of Colonel Emory Upton, Root had little confidence in the fighting efficacy of the National Guard or of volunteer units organized by the states. He wanted the United States to rely more on the trained professionals of the regular army. In his speech Root heaped praise on the regulars and attempted to refute, point by point, the common charges against them—that they were foreign born, uneducated, and morally deficient, for instance. Perhaps in order to counter the image of regular troops as "hirelings" or as desperate characters who entered the military as an alternative to jail, Root described them as "volunteers"—a more positive term usually reserved for those who served in state volunteer regiments created in wartime. The secretary also tried to reassure those who saw a standing army as a threat to liberty and democracy by emphasizing the military's tradition of obedience to civil authority.

Elihu Root, "The Character and Office of the American Army: An Address at a Banquet at Canton, Ohio, January 27, 1903, in honor of the birthday of the late President McKinley"

. . . It is noteworthy that the greatest American presidents who have passed into history have been the most patient, most peaceable, and most just of all the men whose names are found upon the pages of our national life; and yet, that each one of them, Washington, Lincoln, and McKinley, led his country through the dark and bloody paths of war. . . .

Do not forget or be deaf to the lesson. No sense of justice, no desire for peace, no kindliness of heart can turn aside the inexorable decrees of the overwhelming powers that bring war and will bring war in the future, as they brought it in the past. . . . Controversies will arise as they have arisen, when each side believes itself to be right and the weak and feeble will go to the wall. Great and overbearing injustice walks the earth still, and the people who are unable or unwilling to strive for their rights will find small respect. . . .

The nation least able to defend itself most invites aggression. It is to repel and prevent aggression and to defend and assert the right, that the army of the United States exists. Not because we love war or seek war; not because we would infringe upon the rights of any other power or of any other people, but because we have that manhood in us, and we have that respect and love for the right to make us willing to defend it with life itself, we have the army of the United States. It is an insurance against aggression. Among the eighty million people of the United States the cost of this insurance is less than a dollar apiece. . . .

The character of the army of the United States conforms to the high and pacific purpose for which it exists. It is an army of citizens of the United States—volunteers all of them. It is a volunteer army. It is an army of citizens, each of whom is educated, for there is an educational test upon admission. It is an army in which the door of opportunity, the open door of opportunity to youth which is the crowning and chief glory of our American institutions, is never closed, for up from the ranks each common soldier may pass by promotion to the highest rank. . . .

The officers of the army conform in their character and conduct to the purpose for which the army is maintained, and the character of the people from whom they come. . . . [T]hey are free to a degree which I never dreamed of, until I commenced to know of them, from the vices which have prevailed in most armies of the world during all history. They are a temperate set of men. They are freer from the vice of drinking to excess than almost any other class I know of in this country. They are free of the vice of gambling. No such thing as dueling, which disgraces and deforms many military services, obtains in our army. The man who is dissipated is out of favor, and the public sentiment of the officers of the army is opposed to dissipation and excess. . . .

No one ever knew of the American army seeking to make itself a political agent. No one ever knew of the American army seeking to make itself a Praetorian guard to set up a president or an emperor. No one ever knew of the American army seeking to throw off that civil control of the military arm which our fathers inherited from England and which is ingrained in the desires, the prejudices and the instincts of the Anglo-Saxon race. It does its duty under presidents, Republican or Democratic. Whatever the political policy of the American people may be, when the army is called upon it does its duty, asking no questions, doubting not, begrudging no sacrifice, fearing no danger, and hesitating not at death itself. . . .

Source: Elihu Root, *The Military and Colonial Policy of the United States; Addresses and Reports by Elihu Root*, collected and edited by Robert Bacon and James Brown Scott (Cambridge: Harvard University Press, 1916), 15–19.

10. COMMANDER FISKE ON THE NEED FOR A NAVAL GENERAL STAFF, 1906

By the early twentieth century, the increased professionalization of the military—that is, the development of an officer corps that possessed a high level of specialized training and that adhered to a set of common values—had led some officers to question the role that civilians played in the making of military policy. While these officers generally accepted the principle of civilian control of the military, they came to believe that the military should have greater autonomy in how it carried out the tasks assigned to it. The military should have control over its day-to-day affairs, they argued, and over "purely military acts," as Commander Bradley A. Fiske put it in the following article. Like Fiske, many officers thought that the establishment of a general staff system would solve many of the problems caused by what they saw as excessive civilian involvement in military affairs. Above all, they wanted a general staff capable of commanding the bureaus that often seemed to function as agencies of Congress rather than as departments serving the army or navy. As discussed in Chapter 5, Congress passed legislation giving the army a general staff in 1903. Legislation to create a similar body for the navy, however, failed to pass the Naval Affairs Committees of the House and Senate. In the article excerpted below, Commander Fiske presented the case for a naval general staff and called upon the government to hand more of the responsibility for military policy to the professionals—the officers of the army and navy.

At the time of the article's publication in 1906, Fiske was an officer on the rise. A prolific inventor and writer—he held nearly sixty patents for his inventions and wrote six books—Fiske ascended to the rank of rear admiral and held the important post of aide for operations during the presidency of Woodrow Wilson. Fiske's obvious disrespect for civilian leaders such as Secretary of the Navy Josephus Daniels and his increasingly agitated calls for an accelerated naval buildup brought him into disfavor in the Wilson administration, and by 1915 he had lost both his influence and his position as aide for operations. Fiske retired from the navy in 1916.[3]

Bradley A. Fiske, "The Civil and the Military Authority"

It is a common saying that, in the United States, the military is subordinate to the civil authority. But, in every civilized country, the military is subordinate to the civil authority; that is, to the central authority of the government. In every civilized country, including our own, the Sovereign is the chief of every department; and our own President is as much commander-in-chief of the army and the navy as is the Emperor of Germany or the Mikado of Japan—but no more so. . . .

Yet, when we compare the importance which the military authority has, in this country, in time of peace, with the importance which it has in other countries, in time of peace, we find that it has very much less importance in this country. Of course, the simple reason is that this country has never had a serious foreign war since the Revolution, and has never had to develop the military arts: it has been allowed to grow to maturity far away from other countries and undisturbed by them; whereas other countries have grown up close together, and have had to be fighting, or getting ready for fighting, most of the time. In this respect we have grown up in luxury, like the son of a millionaire.

But the time comes, even to the son of a millionaire, when he must put on the armor of manhood, or decide to dawdle away his life. Perhaps this time has now come to the United States. We have already decided not to dawdle, but to take part in the world's struggles. Shall we have to put on a little armor? Every other nation has had to do so. If so, we may not need very heavy armor; but it is clear that the armor should be good. We may not need a very big army and navy, but it is clear that they should be good.

In order that they may become good, the proper means must be allowed. The first means is the correct application to the army and navy of the fundamental military principles. If these principles be mastered thoroughly by the civil authorities, and if the proper application of the principles be understood by them, and if the conditions to which the principles are to be applied be perfectly clear to them, then the army and navy can be perfectly directed by them, as were the army and navy by Napoleon. But if those principles, and the means and conditions governing their application, be not thoroughly mastered by the civil authorities, then common sense and all experience show that interference by the civil authorities with the military authorities should be restricted to cases in which other conditions besides military conditions have to be considered. . . .

It seems improbable that the civil authorities of this government will ever be able to get the time to devote to the study of military principles and conditions which is needed to master them; and yet it is clear that nothing short of absolute mastery can suffice. "A little knowledge" may not be a very dangerous thing when possessed by a mediocre man; but when it is possessed by an official of ability and force, it becomes a menace to the State. Alexander, Caesar, Peter the Great, Washington, and Napoleon were all able to direct the military as well as the civil departments of the government; but they were all geniuses and had military training too. Theirs was not the "little knowledge."

Since the coming of such men cannot be predicted, it would seem unwise to base any system on it. Therefore, it would seem unwise to neglect the only other system by which an army and navy can be made really good, a system by which the lifelong members of those services control their purely military acts, by means of a general staff. This fact has just been recognized, so far as the army is concerned; and it implies no surrender by the civil authorities of perfect control over the army; it simply implies abstention from interference with details, details which are purely technical. It simply implies recognizing army officers as members of a real profession, in the same sense that doctors and clergymen and lawyers are recognized as members of real professions. The civil authorities lose no dignity by not interfering with matters that are purely technical, any more than an admiral does by not interfering with the internal administration of his flagship.

No boy can become an efficient man, if he be kept "tied to his mother's apron strings." No organization can become efficient, unless it be allowed to make and enforce rules for its own government, subject to the laws of the community. No navy can become efficient, unless it be allowed to work out, and to carry out, its own rules of strategy, tactics, and discipline; subject, of course, to the general control of the civil authority, to which it must render absolute obedience. No person, no organization, can become efficient, unless it be made responsible: our own President has often declared that responsibility and authority go together.

The refusal of the civil authorities to give the navy the responsibility and authority which it needs, to be efficient, and the fact that the navy needs them even more than the army does, are both due to the same cause: the non-acquaintance of civilians with naval conditions, especially now when naval conditions are changing with such dizzying rapidity. But, the very difficulty of applying principles to modern naval conditions necessitates professional study of the subject; because the nation which succeeds in learning will acquire a decisive advantage. So clearly is this true, that one can declare with certainty that, if two navies fight, of equal strength, one directed by a general staff, and the other not, the one that is directed by a general staff will whip the other.

Source: Bradley A. Fiske, "The Civil and the Military Authority," *Proceedings of the United States Naval Institute* 32 (1906), 127–30.

11. "OUR UNHAPPY SOLDIERS": A NEWSPAPER COMMENTS ON THE ARMY'S DISCONTENT, 1911

In the early years of the twentieth century military reformers such as General Leonard Wood were interested in changing the regular army—still organized as a frontier constabulary with small units scattered in posts around the country—into a force capable of concerted action in large, division-sized units. In 1911 President William Howard Taft gave the army an opportunity to test its ability to organize into large units when he authorized the concentration of 20,000 troops in Texas. There the troops would be available to intervene in Mexico should its revolution develop in ways that endangered American interests. To the chagrin of its leaders, the army had trouble putting together the "Maneuver Division." The movement of troops and supplies seemed to require endless orders, and after three months the army had assembled only about two-thirds of the soldiers it had promised to provide.

Military reformers bewailed the poor performance, but some saw the episode as an opportunity to strengthen the reform cause. They could point to the lethargic mobilization as evidence that civilian leaders had not yet done enough to provide the army with the organizational reforms and resources that would make it a force capable of fighting in the conditions of modern warfare.

Some critics of the military understood that the lamentations that followed the mobilization were partly for the benefit of civilian policymakers. In the editorial reproduced below, the *New York Evening Post* ridiculed what it saw as the military's exaggerated alarm over the Texas maneuvers. Edited by Oswald Garrison Villard, a staunch anti-imperialist, the *Evening Post* often expressed skepticism about the need to enlarge the military and warned against what it perceived as the increasing influence of the military in the making of public policy. The *Evening Post*'s editorial writers chose as their foil the *Journal of the United States Infantry Association*—commonly known as the *Infantry Journal*—one of the growing number of publications devoted to promoting professional development in the armed services. To its credit, the *Infantry Journal* reprinted the *Post*'s editorial.

New York Evening Post, "Our Unhappy Soldiers"

That soldiers, being but men, never are but always to be blest, everybody recognizes. Indeed, there has come over the world in recent years an understanding that the only way the several armies could be rendered really happy, and freed from the most terrifying fears, would be by turning over to them all the Parliaments, so that they could legislate to their hearts' content on matters military. With superb indifference to merely financial questions, they . . . would vote universal conscription, place a rifle in every boy's hands, and a dynamite bomb by the side of every cradle. Even then, it is hinted, there would be some military men who would see in Germany's or Japan's preparations a menace to our lives and liberties, and have something else to suggest in the way of fortifying our ever defenseless shores. . . .

In this country one thing is certain, never before have our military men been in such depths of woe or prey of such fearful pessimism. Before us lies a copy of the *Infantry Journal*, one of the ablest service organs in this country, bound, as befits its present frame of mind, in a cover of deep blue. It fairly drips unhappiness. Why? All because of our Texas maneuvers. Intended originally by [President William Howard] Taft to deceive the public as to the real reason for assembling troops near Mexico, it seems that they have undeceived the army very thoroughly, for here is what the *Infantry Journal* has to say about them:

> It is a pitiable thing to rejoice at a display of our own weakness, but the concentration in Texas has been such a pitiable display of that weakness that . . . the great mass of the line officers of the army have faced the facts unshrinkingly and declared our whole military organization inefficient and our whole military system extravagant and useless.

This would seem, in all charity, like rather a sweeping assertion—this placing of the whole United States army on the scrap-heap at one time. But worse is yet to come. The same editorial writer positively asserts that heretofore no alarmists had "dared to think" that "our weakness was so great" and "our system so pitiably futile." More than that:

> We have exposed our shame unhesitatingly. Foreign military attaches were invited to witness it, and they came and saw and laughed; national guard officers from all over the country were welcomed, and they came and saw, and, we may hope, understood; for whatever has been displayed of the army is weakness of the National Guard in still greater measure, and whatever there is in this combined weakness is all there is to the military system that supports this nation in its claim as a world power. . . .

And so on for many pages, with copious footnotes of citations from authorities. And if there were no end to the darkness of its despair, the *Infantry Journal* tops it all off with an article by an officer with a highly interesting name—Jens Bugge—which gives us the comforting assurance that "to begin with, we must recognize that we have no army except in name, a natural result of the past and present lack of any military policy." After this, why should not the Mikado and the Kaiser jointly declare war upon us? As for the editor, so great is his distress that there is only one thing left—an appeal to a higher power. "The task is heavy, the confusion great." Hence he says let us pray—to the Prince of Peace. . . .

Meanwhile, we would offer a few crumbs of comfort to our despairing brother journalist. The army is three times as large as in 1898. Promotion swift enough to suit any reasonable man has come to officers who, but for the war with Spain, would have retired as humble captains and majors. . . . The pay of every officer has increased, and the number of officers in every corps and every rank doubled and trebled, if not quadrupled, until ours is the most over-officered army in the world. New and interesting duties, broadening Foreign Service, and special advancement of all kinds have been given to officers—their social and professional prestige enhanced. Within the last eight years we have spent $1,072,000,000 more upon the army and navy than we did in the eight years prior to 1898, which sum would have paid off the national debt and left a tidy balance of $158,000,000 in the bank. We admit these are but trifling crumbs of comfort; the soldiers and sailors only get 70 cents on every dollar the Government spends. Shall we not vote to make it 99 cents?

Source: "Reprints and Reports: Our Unhappy Soldiers," *Infantry Journal* 8 (July–August 1911): 124–33.

Notes

CHAPTER 1: AMERICANS LOOK AT THEIR MILITARY, 1865–1917

1. Peter Cozzens, *General John Pope: A Life for the Nation* (Urbana and Chicago: University of Illinois Press, 2000), 324.

2. Michael Fellman, *Citizen Sherman: A Life of William Tecumseh Sherman* (New York: Random House, 1995), 280; "Representation that Does Not Represent," *Army and Navy Journal*, October 6, 1883, 191.

3. James S. Pettit, "How Far Does Democracy Affect the Organization and Discipline of Our Armies, and How Can Its Influence Be Most Effectively Utilized?" *Journal of the Military Service Institute of the United States* 38 (January–February 1906): 29. A good discussion of the roots of American attitudes about standing armies is found in Arthur A. Ekirch, Jr., *The Civilian and the Military* (New York: Oxford University Press, 1956), 3–73.

4. Edward Berwick, "American Militarism," *The Century* 47 (December 1893): 316–17; Frederic Bancroft, ed., *Speeches, Correspondence and Political Papers of Carl Schurz*, vol. 6 (New York: G. P. Putnam's Sons, 1913), 53.

5. Mark R. Grandstaff, "Preserving the 'Habits and Usages of War': William Tecumseh Sherman, Professional Reform, and the U.S. Army Officer Corps, 1865–1881, Revisited," *Journal of Military History* 62 (July 1998): 533–34.

6. John A. Logan, *The Volunteer Soldier of America* (Chicago: R. S. Peale, 1887), 91; Peter Karsten, "Armed Progressives: The Military Reorganizes for the American Century," in *The Military in America: From the Colonial Era to the Present*, ed. Peter Karsten (New York: Free Press, 1980), 248; Stuart Creighton Miller, *"Benevolent Assimilation": The American Conquest of the Philippines, 1899–1903* (New Haven, CT: Yale University Press, 1982), 141; "Some National Guard Tendencies," *Infantry Journal* 8 (July 1911): 102.

7. C. Robert Kemble, *The Image of the Army Officer in America: Background for Current Views* (Westport, CT: Greenwood Press, 1973), 106–11; Samuel P. Huntington, *The Soldier and the State: The Theory and Politics of Civil-Military*

Relations (Cambridge, MA: Harvard University Press, 1957), 223–30; Russell F. Weigley, *History of the United States Army* (1967; enlarged edition, Bloomington: Indiana University Press, 1984), 271.

8. Robert M. Utley, *Frontier Regulars: The United States Army and the Indian* (New York: Macmillan Publishing, 1973), 23; *Army and Navy Journal*, August 16, 1879, 26.

9. Edward M. Coffman, *The Old Army: A Portrait of the American Army in Peacetime, 1784–1898* (Oxford: Oxford University Press, 1986), 401–2; Henry P. Walker, ed., "The Reluctant Corporal: The Autobiography of William Bladen Jett, Part I," *Journal of Arizona History* 12 (Spring 1971): 22; Richard E. Lingenfelter, Richard A. Dwyer, and David Cohen, *Songs of the American West* (Berkeley: University of California Press, 1968), 280.

10. "Slander's Mask of Humor," *New York Times*, March 24, 1901, 22; Mark Russell Shulman, *Navalism and the Emergence of American Sea Power, 1882–1893* (Annapolis, MD: Naval Institute Press, 1995), 40; Coffman, *Old Army*, 330–32.

11. Gerald F. Linderman, *Embattled Courage: The Experience of Combat in the American Civil War* (New York: Free Press, 1987), 273; Kemble, *Image*, 107, 111–13.

12. Logan, *Volunteer Soldier*, 406–7; John W. Pullman, "The American Citizen *Versus* the American Soldier and Sailor," *Journal of the Military Service Institution of the United States* 39 (November–December 1906): 332.

13. Coffman, *Old Army*, 306–7.

14. William S. McFeely, *Grant: A Biography* (New York: W. W. Norton, 1981), 280–82; Ekirch, *Civilian and Military*, 109.

15. McFeely, *Grant*, 247; James E. Sefton, *The United States Army and Reconstruction, 1865–1877* (Baton Rouge: Louisiana State University Press, 1967), 49–54, 95–96.

16. Brooks D. Simpson, *Let Us Have Peace: Ulysses S. Grant and the Politics of War and Reconstruction, 1861–1868* (Chapel Hill: University of North Carolina Press, 1991), 172–73, 186.

17. Eric Foner, *Reconstruction: America's Unfinished Revolution, 1863–1877* (New York: Harper and Row, 1988), 154, 308; Joseph G. Dawson, III, *Army Generals and Reconstruction: Louisiana, 1862–1877* (Baton Rouge: Louisiana State University Press, 1982), 87–89, 133; Sefton, *Army and Reconstruction*, 55–59, 140–46, 173, 183–84.

18. James D. Richardson, ed., *A Compilation of the Messages and Papers of the Presidents, 1789–1897*, vol. 6 (Washington, DC: Government Printing Office, 1897), 502; Simpson, *Peace*, 248–49; Dawson, *Army Generals*, 206.

19. Foner, *Reconstruction*, 454–59; Gregory J. W. Urwin, *The United States Infantry: An Illustrated History, 1775–1918* (New York: Sterling Publishing, 1988), 118; Allen W. Trelease, *White Terror: The Ku Klux Klan Conspiracy and Southern Reconstruction* (New York: Harper and Row, 1971), 399–418.

20. Dawson, *Army Generals*, 200–210.

21. Bernarr Cresap, *Appomattox Commander: The Story of General E.O.C. Ord* (San Diego, CA: A. S. Barnes, 1981), 268, 294; Sefton, *Army and Reconstruction*, 253–54.

22. Paul Andrew Hutton, *Phil Sheridan and His Army* (Norman: University of Oklahoma Press, 1985), 195.

23. Robert M. Utley, *The Indian Frontier of the American West, 1846–1890* (Albuquerque: University of New Mexico Press, 1984), 101–7, 138, 189–91; Robert Wooster, *The Military and United States Indian Policy, 1865–1903* (New Haven: Yale University Press, 1988; Lincoln: University of Nebraska Press, 1995), 149–50; Hutton, *Sheridan*, 363–64.

24. Utley, *Indian Frontier*, 203–9; Francis Paul Prucha, *The Great Father: The United States Government and the American Indians*, vol. 1 (Lincoln: University of Nebraska Press, 1984), 554–55; Hutton, *Sheridan*, 95–99, 186–97.

25. Linderman, *Embattled Courage*, 275–79; Utley, *Frontier Regulars*, 68–69; Coffman, *Old Army*, 285; Berwick, "American Militarism," 316.

26. Stephen Skowronek, *Building a New American State: The Expansion of National Administrative Capacities, 1877–1920* (Cambridge: Cambridge University Press, 1982), 98–102; Allan R. Millett and Peter Maslowski, *For the Common Defense: A Military History of the United States of America* (New York: Free Press, 1984), 247–48.

27. Robert V. Bruce, *1877: Year of Violence* (Indianapolis, IN: Bobbs-Merrill Company, 1959; Chicago: Ivan R. Dee, 1989), 213, 290, 309–10; Jerry M. Cooper, *The Rise of the National Guard: The Evolution of the American Militia, 1865–1920* (Lincoln: University of Nebraska Press, 1997), 49–50; Jerry M. Cooper, *The Army and Civil Disorder: Federal Military Intervention in Labor Disputes, 1877–1900* (Westport, CT: Greenwood Press, 1980), 61, 82; Coffman, *Old Army*, 252.

28. Cooper, *Civil Disorder*, 126–27, 219.

29. Ibid., 222–26.

30. Ibid., 210–15.

31. Peter Karsten, *The Naval Aristocracy: The Golden Age of Annapolis and the Emergence of Modern American Navalism* (New York: Free Press, 1972), 390; Shulman, *Navalism*, 122.

32. Stephen Howarth, *To Shining Sea: A History of the United States Navy, 1775–1991* (New York: Random House, 1991), 216; Homer E. Socolofsky and Allan B. Spetter, *The Presidency of Benjamin Harrison* (Lawrence: University Press of Kansas, 1987), 97.

33. Shulman, *Navalism*, 46–57.

34. Kenneth Wimmel, *Theodore Roosevelt and the Great White Fleet: American Sea Power Comes of Age* (Washington, DC: Brassey's, 1998), 126, 147–48; Ronald Spector, *Admiral of the New Empire: The Life and Career of George Dewey* (Baton Rouge: Louisiana State University Press, 1974), 102–5.

35. Graham A. Cosmas, *An Army for Empire: The United States Army in the Spanish-American War* (Columbia: University of Missouri Press, 1971; College Station: Texas A&M Press, 1994), 278–81; Millett and Maslowski, *Common Defense*, 309.

36. Cosmas, *Army for Empire*, 160–67; Weigley, *U.S. Army*, 295–303.

37. Ivan Musicant, *Empire by Default: The Spanish-American War and the Dawn of the American Century* (New York: Henry Holt, 1998), 642–52; Millett and Maslowski, *Common Defense*, 284–85; Cosmas, *Army for Empire*, 254–78.

38. Cosmas, *Army for Empire*, 284–86, 297–98.

39. Ibid., 286–96; Peter R. DeMontravel, *A Hero to His Fighting Men: Nelson A. Miles, 1839–1925* (Kent, OH: Kent State University Press, 1998), 310–23.

40. Brian McAllister Linn, *The Philippine War, 1899–1902* (Lawrence: University Press of Kansas, 2000), 29–31, 200–3; Millett and Maslowski, *Common Defense*, 287.

41. Max Boot, *The Savage Wars of Peace: Small Wars and the Rise of American Power* (New York: Basic Books, 2002), 69–70.

42. Millett and Maslowski, *Common Defense*, 296; Linn, *Philippine War*, 139–59, 275; Miller, *Benevolent Assimilation*, 167–69.

43. Miller, *Benevolent Assimilation* and Linn, *Philippine War* contain extensive discussions of the atrocity allegations and the conduct of the campaign against the insurgents.

44. DeMontravel, *Miles*, 337–52.

45. Ibid.; Linn, *Philippine War*, 311–21; Miller, *Benevolent Assimilation*, 238, 258–59; Millett and Maslowski, *Common Defense*, 295–96.

46. Bancroft, *Speeches of Carl Schurz*, vol. 6, 72; Ray Ginger, ed., *William Jennings Bryan: Selections* (Indianapolis, IN: Bobbs-Merrill, 1967), 64. See also Hans L. Trefousse, *Carl Schurz: A Biography* (Knoxville: University of Tennessee Press, 1982), 284; Miller, *Benevolent Assimilation*, 104.

47. Robert H. Noble, "The Army, the National Guard, and the Nation," *Infantry Journal* 6 (September 1909): 174; Miller, *Benevolent Assimilation*, 141.

48. Edward M. Coffman, *The Regulars: The American Army, 1898–1941* (Cambridge, MA: Harvard University Press, 2004), 96; Thomas C. Leonard, *Above the Battle: War-Making in America from Appomattox to Versailles* (New York: Oxford University Press, 1978), 35; Frederick S. Harrod, *Manning the New Navy: The Development of a Modern Naval Enlisted Force, 1899–1940* (Westport, CT: Greenwood Press, 1978), 159; "Disrespect to the Uniform," *Army and Navy Journal*, September 28, 1907, 93. For examples of officers expressing their resentment of negative stereotypes about the military, see I. L. Hunt, "Public Opinion and the American Army," *Infantry Journal* 3 (January 1907): 69–76; Pullman, "American Citizen," 329–40.

CHAPTER 2: CONGRESS, POPULAR OPINION, AND THE MAKING OF MILITARY POLICY

1. Samuel P. Huntington, *The Soldier and the State: The Theory and Politics of Civil-Military Relations* (Cambridge, MA: Harvard University Press, 1957), 177–80.

2. Ari Hoogenboom, *The Presidency of Rutherford B. Hayes* (Lawrence: University Press of Kansas, 1988), 173–74.

3. "Biographical Directory of the United States Congress," http://bioguide.congress.gov

4. James Pickett Jones, *John A. Logan: Stalwart Republican from Illinois* (Tallahassee: University Presses of Florida, 1982), 41.

5. Robert Wooster, *The Military and United States Indian Policy, 1865–1903* (Lincoln: University of Nebraska Press, 1988), 99; Kenneth Wimmel, *Theodore Roosevelt and the Great White Fleet: American Sea Power Comes of Age* (Washington, DC: Brassey's, 1998), 11; Robert G. Albion, "George M. Robeson," in *American Secretaries of the Navy*, vol. 1, ed. Paolo E. Coletta (Annapolis, MD: Naval Institute Press, 1980), 374–75; Benjamin Franklin Cooling, *Grey Steel and Blue Water Navy: The Formative Years of America's Military-Industrial Complex, 1881–1917* (Hamden,

CT: Archon Books, 1979), 55; Elting E. Morison, *Turmoil and Tradition: A Study of the Life and Times of Henry L. Stimson* (New York: Houghton Mifflin, 1960), 120.

6. Edward M. Coffman, *The Old Army: A Portrait of the American Army in Peacetime, 1784–1898* (Oxford: Oxford University Press, 1986), 345–46; Morison, *Stimson*, 126–27; Jack C. Lane, *Armed Progressive: General Leonard Wood* (San Rafael, CA: Presidio Press, 1978), 171–72.

7. Albert Bigelow Paine, *Thomas Nast: His Period and His Pictures* (New York: Macmillan, 1904; New York: Chelsea House Publishers, 1980), 293–94, 297–98; James A. Garfield, "The Army of the United States, Part II," *The North American Review* 126 (May 1878): 463; Robert M. Utley, *Frontier Regulars: The United States Army and the Indian* (New York: Macmillan Publishing, 1973), 67.

8. Utley, *Frontier Regulars*, 13; Russell F. Weigley, *History of the United States Army* (1967; enlarged edition, Bloomington: Indiana University Press, 1984), 262; Theodore Clarke Smith, *The Life and Letters of James Abram Garfield* (New Haven, CT: Yale University Press, 1925), 420–21.

9. Thomas S. Langston, *Uneasy Balance: Civil-Military Relations in Peacetime America Since 1783* (Baltimore: Johns Hopkins University Press, 2003), 75–76; Utley, *Frontier Regulars*, 16; Gregory J. W. Urwin, *The United States Infantry: An Illustrated History, 1775–1918* (New York: Sterling Publishing, 1988), 118; Wooster, *Indian Policy*, 87; Jones, *Logan*, 39–40.

10. Utley, *Frontier Regulars*, 63–64.

11. Ibid., 64–65.

12. Ibid., 362; Wooster, *Indian Policy*, 88, 93–95.

13. Stephen Skowronek, *Building a New American State: The Expansion of National Administrative Capacities, 1877–1920* (Cambridge: Cambridge University Press, 1982), 102–3.

14. Brooks D. Simpson, *The Reconstruction Presidents* (Lawrence: University Press of Kansas, 1998), 220–23.

15. Jerry M. Cooper, *The Army and Civil Disorder: Federal Military Intervention in Labor Disputes, 1877–1900* (Westport, CT: Greenwood Press, 1980), 217–18; Allan R. Millett and Peter Maslowski, *For the Common Defense: A Military History of the United States of America* (New York: Free Press, 1984), 248–49.

16. Edward Ranson, "The Endicott Board of 1885–86 and the Coast Defenses," *Military Affairs* 31 (Summer 1967): 74–77.

17. Skowronek, *Building a New American State*, 111; James L. Abrahamson, *America Arms for a New Century: The Making of a Great Military Power* (New York: Free Press, 1981), 136.

18. Ranson, "Endicott," 77–78; Weigley, *U.S. Army*, 284.

19. Francis Paul Prucha, *The Great Father: The United States Government and the American Indians*, vol. 1 (Lincoln: University of Nebraska Press, 1984), 549–51; Robert M. Utley, *The Indian Frontier of the American West, 1846–1890* (Albuquerque: University of New Mexico Press, 1984), 41–42.

20. Paul Andrew Hutton, *Phil Sheridan and His Army* (Norman: University of Oklahoma Press, 1999), 181–82; James Joseph Talbot, "The Indian Question," *The United Service: A Quarterly Review of Military and Naval Affairs* 1 (January 1879): 141–51.

21. Utley, *Indian Frontier*, 207–9; Prucha, *Great Father*, 553–57.

22. Prucha, *Great Father*, 553–57.

23. Ibid., 550–51; Hutton, *Sheridan*, 191–98.

24. Prucha, *Great Father*, 554–58; Rachel Sherman Thorndike, ed., *The Sherman Letters: Correspondence Between General and Senator Sherman from 1837 to 1891* (New York: Charles Scribner's Sons, 1894), 344; Hans L. Trefousse, *Carl Schurz: A Biography* (Knoxville: University of Tennessee Press, 1982), 242–44.

25. Millett and Maslowski, *Common Defense*, 234; Stephen Howarth, *To Shining Sea: A History of the United States Navy, 1775–1991* (New York: Random House, 1991), 218.

26. Abrahamson, *Arms*, 48; Albion, "Robeson," 372–73.

27. Mark Russell Shulman, *Navalism and the Emergence of American Sea Power, 1882–1893* (Annapolis, MD: Naval Institute Press, 1995), 46–52; Justus D. Doenecke, *The Presidencies of James A. Garfield and Chester A. Arthur* (Lawrence: Regents Press of Kansas, 1981), 146; John B. Hattendorf, "Stephen B. Luce: Intellectual Leader of the New Navy," in *Admirals of the New Steel Navy: Makers of the American Naval Tradition, 1880–1930*, ed. James C. Bradford (Annapolis, MD: Naval Institute Press, 1990), 10–11; Walter R. Herrick, "Benjamin F. Tracy," in *American Secretaries of the Navy*, vol. 1, ed. Coletta, 417; Wimmel, *Great White Fleet*, 1.

28. Herrick, "William H. Hunt," in Coletta, *American Secretaries of the Navy*, 391–93; James D. Richardson, ed., *A Compilation of the Messages and Papers of the Presidents, 1789–1897*, vol. 8 (Washington, DC: Government Printing Office, 1898), 51; Howarth, *Shining Sea*, 224, 232–33.

29. Herrick, "William E. Chandler," in Coletta, *American Secretaries of the Navy*, 398–99; Howarth, *Shining Sea*, 240–43.

30. Shulman, *Navalism*, 118–29; Herrick, "Tracy," in Coletta, *American Secretaries of the Navy* 416–18; Ivan Musicant, *Empire by Default: The Spanish-American War and the Dawn of the American Century* (New York: Henry Holt, 1998), 15–16; Paolo E. Coletta, "John Davis Long," in Coletta, *American Secretaries of the Navy*, 432.

31. Cooling, *Grey Steel*, 122, 217; Abrahamson, *Arms*, 137–39; Musicant, *Empire*, 14–15; Howarth, *Shining Sea*, 242.

32. Wimmel, *Great White Fleet*, 65–66; Shulman, *Navalism*, 105; Homer E. Socolofsky and Allan B. Spetter, *The Presidency of Benjamin Harrison* (Lawrence: University Press of Kansas, 1987), 100–102.

33. Wimmel, *Great White Fleet*, 155; Millett and Maslowski, *Common Defense*, 270.

34. Howarth, *Shining Sea*, 279–82.

35. Peter Karsten, *The Naval Aristocracy: The Golden Age of Annapolis and the Emergence of Modern American Navalism* (New York: Free Press, 1972), 367–69; Howarth, *Shining Sea*, 298.

36. Howarth, *Shining Sea*, 288; Wimmel, *Great White Fleet*, xi–xii.

37. Wimmel, *Great White Fleet*, 189; Matthew M. Oyos, "Theodore Roosevelt, Congress, and the Military: U.S. Civil-Military Relations in the Early Twentieth Century," *Presidential Studies Quarterly* 30 (January 2000): 314–15.

38. Ronald Spector, *Admiral of the New Empire: The Life and Career of George Dewey* (Baton Rouge: Louisiana State University Press, 1974), 152–53; Wimmel, *Great White Fleet*, 238; Paolo E. Coletta, "George von Lengerke Meyer," in Coletta, *American Secretaries of the Navy*, 503–5.

39. Graham A. Cosmas, *An Army for Empire: The United States Army in the Spanish-American War* (College Station: Texas A&M Press, 1994), 82–101.

40. Lewis L. Gould, *The Presidency of William McKinley* (Lawrence: University Press of Kansas, 1980), 172–74; Cosmas, *Army for Empire*, 304–6; Weigley, *U.S. Army*, 317–18.

41. Weigley, *U.S. Army*, 599; Arthur S. Link, *Wilson: The Struggle for Neutrality, 1914–1915* (Princeton, NJ: Princeton University Press, 1960), 136–40.

42. Skowronek, *Building a New American State*, 228–32; Arthur S. Link, *Wilson: Confusions and Crises, 1915–1916* (Princeton, NJ: Princeton University Press, 1964), 332–33.

CHAPTER 3: THE MILITARY EXPERIENCE, 1865–1917

1. Henry P. Walker, ed., "The Reluctant Corporal: The Autobiography of William Bladen Jett, Part I," *Journal of Arizona History* 12 (Spring 1971): 1–44.

2. Edward M. Coffman, *The Old Army: A Portrait of the American Army in Peacetime, 1784–1898* (Oxford: Oxford University Press, 1986), 404; Frederick S. Harrod, *Manning the New Navy: The Development of a Modern Naval Enlisted Force, 1899–1940* (Westport, CT: Greenwood Press, 1978), 5–7, 70; Peter Karsten, *The Naval Aristocracy: The Golden Age of Annapolis and the Emergence of Modern American Navalism* (New York: Free Press, 1972), 53–58, 278–79.

3. Harrod, *Manning*, 8–11, 14.

4. Coffman, *Old Army*, 329–35.

5. Ibid., 330; Harrod, *Manning*, 15–17.

6. Coffman, *Old Army*, 371–73; Harrod, *Manning*, 13–15; Karsten, *Aristocracy*, 83.

7. Coffman, *Old Army*, 346–48; Karsten, *Aristocracy*, 81; Gregory J. W. Urwin, *The United States Infantry: An Illustrated History, 1775–1918* (New York: Sterling Publishing, 1988), 126.

8. Harrod, *Manning*, 11–12; Coffman, *Old Army*, 340–46.

9. Coffman, *Old Army*, 340–46, 356–57, 375.

10. Ibid., 374–75.

11. Urwin, *U.S. Infantry*, 133–34; Coffman, *Old Army*, 331.

12. Mark Russell Shulman, *Navalism and the Emergence of American Sea Power, 1882–1893* (Annapolis, MD: Naval Institute Press, 1995), 40–41; Harrod, *Manning*, 19–23, 34; Karsten, *Aristocracy*, 83–92.

13. Harrod, *Manning*, 185, 198; Edward M. Coffman, *The Regulars: The American Army, 1898–1941* (Cambridge, MA: Harvard University Press, 2004), 114.

14. Shulman, *Navalism*, 40–41; Karsten, *Aristocracy*, 88–92.

15. Harrod, *Manning*, 15–18, 34–36, 181.

16. Ibid., 10–11, 183; Bernard C. Nalty, *Strength for the Fight: A History of Black Americans in the Military* (New York: Free Press, 1986), 80–84.

17. Coffman, *Old Army*, 331–32; Robert M. Utley, *Frontier Regulars: The United States Army and the Indian* (New York: Macmillan Publishing, 1973), 11–12; Gerald Astor, *The Right to Fight: A History of the African Americans in the Military* (Novato, CA: Presidio Press, 1998), 43–44.

18. W. Thornton Parker, "The Evolution of the Colored Soldier," *The North*

American Review 168 (February 1899): 223–24; Utley, *Frontier Regulars*, 28–29; Coffman, *Old Army*, 370–71; Astor, *Right to Fight*, 43–45.

19. Coffman, *Old Army*, 332, 366–69; Parker, "Colored Soldier," 228.

20. Nalty, *Strength*, 59; Astor, *Right to Fight*, 47–49, Coffman, *Old Army*, 226–29.

21. John F. Marszalek, Jr., *Court-Martial: A Black Man in America* (New York: Charles Scribner's Sons, 1972), 248–49; Coffman, *Old Army*, 227–28; Michael Fellman, *Citizen Sherman: A Life of William Tecumseh Sherman* (New York: Random House, 1995), 296–97; John M. Schofield, *Forty-Six Years in the Army* (New York: Century Company, 1897; Norman: University of Oklahoma Press, 1998), 445–46.

22. Graham A. Cosmas, *An Army for Empire: The United States Army in the Spanish-American War* (College Station: Texas A&M Press, 1994), 129–32; Astor, *Right to Fight*, 59–75.

23. Coffman, *Regulars*, 126–29.

24. Ann J. Lane, *The Brownsville Affair: National Crisis and Black Reaction* (Port Washington, NY: Kennikat Press, 1971), 22–23; Coffman, *Regulars*, 129–30.

25. Lane, *Brownsville*, 31–38, 167; Coffman, *Regulars*, 130–33.

26. Karsten, *Aristocracy*, 7–16; Coffman, *Old Army*, 222–23.

27. Karsten, *Aristocracy*, 13; Coffman, *Old Army*, 223–25; *Army and Navy Journal*, August 16, 1879, 26.

28. Utley, *Frontier Regulars*, 20–22; Karsten, *Aristocracy*, 280–81.

29. Karsten, *Aristocracy*, 280–81, 357.

30. Walter R. Herrick, "William E. Chandler," in *American Secretaries of the Navy*, vol. 1, ed. Paolo E. Coletta (Annapolis, MD: Naval Institute Press, 1980), 401; Peter Karsten, "Armed Progressives: The Military Reorganizes for the American Century," in *The Military in America: From the Colonial Era to the Present*, ed. Peter Karsten (New York: Free Press, 1980), 232–35.

31. Karsten, "Armed Progressives," 242–45.

32. Coffman, *Old Army*, 230; Utley, *Frontier Regulars*, 20–21.

33. Robert Wooster, *Nelson A. Miles and the Twilight of the Frontier Army* (Lincoln: University of Nebraska Press, 1993), 130–31, 174–75; Ari Hoogenboom, *The Presidency of Rutherford B. Hayes* (Lawrence: University Press of Kansas, 1988), 215.

34. Allan R. Millett and Peter Maslowski, *For the Common Defense: A Military History of the United States of America* (New York: Free Press, 1984), 262; Coffman, *Old Army*, 233, 281.

35. Cosmas, *Army for Empire*, 93.

36. Ibid., 141–46.

37. Coffman, *Regulars*, 50–51.

38. Matthew M. Oyos, "Theodore Roosevelt, Congress, and the Military: U.S. Civil-Military Relations in the Early Twentieth Century," *Presidential Studies Quarterly* 30 (January 2000): 321–23; Donald Smythe, *Guerrilla Warrior: The Early Life of John J. Pershing* (New York: Charles Scribner's Sons, 1973), 125; Jack C. Lane, *Armed Progressive: General Leonard Wood* (San Rafael, CA: Presidio Press, 1978), 115.

39. Allan R. Millett, *The General: Robert L. Bullard and Officership in the United States Army, 1881–1925* (Westport, CT: Greenwood Press, 1975), 255, 261.

40. Allan R. Millett, "Military Professionalism and Officership in America," in *In Defense of the Republic: Readings in American Military History*, ed. David Curtis

Skaggs and Robert S. Browning III (Belmont, CA: Wadsworth Publishing Company, 1991), 159–62; Coffman, *Old Army*, 269–70.

41. Coffman, *Old Army*, 269–70.

42. Millett, "Professionalism," 163; John B. Hattendorf, "Stephen B. Luce: Intellectual Leader of the New Navy," in *Admirals of the New Steel Navy: Makers of the American Naval Tradition, 1880–1930*, ed. James C. Bradford (Annapolis, MD: Naval Institute Press, 1990), 14.

43. Coffman, *Old Army*, 270; Edward M. Coffman, "American Command and Commanders in World War I," in Skaggs and Browning, *In Defense of the Republic: Readings in American Military History*, 211.

44. Samuel P. Huntington, *The Soldier and the State: The Theory and Politics of Civil-Military Relations* (Cambridge, MA: Harvard University Press, 1957), 237–44; Millett, "Professionalism," 164; Hattendorf, "Luce," 11–15; Russell F. Weigley, *History of the United States Army* (1967; enlarged edition, Bloomington: Indiana University Press, 1984), 287, 325.

45. Huntington, *Soldier and State*, 260–63.

CHAPTER 4: "AN ANIMATED MACHINE": MILITARY SUBORDINATION TO CIVIL AUTHORITY

1. Samuel P. Huntington, *The Soldier and the State: The Theory and Politics of Civil-Military Relations* (Cambridge, MA: Harvard University Press, 1957), 231, 261; Russell F. Weigley, "The American Military and the Principle of Civilian Control from McClellan to Powell," *Journal of Military History* 57 (October 1993): 39.

2. William B. Skelton, "Samuel P. Huntington and the Roots of the American Military Tradition," *Journal of Military History* 60 (April 1996): 335; Brooks D. Simpson, *Let Us Have Peace: Ulysses S. Grant and the Politics of War and Reconstruction, 1861–1868* (Chapel Hill: University of North Carolina Press, 1991), 256; "Representation that Does Not Represent," *Army and Navy Journal*, October 6, 1883, 191; Huntington, *Soldier and State*, 231–32.

3. Robert Wooster, *The Military and United States Indian Policy, 1865–1903* (Lincoln: University of Nebraska Press, 1995), 75–76; John A. Carpenter, *Sword and Olive Branch: Oliver Otis Howard* (Pittsburgh, PA: University of Pittsburgh Press, 1964), 290–91; David M. Jordan, *Winfield Scott Hancock: A Soldier's Life* (Bloomington: Indiana University Press, 1988), 228; Bernarr Cresap, *Appomattox Commander: the Story of General E.O.C. Ord* (San Diego: A. S. Barnes, 1981), 330; John B. Hattendorf, "Stephen B. Luce: Intellectual Leader of the New Navy," in *Admirals of the New Steel Navy: Makers of the American Naval Tradition, 1880–1930*, ed. James C. Bradford (Annapolis, MD: Naval Institute Press, 1990), 10–11; Jerry M. Cooper, *The Army and Civil Disorder: Federal Military Intervention in Labor Disputes, 1877–1900* (Westport, CT: Greenwood Press, 1980), 247–48.

4. Wooster, *Indian Policy*, 109; Lee Kennett, *Sherman: A Soldier's Life* (New York: HarperCollins, 2001), 310; James L. Abrahamson, *America Arms for a New Century: The Making of a Great Military Power* (New York: Free Press, 1981), 75; Richard D. Challener, *Admirals, Generals, and American Foreign Policy, 1898–1914* (Princeton, NJ: Princeton University Press, 1973), 58.

5. Wooster, *Indian Policy*, 77–82; Challener, *Admirals*, 54–57.

6. James L. McDonough, *Schofield: Union General in the Civil War and Reconstruction* (Tallahassee: Florida State University Press, 1972), 180–83; Cresap, *Ord*, 257–58; Joseph G. Dawson III, *Army Generals and Reconstruction: Louisiana, 1862–1877* (Baton Rouge: Louisiana State University Press, 1982), 84–89; Edward M. Coffman, *The Old Army: A Portrait of the American Army in Peacetime, 1784–1898* (Oxford: Oxford University Press, 1986), 243; Jeffry D. Wert, *Custer: The Controversial Life of George Armstrong Custer* (New York: Simon and Schuster, 1996), 242.

7. Robert Wooster, *Nelson A. Miles and the Twilight of the Frontier Army* (Lincoln: University of Nebraska Press, 1993), 53; Jordan, *Hancock*, 202; James E. Sefton, *The United States Army and Reconstruction, 1865–1877* (Baton Rouge: Louisiana State University Press, 1967), 195–97; Richard Nelson Current, *Those Terrible Carpetbaggers: A Reinterpretation* (New York: Oxford University Press, 1988), 179; Wooster, *Indian Policy*, 107.

8. Carpenter, *Howard*, 142.

9. Simpson, *Peace*, 170–95; Paul Andrew Hutton, *Phil Sheridan and His Army* (Norman: University of Oklahoma Press, 1999), 25–27.

10. Simpson, *Peace*, 165–66.

11. Ibid., 236; William S. McFeely, *Grant: A Biography* (New York: W. W. Norton, 1981), 369–73; Dawson, *Army Generals*, 243–44.

12. Jordan, *Hancock*, 200–205; Dawson, *Army Generals*, 69–70.

13. Ari Hoogenboom, *The Presidency of Rutherford B. Hayes* (Lawrence: University Press of Kansas, 1988), 79–83.

14. Cooper, *Civil Disorder*, 62–64; Jordan, *Hancock*, 246; Elwell S. Otis, "The Army in Connection with the Labor Riots of 1877," *Journal of the Military Service Institute of the United States* 6 (June 1885): 123–25.

15. Stephen Skowronek, *Building a New American State: The Expansion of National Administrative Capacities, 1877–1920* (Cambridge: Cambridge University Press, 1982), 100–101; Cooper, *Civil Disorder*, 248–51, 262–63; Coffman, *Old Army*, 247–48; Jordan, *Hancock*, 249; Robert V. Bruce, *1877: Year of Violence* (Indianapolis, IN: Bobbs-Merrill Company, 1959; Chicago: Ivan R. Dee, 1989), 214–16.

16. Cooper, *Civil Disorder*, 76–80; Wallis O. Clark, "The Use of Regulars during Civil Disorders," *Infantry Journal* 1 (January 1905): 41.

17. Skowronek, *Building a New American State*, 102–3; Cooper, *Civil Disorder*, 83; Charles B. Hall, "The Relation of the Military to the Civil Authority," *Infantry Journal* 5 (September 1908): 153.

18. M. A. DeWolfe Howe, ed., *Home Letters of General Sherman* (New York: Charles Scribner's Sons, 1909), 387; Cooper, *Civil Disorder*, 84–85; Skowronek, *Building a New American State*, 103; Hutton, *Sheridan*, 177; William Wallace, "The Army and the Civil Power," *Journal of the Military Service Institution of the United States* 17 (September 1895): 235–66.

19. Craig Storti, *Incident at Bitter Creek: The Story of the Rock Springs Chinese Massacre* (Ames: Iowa State University Press, 1991), 131–37; Cooper, *Civil Disorder*, 86–88.

20. Cooper, *Civil Disorder*, 88–90.

21. Richard E. Welch, Jr., *The Presidencies of Grover Cleveland* (Lawrence: University Press of Kansas, 1988), 142–48.

22. John M. Schofield, *Forty-Six Years in the Army* (New York: Century Company, 1897; Norman: University of Oklahoma Press, 1998), 491–509; Cooper, *Civil Disorder*, 104–8, 113, 126–30, 150–51; Peter R. DeMontravel, *A Hero to His Fighting Men: Nelson A. Miles, 1839–1925* (Kent, OH: Kent State University Press, 1998), 215–23.

23. Cooper, *Civil Disorder*, 126–27, 151, 247–49.

24. Hutton, *Sheridan*, 177–78; Wallace, "Civil Power," 235–66; Cooper, *Civil Disorder*, 249–53.

25. Cooper, *Civil Disorder*, 192–93, 216, 244–45.

26. Ibid., 172–78.

27. Ibid., 192–93.

28. Hall, "Relation of the Military," 152–54.

29. Cooper, *Civil Disorder*, 240–41; Jerry Cooper, *The Rise of the National Guard: The Evolution of the American Militia, 1865–1920* (Lincoln: University of Nebraska Press, 1997), 148–50; Arthur S. Link, *Wilson: The New Freedom* (Princeton, NJ: Princeton University Press, 1956), 457–59.

30. Lewis L. Gould, *The Presidency of William McKinley* (Lawrence: University Press of Kansas, 1980), 91–102; Graham A. Cosmas, *An Army for Empire: The United States Army in the Spanish-American War* (College Station: Texas A&M Press, 1994), 94–101, 201–2; Wooster, *Miles*, 217–21; Ivan Musicant, *Empire by Default: The Spanish-American War and the Dawn of the American Century* (New York: Henry Holt, 1998), 297–98.

31. Gould, *McKinley*, 91; Cosmas, *Army for Empire*, 104–22.

32. Musicant, *Empire*, 213, 232–33; Stephen Howarth, *To Shining Sea: A History of the United States Navy, 1775–1991* (New York: Random House, 1991), 262.

33. Challener, *Admirals*, 203; Max Boot, *The Savage Wars of Peace: Small Wars and the Rise of American Power* (New York: Basic Books, 2002), 74–78.

34. Challener, *Admirals*, 201–4.

35. Kenneth Wimmel, *Theodore Roosevelt and the Great White Fleet: American Sea Power Comes of Age* (Washington, DC: Brassey's, 1998), 154–55.

36. Challener, *Admirals*, 52–53, 164–65, 269.

37. Ibid., 54, 172–73, 268–69.

38. Lester D. Langley, *The Banana Wars: United States Intervention in the Caribbean, 1898–1934* (Lexington: University Press of Kentucky, 1983; Wilmington, DE: Scholarly Resources, 2002), 82–84.

39. Langley, *Banana Wars*, 84; Joseph L. Morrison, *Josephus Daniels: The Small-d Democrat* (Chapel Hill: University of North Carolina Press, 1966), 62.

40. Langley, *Banana Wars*, 82–101.

41. Challener, *Admirals*, 366, 394–96.

42. Arthur S. Link, *Wilson: Confusions and Crises, 1915–1916* (Princeton, NJ: Princeton University Press, 1964), 209–16; Donald Smythe, *Guerrilla Warrior: The Early Life of John J. Pershing* (New York: Charles Scribner's Sons, 1973), 220–21.

43. Link, *Confusions and Crises*, 284–86; Smythe, *Pershing*, 241–54, 275.

44. Smythe, *Pershing*, 255–60; Arthur S. Link, *Woodrow Wilson and the Progressive Era, 1910–1917* (New York: Harper and Row, 1954), 141–44.

45. Smythe, *Pershing*, 278–79.

46. Wooster, *Miles*, 242–46; Stuart Creighton Miller, *"Benevolent Assimilation": The American Conquest of the Philippines, 1899–1903* (New Haven, CT: Yale

University Press, 1982), 233–35; Paolo E. Coletta, "George von Lengerke Meyer," in *American Secretaries of the Navy*, vol. 1, ed. Paolo E. Coletta (Annapolis, MD: Naval Institute Press, 1980), 509–10.

47. Benjamin Franklin Cooling, "Bradley Allen Fiske: Inventor and Reformer in Uniform," in Bradford, *Admirals of the New Steel Navy*, 133–35; Jack C. Lane, *Armed Progressive: General Leonard Wood* (San Rafael, CA: Presidio Press, 1978), 204–5; Abrahamson, *Arms*, 149–50.

48. Link, *New Freedom*, 77–78.

49. Challener, *Admirals*, 53; Link, *New Freedom*, 78–79.

CHAPTER 5: CIVIL-MILITARY RELATIONS AND THE CAMPAIGN FOR MILITARY REFORM

1. John M. Schofield, *Forty-Six Years in the Army* (New York: Century Company, 1897; Norman: University of Oklahoma Press, 1998), 410.

2. Robert M. Utley, *Frontier Regulars: The United States Army and the Indian* (New York: Macmillan Publishing, 1973), 30; Allan R. Millett, *The General: Robert L. Bullard and Officership in the United States Army, 1881–1925* (Westport, CT: Greenwood Press, 1975), 49–50; Russell F. Weigley, *History of the United States Army* (1967; enlarged edition, Bloomington: Indiana University Press, 1984), 288.

3. James A. Garfield, "The Army of the United States, Part II," *The North American Review* 126 (May 1878): 446.

4. William T. Sherman, *Memoirs of General William T. Sherman*, vol. 2 (New York: D. Appleton, 1891), 931–44; Brooks D. Simpson, *Let Us Have Peace: Ulysses S. Grant and the Politics of War and Reconstruction, 1861–1868* (Chapel Hill: University of North Carolina Press, 1991), 172; James E. Sefton, *The United States Army and Reconstruction, 1865–1877* (Baton Rouge: Louisiana State University Press, 1967), 110–11.

5. Michael Fellman, *Citizen Sherman: A Life of William Tecumseh Sherman* (New York: Random House, 1995), 278–81; Sherman, *Memoirs*, 931–33.

6. Sherman, *Memoirs*, 933–45; Fellman, *Sherman*, 280–83.

7. Graham A. Cosmas, *An Army for Empire: The United States Army in the Spanish-American War* (College Station: Texas A&M Press, 1994), 10–16.

8. Millett, *Bullard*, 49–50.

9. Stephen E. Ambrose, *Upton and the Army* (Baton Rouge: Louisiana State University Press, 1964; reprint 1992), 100–104; Edward M. Coffman, *The Old Army: A Portrait of the American Army in Peacetime, 1784–1898* (Oxford: Oxford University Press, 1986), 272–73.

10. Stephen Skowronek, *Building a New American State: The Expansion of National Administrative Capacities, 1877–1920* (Cambridge: Cambridge University Press, 1982), 108–9; Ambrose, *Upton*, 116–18.

11. Fellman, *Sherman*, 281; Paul Andrew Hutton, *Phil Sheridan and His Army* (Norman: University of Oklahoma Press, 1999), 349–50.

12. Hutton, *Sheridan*, 350; Schofield, *Forty-Six Years*, 471–72.

13. Cosmas, *Army for Empire*, 24, 27–28.

14. Schofield, *Forty-Six Years*, 480; Peter R. DeMontravel, *A Hero to His Fighting Men: Nelson A. Miles, 1839–1925* (Kent, OH: Kent State University Press,

1998), 306–7; Ronald J. Barr, *The Progressive Army: U.S. Army Command and Administration, 1870–1914* (New York: St. Martin's Press, 1998), 43.

15. Cosmas, *Army for Empire*, 136; Robert Wooster, *Nelson A. Miles and the Twilight of the Frontier Army* (Lincoln: University of Nebraska Press, 1993), 214–21.

16. Allan R. Millett and Peter Maslowski, *For the Common Defense: A Military History of the United States of America* (New York: Free Press, 1984), 304; Ronald Spector, *Admiral of the New Empire: The Life and Career of George Dewey* (Baton Rouge: Louisiana State University Press, 1974), 122–23.

17. Robert W. Love, Jr., *History of the United States Navy, 1775–1941* (Harrisburg, PA: Stackpole Books, 1992), 417; Vernon L. Williams, "George Dewey: Admiral of the Navy," in *Admirals of the New Steel Navy: Makers of the American Naval Tradition, 1880–1930*, ed. James C. Bradford (Annapolis, MD: Naval Institute Press, 1990), 237–38; Spector, *Dewey*, 123–25; Richard D. Challener, *Admirals, Generals, and American Foreign Policy, 1898–1914* (Princeton, NJ: Princeton University Press, 1973), 47.

18. Barton C. Hacker, "The United States Army as a National Police Force: The Federal Policing of Labor Disputes, 1877–1898," *Military Affairs* 33 (April 1969): 262; Millett and Maslowski, *Common Defense*, 310; Philip L. Semsch, "Elihu Root and the General Staff," *Military Affairs* 27 (Spring 1963): 17–19.

19. Skowronek, *Building a New American State*, 220–21; Millett and Maslowski, *Common Defense*, 310–11; Semsch, "Root," 20–21.

20. Elihu Root, *The Military and Colonial Policy of the United States*, eds. Robert Bacon and James Brown Scott (Cambridge, MA: Harvard University Press, 1916), 429.

21. Semsch, "Root," 23–24; Wooster, *Miles*, 242–43.

22. Semsch, "Root," 23; Wooster, *Miles*, 243; Kenneth Ray Young, *The General's General: The Life and Times of Arthur MacArthur* (Boulder, CO: Westview Press, 1994), 305.

23. Semsch, "Root," 23–25; Barr, *Progressive Army*, 105–6.

24. Barr, *Progressive Army*, 116; Millett and Maslowski, *Common Defense*, 311; Wooster, *Miles*, 247.

25. Young, *MacArthur*, 329; Allan R. Millett, "The General Staff and the Cuban Intervention of 1906," *Military Affairs* 31 (Autumn 1967): 113–18; Jack C. Lane, *Armed Progressive: General Leonard Wood* (San Rafael, CA: Presidio Press, 1978), 169–70.

26. Skowronek, *Building a New American State*, 221–22; Matthew M. Oyos, "Theodore Roosevelt, Congress, and the Military: U.S. Civil-Military Relations in the Early Twentieth Century," *Presidential Studies Quarterly* 30 (January 2000): 316.

27. Skowronek, *Building a New American State*, 221–22; Lane, *Wood*, 156–59.

28. Weigley, *U.S. Army*, 327–32; Skowronek, *Building a New American State*, 223–25.

29. Weigley, *U.S. Army*, 331–32; Lane, *Wood*, 162–67, 171–73.

30. Lane, *Wood*, 165–67; Weigley, *U.S. Army*, 333; Skowronek, *Building a New American State*, 225–28.

31. Spector, *Dewey*, 154–57; Kenneth Wimmel, *Theodore Roosevelt and the Great White Fleet: American Sea Power Comes of Age* (Washington, DC: Brassey's, 1998), 233–34; Oyos, "Roosevelt," 318–20.

32. Bradley A. Fiske, "The Civil and the Military Authority," *Proceedings of the United States Naval Institute* 32 (1906): 129.

33. Oyos, "Roosevelt," 319–21.

34. Paolo Coletta, *The Presidency of William Howard Taft* (Lawrence: University Press of Kansas, 1973): 212–13; Spector, *Dewey*, 181–82.

35. Challener, *Admirals*, 59–60; Spector, *Dewey*, 188–89.

36. James L. Abrahamson, *America Arms for a New Century: The Making of a Great Military Power* (New York: Free Press, 1981), 124–27; Challener, *Admirals*, 59–60; Spector, *Dewey*, 188–89.

37. Spector, *Dewey*, 191; Benjamin Franklin Cooling, "Bradley Allen Fiske: Inventor and Reformer in Uniform," in *Admirals of the New Steel Navy: Makers of the American Naval Tradition, 1880–1930*, ed. James C. Bradford (Annapolis, MD: Naval Institute Press, 1990), 128–34.

38. Arthur S. Link, *Wilson: The Struggle for Neutrality, 1914–1915* (Princeton, NJ: Princeton University Press, 1960), 141–43; Joseph L. Morrison, *Josephus Daniels: The Small-d Democrat* (Chapel Hill: University of North Carolina Press, 1966), 69; Cooling, "Fiske," 132–34.

39. Cooling, "Fiske," 134; Spector, *Dewey*, 198–99; Mary Klachko, "William Shepherd Benson: Naval General Staff American Style," in Bradford, *Admirals of the New Steel Navy*.

40. Klachko, "Benson," 301–5.

41. Two works that discuss the relationship between military reformers and other reform movements active in the turn-of-the-century United States are Peter Karsten, "Armed Progressives: The Military Reorganizes for the American Century," in *The Military in America: From the Colonial Era to the Present*, ed. Peter Karsten (New York: Free Press, 1980), 229–71 and Skowronek, *Building a New American State*.

CHAPTER 6: MILITARY DISAFFECTION AND CHALLENGES TO CIVIL AUTHORITY

1. William T. Sherman, *Memoirs of General William T. Sherman*, vol. 2 (New York: D. Appleton, 1891), 944; Michael Fellman, *Citizen Sherman: A Life of William Tecumseh Sherman* (New York: Random House, 1995), 283–98.

2. Russell F. Weigley, "The American Civil-Military Cultural Gap: A Historical Perspective, Colonial Times to the Present," in *Soldiers and Civilians: The Civil-Military Gap and American National Security*, ed. Peter D. Feaver and Richard H. Kohn (Cambridge, MA: MIT Press, 2001), 216.

3. Walter Millis, ed., *American Military Thought* (Indianapolis, IN: Bobbs-Merrill Company, 1966), 171; James L. Abrahamson, *America Arms for a New Century: The Making of a Great Military Power* (New York: Free Press, 1981), 84.

4. Edward M. Coffman, *The Old Army: A Portrait of the American Army in Peacetime, 1784–1898* (Oxford: Oxford University Press, 1986), 241–43; Fellman, *Sherman*, 292–93; John M. Schofield, *Forty-Six Years in the Army* (New York: Century Company, 1897; Norman: University of Oklahoma Press, 1998), 374; Bernarr Cresap, *Appomattox Commander: the Story of General E.O.C. Ord* (San Diego: A. S. Barnes, 1981), 244–46, 268; Eric Foner, *Reconstruction: America's Unfinished Revolution, 1863–1877* (New York: Harper and Row, 1988), 307–8.

5. Cresap, *Ord*, 294; James E. Sefton, *The United States Army and Reconstruction, 1865–1877* (Baton Rouge: Louisiana State University Press, 1967), 8.

6. Robert M. Utley, *The Indian Frontier of the American West, 1846–1890* (Albuquerque: University of New Mexico Press, 1984), 101, 165; Thomas C. Leonard, *Above the Battle: War-Making in America from Appomattox to Versailles* (New York: Oxford University Press, 1978), 44; Sherry L. Smith, *The View from Officers' Row: Army Perceptions of the Western Indians* (Tucson: University of Arizona Press, 1990), 92–112; Robert Wooster, *The Military and United States Indian Policy, 1865–1903* (Lincoln: University of Nebraska Press, 1988), 215.

7. Robert M. Utley, *Frontier Regulars: The United States Army and the Indian* (New York: Macmillan Publishing, 1973), 137.

8. "Representation that Does Not Represent," *Army and Navy Journal*, October 6, 1883, 191; Fellman, *Sherman*, 261–63; Wooster, *Indian Policy*, 108.

9. Paul Andrew Hutton, *Phil Sheridan and His Army* (Norman: University of Oklahoma Press, 1985), 98; Wooster, *Indian Policy*, 122.

10. Fellman, *Sherman*, 263; "Representation that Does Not Represent," *Army and Navy Journal*, October 6, 1883, 191; Leonard, *Above the Battle*, 44.

11. Abrahamson, *Arms*, 74–76, 84–86.

12. Sefton, *Army and Reconstruction*, 213–15.

13. Ibid., 215–18; Joseph G. Dawson III, *Army Generals and Reconstruction: Louisiana, 1862–1877* (Baton Rouge: Louisiana State University Press, 1982), 123–27; James D. Richardson, ed., *A Compilation of the Messages and Papers of the Presidents, 1789–1897*, vol. 7 (Washington: Government Printing Office, 1898), 314.

14. Graham A. Cosmas, *An Army for Empire: The United States Army in the Spanish-American War* (Columbia: University of Missouri Press, 1971; College Station: Texas A&M Press, 1994), 68, 186–88; Brian McAllister Linn, *The Philippine War, 1899–1902* (Lawrence: University Press of Kansas, 2000), 5–6, 26–27.

15. Donald Smythe, *Guerrilla Warrior: The Early Life of John J. Pershing* (New York: Charles Scribner's Sons, 1973), 270–72, 276–78.

16. Samuel P. Huntington, *The Soldier and the State: The Theory and Politics of Civil-Military Relations* (Cambridge, MA: Harvard University Press, 1957), 7–18, 230–45; Bradley A. Fiske, "The Civil and the Military Authority," *Proceedings of the United States Naval Institute* 32 (1906): 129.

17. Stephen Howarth, *To Shining Sea: A History of the United States Navy, 1775–1991* (New York: Random House, 1991), 219; William S. McFeely, *Grant: A Biography* (New York: W. W. Norton, 1981), 428–33; James S. Pettit, "How Far Does Democracy Affect the Organization and Discipline of Our Armies, and How Can Its Influence Be Most Effectively Utilized?" *Journal of the Military Service Institute of the United States* 38 (January–February 1906): 25.

18. Utley, *Frontier Regulars*, 117–18, 213–19, 341–51.

19. Ivan Musicant, *Empire by Default: The Spanish-American War and the Dawn of the American Century* (New York: Henry Holt, 1998), 297–98; Allan R. Millett and Peter Maslowski, *For the Common Defense: A Military History of the United States of America* (New York: Free Press, 1984), 271.

20. Kenneth Ray Young, *The General's General: The Life and Times of Arthur MacArthur* (Boulder, CO: Westview Press, 1994), 261–73; Rowland T. Berthoff, "Taft and MacArthur, 1900–1901: A Study in Civil-Military Relations," *World*

Politics 5 (January 1953): 196–213; Linn, *Philippine War*, 216–17; Stuart Creighton Miller, *"Benevolent Assimilation": The American Conquest of the Philippines, 1899–1903* (New Haven, CT: Yale University Press, 1982), 205.

21. Linn, *Philippine War*, 187; Miller, *Benevolent Assimilation*, 145–46, 184–86.

22. Huntington, *Soldier and State*, 259; Russell F. Weigley, *History of the United States Army* (1967; enlarged edition, Bloomington: Indiana University Press, 1984), 280–81; Peter Karsten, *The Naval Aristocracy: The Golden Age of Annapolis and the Emergence of Modern American Navalism* (New York: Free Press, 1972), 204–5.

23. M. A. DeWolfe Howe, ed., *Home Letters of General Sherman* (New York: Charles Scribner's Sons, 1909), 386; A. H. Russell, "What is the Use of a Regular Army in this Country?" *Journal of the Military Service Institution of the United States* 24 (March 1899): 220–21.

24. Pettit, "Democracy," 4.

25. Weigley, *U.S. Army*, 335–36; Leonard, *Above the Battle*, 146; "Reprints and Reports: Our Unhappy Soldiers," *Infantry Journal* 8 (July–August 1911): 125.

26. Emory Upton, *The Military Policy of the United States* (Washington, DC: Government Printing Office, 1904), vii–xv; Stephen E. Ambrose, *Upton and the Army* (Baton Rouge: Louisiana State University Press, 1964; reprint 1992), 129–32.

27. Russell F. Weigley, "The George C. Marshall Lecture in Military History: The Soldier, the Statesman, and the Military Historian," *Journal of Military History* 63 (October 1999): 813; Pettit, "Democracy," 1–38.

28. Russell, "Regular Army," 220; John W. Pullman, "The American Citizen *Versus* the American Soldier and Sailor," *Journal of the Military Service Institution of the United States* 39 (November–December 1906): 329, 340.

29. Karsten, *Aristocracy*, 207–9; Leonard, *Above the Battle*, 53–54; Hutton, *Sheridan*, 142–43; Huntington, *Soldier and State*, 258–69.

30. Weigley, *U.S. Army*, 336; Richard Stockton, Jr., *Peace Insurance* (Chicago: A.C. McClurg and Company, 1915), 132–33.

31. William Wallace, "Our Military Decline," *Infantry Journal* 9 (March–April 1913): 625–38.

32. Abrahamson, *Arms*, 32; Jerry M. Cooper, *The Army and Civil Disorder: Federal Military Intervention in Labor Disputes, 1877–1900* (Westport, CT: Greenwood Press, 1980), 35; Huntington, *Soldier and State*, 279; Allan R. Millett, *The General: Robert L. Bullard and Officership in the United States Army, 1881–1925* (Westport, CT: Greenwood Press, 1975), 200.

33. Brooks D. Simpson, *Let Us Have Peace: Ulysses S. Grant and the Politics of War and Reconstruction, 1861–1868* (Chapel Hill: University of North Carolina Press, 1991), 136–54.

34. Ibid., 155–57.

35. Ibid., 162–71.

36. Ibid., 182–87.

37. Ibid., 186–87; McFeely, *Grant*, 262–63.

38. Miles did inspect the camp at Tampa, Florida, as Alger had ordered him to do. Peter R. DeMontravel, *A Hero to His Fighting Men: Nelson A. Miles, 1839–1925* (Kent, OH: Kent State University Press, 1998), 242, 294–95; Robert Wooster, *Nelson A. Miles and the Twilight of the Frontier Army* (Lincoln: University of Nebraska Press, 1993), 220.

39. Wooster, *Miles*, 240–41; Edmund Morris, *Theodore Rex* (New York: Random House, 2001), 78–79, 97–99.

40. Thomas J. Knock, *To End All Wars: Woodrow Wilson and the Quest for a New World Order* (New York: Oxford University Press, 1992), 59; Arthur S. Link, *Wilson: The New Freedom* (Princeton, NJ: Princeton University Press, 1956), 122–23.

41. Link, *New Freedom*, 122–24; Joseph L. Morrison, *Josephus Daniels: The Small-d Democrat* (Chapel Hill: University of North Carolina Press, 1966), 60–65; Knock, *End*, 59.

42. Link, *New Freedom*, 78–79; Richard D. Challener, *Admirals, Generals, and American Foreign Policy, 1898–1914* (Princeton, NJ: Princeton University Press, 1973), 368–70.

43. Link, *New Freedom*, 298–99; Challener, *Admirals*, 47–48, 368–78.

44. Challener, *Admirals*, 376–78; Link, *New Freedom*, 299.

45. Arthur S. Link, *Wilson: The Struggle for Neutrality, 1914–1915* (Princeton, NJ: Princeton University Press, 1960), 137–41.

46. Benjamin Franklin Cooling, "Bradley Allen Fiske: Inventor and Reformer in Uniform," in *Admirals of the New Steel Navy: Makers of the American Naval Tradition, 1880–1930*, ed. James C. Bradford (Annapolis, MD: Naval Institute Press, 1990), 132–34.

47. Cooling, "Fiske," 134–35; Mary Klachko, "William Shepherd Benson: Naval General Staff American Style," in Bradford, *Admirals of the New Steel Navy*, 302–3.

48. Jack C. Lane, *Armed Progressive: General Leonard Wood* (San Rafael, CA: Presidio Press, 1978), 184–88.

49. Ibid., 188–92.

50. Ibid., 189–95.

51. Ibid., 205–8.

52. Ibid., 208–17.

53. Cooling, "Fiske," 140.

DOCUMENTS

1. Patricia L. Faust, ed., *Historical Times Illustrated Encyclopedia of the Civil War* (New York: HarperCollins, 1991), 510.

2. See Hans L. Trefousse, *Carl Schurz: A Biography* (Knoxville: University of Tennessee Press, 1982).

3. Benjamin Franklin Cooling, "Bradley Allen Fiske: Inventor and Reformer in Uniform," in *Admirals of the New Steel Navy: Makers of the American Naval Tradition, 1880–1930*, ed. James C. Bradford (Annapolis, MD: Naval Institute Press, 1990), 120–45.

Bibliographical Essay

Although published nearly a half a century ago, Samuel P. Huntington's *The Soldier and the State: The Theory and Politics of Civil-Military Relations* (Cambridge, MA: Harvard University Press, 1957) remains a good starting point for anyone interested in the topic of civil-military relations in the United States. Huntington provides a helpful theoretical framework for understanding civil-military relations, and his discussion of the effects of the professionalization of the officer corps on those relations is invaluable. Some of Huntington's interpretations require revision, however. Edward M. Coffman's article, "The Long Shadow of *The Soldier and the State*," *Journal of Military History* 55 (January 1991), and William B. Skelton's "Samuel P. Huntington and the Roots of the American Military Tradition," *Journal of Military History* 60 (April 1996), offer useful critiques. Russell F. Weigley published two fine interpretative essays regarding civil-military relations in the United States, "The American Military and the Principle of Civilian Control from McClellan to Powell," *Journal of Military History* 57 (October 1993), and "The American Civil-Military Cultural Gap: A Historical Perspective, Colonial Times to the Present," in Peter D. Feaver and Richard H. Kohn, eds., *Soldiers and Civilians: The Civil-Military Gap and American National Security* (Cambridge, MA: MIT Press, 2001). Thomas S. Langston's *Uneasy Balance: Civil-Military Relations in Peacetime America Since 1783* (Baltimore: Johns Hopkins University Press, 2003) is a first-rate study of the extent to which the American political system established a proper balance between military effectiveness and civilian control of the military in the periods following the country's major wars. Langston's observations about the troubled relationship between the civilian government and the military after the Civil War and the comparatively harmonious civil-military relations that followed the Spanish-American War are valuable, although he tends to overlook some of the strife that marked civil-military relations in the early twentieth century.

Important works that discuss military developments of the late nineteenth and early twentieth centuries include Allan R. Millett and Peter Maslowski, *For the Common Defense: A Military History of the United States of America* (New York: Free Press, 1984) and James L. Abrahamson, *America Arms for a New Century: The Making of a Great Military Power* (New York: Free Press, 1981). Edward M. Coffman's two books on the social history of the army, *The Old Army: A Portrait of the American Army in Peacetime, 1784–1898* (Oxford: Oxford University Press, 1986) and *The Regulars: The American Army, 1898–1941* (Cambridge, MA: Belknap Press of Harvard University Press, 2004), are superb; no one has produced a better historical study of the experiences of the army's officers, enlisted men, and their families. Russell F. Weigley's *History of the United States Army* (Bloomington: Indiana University Press, enlarged edition, 1984) remains the preeminent history of that institution.

A number of biographies of important army officers of the era stand out. William S. McFeely's *Grant: A Biography* (New York: W. W. Norton, 1981) offers judicious interpretations of Grant as a military leader and politician. Stephen E. Ambrose, *Upton and the Army* (Baton Rouge: Louisiana State University Press, 1964) discusses the experiences and ideas of Emory Upton, an officer whose critique of the American military system's reliance on volunteers and civilian leadership was influential in the army. Michael Fellman's *Citizen Sherman: A Life of William Tecumseh Sherman* (New York: Random House, 1995) does an effective job of unraveling Sherman's complex views on matters such as Reconstruction and the conflict between whites and Indians and makes a good argument that Sherman was mostly ineffective as commanding general. David M. Jordan, *Winfield Scott Hancock: A Soldier's Life* (Bloomington: Indiana University Press, 1988) and Peter Cozzens, *General John Pope: A Life for the Nation* (Urbana: University of Illinois Press, 2000) examine the careers of two generals who had significant roles in Reconstruction and the Indian wars. General Nelson Miles is the subject of two recent biographies, Robert Wooster, *Nelson A. Miles and the Twilight of the Frontier Army* (Lincoln: University of Nebraska Press, 1993) and Peter R. DeMontravel, *A Hero to His Fighting Men: Nelson A. Miles, 1839–1925* (Kent, OH: Kent State University Press, 1998). Of the two biographers, DeMontravel is less critical of the general. Jack C. Lane, *Armed Progressive: General Leonard Wood* (San Rafael, CA: Presidio Press, 1978) provides a thorough account of the controversial general's career and, as the title suggests, ties Wood's reform interests to important political and intellectual developments of the progressive era.

Capable surveys of the history of the U.S. Navy can be found in Stephen Howarth, *To Shining Sea: A History of the United States Navy, 1775–1991*

(New York: Random House, 1991) and Robert W. Love, Jr., *History of the United States Navy, 1775–1941* (Harrisburg, PA: Stackpole Books, 1992). Two works that focus on the political and technological developments that gave rise to the modern navy in the late nineteenth century are Benjamin Franklin Cooling, *Grey Steel and Blue Water Navy: The Formative Years of the Military-Industrial Complex, 1881–1917* (Hamden, CT: Archon Books, 1979) and Mark Russell Shulman, *Navalism and the Emergence of American Sea Power, 1882–1893* (Annapolis, MD: Naval Institute Press, 1995). Frederick S. Harrod's *Manning the New Navy: The Development of a Modern Naval Enlisted Force, 1899–1940* (Westport, CT: Greenwood Press, 1978) explains the important shift in the navy's recruiting policies. Peter Karsten's *The Naval Aristocracy: The Golden Age of Annapolis and the Emergence of Modern American Navalism* (New York: Free Press, 1972) is a well-researched and engagingly written study of the social background and political attitudes of the navy's officer class. Kenneth Wimmel's *Theodore Roosevelt and the Great White Fleet: American Sea Power Comes of Age* (Washington, DC: Brassey's, 1998) is a highly readable account of the Roosevelt administration's naval policies. Good biographical studies of important figures in the naval history of the period include Benjamin Franklin Cooling's *Benjamin Franklin Tracy: Father of the Modern American Fighting Navy* (Hamden, CT: Archon Books, 1973); Ronald Spector, *Admiral of the New Empire: The Life and Career of George Dewey* (Baton Rouge: Louisiana State University Press, 1974); and Richard W. Turk, *The Ambiguous Relationship: Theodore Roosevelt and Alfred Thayer Mahan* (Westport, CT: Greenwood Press, 1987). Two collections of biographical pieces, James C. Bradford, ed., *Admirals of the New Steel Navy: Makers of the American Naval Tradition, 1880–1930* (Annapolis, MD: Naval Institute Press, 1990) and Paolo E. Coletta, ed., *American Secretaries of the Navy*, vol. 1 (Annapolis, MD: Naval Institute Press, 1980), are especially useful.

James E. Sefton, *The United States Army and Reconstruction, 1865–1877* (Baton Rouge: Louisiana State University Press, 1967) provides a thorough overview of the role of the army in Reconstruction. Joseph G. Dawson III, *Army Generals and Reconstruction: Louisiana, 1862–1877* (Baton Rouge: Louisiana State University Press, 1982) offers an interesting case study of the problems encountered by army commanders in one of the more politically tumultuous southern states. A discerning account of Ulysses S. Grant's role in Reconstruction prior to his time as president is Brooks D. Simpson, *Let Us Have Peace: Ulysses S. Grant and the Politics of War and Reconstruction, 1861–1868* (Chapel Hill: University of North Carolina Press, 1991). William S. McFeely's *Yankee Stepfather: General O. O. Howard and the Freedmen* (New York: W. W. Norton, 1968) examines the important role of army officers in the Freedman's Bureau. Brooks D. Simpson, *The Reconstruction Presidents* (Lawrence: University Press of Kansas, 1998) provides thoughtful analysis of the policies of the four Reconstruction presidents—Lincoln, Johnson, Grant, and Hayes. The best general history of Reconstruction remains Eric Foner's *Reconstruction: America's Unfinished Revolution, 1863–1877* (New York: Harper and Row, 1988).

Robert M. Utley has written two essential books that deal with the role of the army in the West: *Frontier Regulars: The United States Army and the Indian* (New York: Macmillan Publishing, 1973) and *The Indian Frontier of the American West, 1846–1890* (Albuquerque: University of New Mexico Press, 1984). The latter contains an excellent discussion of the beliefs and activities of the eastern humanitarians who became known as "Friends of the Indians." Robert Wooster's *The Military and United States Indian Policy, 1865–1903* (Lincoln: University of Nebraska Press, 1988) includes a perceptive analysis of the culture and organization of the post–Civil War army. The best discussion of the controversy over whether the Indian Bureau should be transferred from the Interior Department to the War Department is in Francis Paul Prucha, *The Great Father: The United States Government and the American Indians*, 2 volumes (Lincoln: University of Nebraska Press, 1984). Paul Andrew Hutton's *Phil Sheridan and His Army* (Norman: University of Oklahoma Press, 1985) is a solid account of Sheridan's military career after the Civil War that focuses on his leadership in the army's war against the Plains tribes. Sherry L. Smith, *The View from Officers' Row: Army Perceptions of Western Indians* (Tucson: University of Arizona Press, 1990) and Thomas C. Leonard, *Above the Battle: War-making in America from Appomatox to Versailles* (New York: Oxford University Press, 1978) offer insightful discussions of the often complicated ways in which army officers viewed their Indian foes and American civil society.

Relatively few scholars have examined the role of the military in the labor-management conflict of late nineteenth and early twentieth centuries. Fortunately there is Jerry M. Cooper's well-researched book, *The Army and Civil Disorder: Federal Military Intervention in Labor Disputes, 1877–1900* (Westport, CT: Greenwood Press, 1980). Barton C. Hacker's "The United States Army as a National Police Force: The Federal Policing of Labor Disputes, 1877–1898," *Military Affairs* 33 (April 1969) contains some good observations. A lively account of the Great Strike of 1877 is Robert V. Bruce, *1877: Year of Violence* (Indianapolis, IN: Bobbs-Merrill, 1959; Chicago: Ivan R. Dee, 1989). Almont Lindsey, *The Pullman Strike: The Story of a Unique Experiment and of a Great Labor Upheaval* (Chicago: University of Chicago Press, 1994) discusses the labor protests of 1894.

On the subject of African Americans in the military in the years after the Civil War, readers should consult Bernard C. Nalty, *Strength for the Fight: A History of Black Americans in the Military* (New York: Free Press, 1986); Gerald Astor, *The Right to Fight: A History of African Americans in the Military* (Novato, CA: Presidio Press, 1998); William A. Dobak and Thomas D. Phillips, *The Black Regulars, 1866–1898* (Norman: University of Oklahoma Press, 2001). John F. Marszalek, Jr., *Court-Martial: A Black Man in America* (New York: Charles Scribner's Sons, 1972) discusses the difficulties encountered by a black cadet, Johnson Whittaker, at West Point in the late nineteenth century. Ann J. Lane, *The Brownsville Affair: National Crisis and Black Reaction* (Port Washington, NY: Kennikat Press, 1971) examines the controversy surrounding the raid on Brownsville, Texas, and the subsequent decision of President Theodore Roosevelt to discharge 167 black soldiers.

David F. Trask's *The War with Spain in 1898* (New York: Macmillan Publishing, 1981) is the best history of the Spanish-American War. Ivan Musicant's *Empire by Default: The Spanish-American War and the Dawn of the American Century* (New York: Henry Holt, 1998) is less scholarly but offers some interesting details. Gerald F. Linderman's *The Mirror of War: American Society and the Spanish-American War* (Ann Arbor: University of Michigan Press, 1974) provides valuable insights and a good account of the revival of interest in things military in the last years of the nineteenth century. Graham A. Cosmas, *An Army for Empire: The United States Army in the Spanish-American War* (College Station: Texas A&M University Press, 1994) is strong in every respect—it is thoroughly researched, soundly reasoned, and clearly written. Lewis L. Gould's *The Presidency of William McKinley* (Lawrence, KA: University Press of Kansas, 1980) effectively presents the diplomatic and political aspects of the war and makes a convincing case for McKinley as an active war leader.

Brian McAllister Linn's *The Philippine War, 1899–1902* (Lawrence: University Press of Kansas, 2000) provides an astute interpretation of the reasons for the army's success in defeating the insurgency in the Philippines and generally defends American soldiers from the charge that they fought the war with particular brutality. John M. Gates, *Schoolbooks and Krags: The United States Army in the Philippines, 1898–1902* (Westport, CT: Greenwood Press, 1973) also has praise for the army's handling of the conflict, especially its civil improvement projects. More critical of the conduct of U.S. forces is Stuart Creighton Miller in his book *"Benevolent Assimilation": The American Conquest of the Philippines, 1899–1903* (New Haven, CT: Yale University Press, 1982). Rowland T. Berthoff, "Taft and MacArthur, 1900–1901: A Study in Civil-Military Relations," *World Politics 5* (January 1953) provides a good account of the conflict between William Howard Taft, the head of the Philippine Commission, and General Arthur MacArthur, commander of U.S. forces in the Philippines, although Berthoff relies heavily on Taft's assessment of the situation. More sympathetic to MacArthur is Kenneth Ray Young, *The General's General: The Life and Times of Arthur MacArthur* (Boulder, CO: Westview Press, 1994).

Useful works on the role of the military in the new American empire are Lester D. Langley, *The Banana Wars: United States Intervention in the Caribbean, 1898–1934* (Wilmington, DE: Scholarly Resources, 2002); Brian

McAllister Linn, *Guardians of Empire: The U.S. Army and the Pacific, 1902–1940* (Chapel Hill: University of North Carolina Press, 1997); and Allan R. Millett, *The Politics of Intervention: The Military Occupation of Cuba, 1906–1909* (Columbus: Ohio State University Press, 1968). Richard D. Challener, *Admirals, Generals, and American Foreign Policy, 1898–1914* (Princeton, NJ: Princeton University Press, 1973) provides a good discussion of the growing importance of the military in the making of American foreign policy by the turn of the century as well as the continuing limitations on the military's role in determining policy. Worthwhile accounts of the American interventions in Mexico during the Wilson administration are Robert E. Quirk, *An Affair of Honor: Woodrow Wilson and the Occupation of Vera Cruz* (Lexington, KY: W. W. Norton, 1962) and Joseph A. Stout, *Border Conflict: Villistas, Carrancistas and the Punitive Expedition, 1915–1920* (Fort Worth: Texas Christian University Press, 1999).

Military professionalism and the campaign for administrative reform in the armed services are discussed in Ronald J. Barr, *The Progressive Army: U.S. Army Command and Administration, 1870–1914* (New York: St. Martin's Press, 1998); Mark R. Grandstaff, "Preserving the 'Habits and Usages of War': William Tecumseh Sherman, Professional Reform, and the U.S. Army Officer Corps, 1865–1881, Revisited," *Journal of Military History* 62 (July 1998); and Peter Karsten, "Armed Progressives: The Military Reorganizes for the American Century," in *The Military in America: From the Colonial Era to the Present*, ed. Peter Karsten (New York: Free Press, 1980). Stephen Skowronek, *Building a New American State: The Expansion of National Administration Capacities, 1877–1920* (Cambridge: Cambridge University Press, 1982) places reform efforts in the military into the broader context of administrative reform in government generally. President Theodore Roosevelt's role in the promotion of military reform is assessed in Matthew M. Oyos, "Theodore Roosevelt, Congress, and the Military: U.S. Civil-Military Relations in the Early Twentieth Century," *Presidential Studies Quarterly* 30 (January 2000).

Index

About the Author

CHARLES A. BYLER is Associate Professor of History at Carroll College.